P9-CKE-047

Aesthetic Paganism
in German Literature

Henry Hatfield is Professor of German at Harvard University. He is the author of *Winckelmann and His German Critics, Thomas Mann,* and *Goethe: A Critical Introduction.*

Aesthetic Paganism in German Literature

From Winckelmann to the Death of Goethe

ⅉⅉⅉⅉⅉⅉⅉⅉⅉⅉⅉⅉⅉⅉⅉⅉⅉⅉⅉⅉⅉⅉⅉⅉ

By HENRY HATFIELD

HARVARD UNIVERSITY PRESS

Cambridge, Massachusetts

1964

LIBRARY

MAY 8   1964

UNIVERSITY OF THE PACIFIC

128558

© *Copyright 1964 by the President and Fellows of Harvard College*

All rights reserved

Distributed in Great Britain by Oxford University Press, London

*Publication of this book has been aided by a grant from the
Ford Foundation*

Library of Congress Catalog Card Number 64-13423

Printed in the United States of America

For Harry and Elena Levin

Preface

The attempt to write a study of aesthetic paganism in German literature confronts one with several hard problems. Focusing on any point of view inevitably causes a distortion of the total picture; I have tried to minimize this, but well realize that one can, at best, portray only one aspect of the truth. Then there is the question of sheer bulk: I have limited myself to writers of real importance, but the mass of their works, from Winckelmann on, is very great. The book does not pretend to discuss new material but hopes to provide, in Lichtenberg's phrase, "new glimpses through the old holes."

The question of where to start is a hard one. It could be plausibly argued that a book on this theme should begin with an account of the impact of the Renaissance on Germany and the writings of the German Humanists of the fifteenth and sixteenth centuries. But there are limits to what one should try to include in a single work; and while my discussion of aesthetic paganism is admittedly incomplete, its scope is still a broad one; I only hope that it is not too broad.

The problem of definition is also difficult. The term "paganism" in this book denotes first of all a "this-worldly" view of life, as opposed to Christian dualism. (In the writers discussed here, "this-worldliness" usually implies a belief in divine forces immanent in nature and man.) The typical modern pagan — of course he is an abstraction — tends to a belief in enjoyment rather than asceticism, and vindicates the physical side of life, often with a special stress on the sexual element. He is likely to insist upon man's just pride in himself, not humility, though he need not exclude altruism. Such concepts as sin and conscience are generally played down or ignored; Goethe and other dominating figures of the time rejected the dogma of original sin. By the late eighteenth century there are instances of that revolt against pity which Nietzsche was to express with such hectic violence. In ethics, the pagan point of view is aristocratic rather than democratic: the strong, great-souled, superior man, *kalos kai agathos*, is glorified. Man is the center of the world as well as its measure. There is a stress both on Epicurean joy and Stoic dignity. Increasingly it is felt that the notion of living virtuously for the sake of rewards and punishments in a life to come is unworthy of man; this attitude stems mainly from Spinoza, but also from the study of Greek literature.

Goethe's description of the pagan spirit, in his essay on Winckelmann, is relevant here. Classical man, the poet maintains, was self-reliant, with interests and ambitions centered on the here-and-now. Although he regarded the gods reverently and disinterestedly, he admired them "only as works of art, as it were." (This predominantly aesthetic approach to religion is generally characteristic of German Hellenism.) Above all, the pagan possessed "indestructible health" of soul, even in disaster. During the course of this essay it becomes clear that Goethe is prescribing as well as describing: he regarded "pagan man" as an archetype, a valid if usually unattainable norm.

Of course one must bear in mind that the attitude just outlined is a relatively recent one and by no means identical with any of the beliefs of antiquity. Neopaganism in its various forms is very much aware of the past; its modern adherents tend to combine, in differing amounts, Epicurean, Platonic, and even Stoic elements, along with conscious or unconscious Christian ones, accenting the "Apollonian" or the "Dionysiac," or trying to form a synthesis. These "pagans" of the Age of Goethe are not only eclectic; they tend to place a greater stress on beauty, and especially on art, than most of the ancients did. Perhaps I should call them neopagans throughout, but this seems unnecessary, as the context makes clear who the objects of discussion are.

Some further definitions: in using terms like "the myth of Greece," I use "myth" in an extended sense to mean a fairly coherent whole, made up of beliefs, intuitions, and (often) historical facts. Such a myth is not a "lie": some of those who propound it believe in it literally, and the majority holds that it is symbolically or at least aesthetically true. "Hellenism" in this book signifies, rather arbitrarily, a belief in the myth of Greece as formulated by Winckelmann and his successors. The word *Humanität* is used to denote the synthesis of humanistic and humanitarian ideals at which Goethe, Schiller, and Lessing aimed.

Two well-known books (and a number of minor or more specialized ones) deal with the myth of Greece in German literature: *The Tyranny of Greece over Germany*, by the late E. M. Butler, and Walther Rehm's *Griechentum und Goethezeit*. My theme is another one: not all the poets inspired by the Greek ideal were pagan by any means, and various pagans turned elsewhere for inspiration. Inevitably there is a good deal of overlapping, but my approach and attitude are quite different from those of Miss Butler on the one hand and Professor Rehm on the other.

As her title implies, Miss Butler regarded the whole Hellenist movement as an aberration, though one which often produced brilliant results. She makes very clear her opinion that it would have been better if the Germans had limited themselves to native themes. (Wotan perhaps?) Her book is witty and contains some keen insights, but it is at times annoyingly superficial. Rehm's book is extraordinarily learned and is written with great historical and literary empathy; it is an excellent work in many respects. Anyone acquainted with the subject will see at once that my debt to Rehm is great but that my approach is a very different one. While Miss Butler's tone is too negative, Rehm's is lacking in critical distance and irony. Although he is by no means a chauvinist, he often seems to imply, perhaps unconsciously, that the Greek-German tradition is more authentic than the Roman-French line, though he finds the latter at times admirable, especially in Racine. From his presuppositions it follows, though it is not flatly stated, that the German interpretation of Greece is truer and "deeper" than any other. (To be sure, the German involvement with Hellenism was more prolonged and passionate than the French or the English; but that is another matter indeed.) One cannot synthesize these two books — it would be like trying to mix oil and water — but one can try to avoid the more extreme positions of both.

German paganism has been both a creative and a destructive force. In its extreme form, as in much of Nietzsche, it has had a disastrous effect. Yet there is great merit in the belief, held by so many from Goethe to Santayana, that the Northerner needs contact with the classical world if he is to be made whole. Gundolf wrote of the "creative belief" of the German interpreters of Hellas, maintaining that even their errors were incomparably more productive than was the work of the conventional philologists. Surely German literature would have been poorer and more provincial without the aesthetic faith which Goethe, Schiller, Hölderlin, and their successors derived from Winckelmann's vision.

My debts to scholars who have written on aspects of aesthetic paganism are recorded in the notes; there is no separate bibliography, but a list of editions most frequently cited is included on page 238. The fine collection of Winckelmann's letters edited by Rehm and Diepolder was especially helpful, as were Justi's still invaluable *Winckelmann und seine Zeitgenossen* and various publications of Ernst Howald, Horst Rüdiger, and Wolfgang Schadewaldt. Among the works not specifically related to my theme, I am most indebted to René Wellek's *A History of Modern Criticism*. Barker Fairley's interpretations of Goethe were both a stimulus and a guide.

I am grateful, for help and encouragement, to Herbert Dieckmann, Hans Eichner, W. M. Frohock, Ruth and Peter Gay, Walter Grossmann, Harlan Hanson, Walther Killy, and Harry Levin; and I must especially thank Herbert Bloch and Jack Stein, who read the entire manuscript and made many very valuable suggestions. Margaret Guenther and the late Arnold Weinberger checked many of my references; Ingeburg Zemmrich also gave me useful assistance. Above all, I must thank Jane Hatfield, who for years bore the brunt of typing the manuscript, from first draft to final revision.

It is a pleasure also to express my gratitude to the staffs of the libraries of Harvard University and Dartmouth College, of the Austrian National Library, and of the university libraries at the Free University of Berlin and in Vienna. At the last named, Hugo Alker and Rudolf Dettelmaier were always extremely gracious and even let me work in the library during an entire month when it was officially closed: certainly a rare triumph of kindness over the bureaucratic spirit. The Zürcher Kunstgesellschaft kindly supplied me with the reproduction of the drawing by Johann Heinrich Füssli which appears on the jacket of this book.

Further, I must thank the administrators of the John Simon Guggenheim Memorial Foundation, the Fulbright Commission, and the Clark Fund at Harvard for generous assistance; C. F. MacIntyre and the University of California Press for permission to quote Mr. MacIntyre's translation of Rilke's "Archaic Torso of Apollo"; and the University of Illinois Press for letting me use an article of mine in the volume *Schiller: 1759–1959* as the basis for a chapter in this book. The rhymed translations of lines of Schiller, in the notes, were made by Bulwer-Lytton; otherwise, the translations are my own.

H. H.

Cambridge, Massachusetts
June 1963

Contents

Aesthetic Paganism
in German Literature

Chapter I

Winckelmann
and the Myth of Greece

Since the middle of the eighteenth century one of the dominant strains in German literature has been the tendency to turn from a Christian view of the world to some belief or myth which appears to its adherents more beautiful, more in keeping with the dignity of man, than the Christian. The most striking and influential of such beliefs, though by no means the only one, has been the cult of Greece. The vision of Greece has changed radically, of course. Winckelmann, Goethe, Schiller, and a host of others were attracted by the serenity and control of the Greeks, but it was the wild, tragic, "Dionysiac" quality of Hellenic culture which primarily fascinated writers from the later nineteenth century to the present. The Greeks were joyful in Schiller's eyes, pathetic in Heine's, tortured in Nietzsche's. To Lessing and Goethe they appeared humane and warmhearted; to the Hofmannsthal of *Elektra*, cruel and perverse; to Stefan George, cool and self-contained. To many writers they have been the paradigm of health, to others the ultimate of fascinating decadence. They have served both as ideals of virtue and exemplars of the hedonistic enjoyment of life. Notoriously, moralists and historians as well as poets have read their own ideals and prejudices into "the Greeks." On one point however writers are in general agreement: the Greek way of life, like Greek art, the Greek gods, and "the Greek man," was more beautiful than its modern counterpart. Precisely for this reason, the aesthetic revolt against Christianity was waged primarily in the name of Hellas.

Other myths and utopias also had their appeal. Italy not only served as a substitute Greece; the Italian landscape [1] and Italian life exerted in their own right the magnetic attraction of the South upon a Northern people. One thinks back beyond Goethe's Mignon to the Hohenstaufens, perhaps even to the earliest Germanic invasions. Most particularly the Italy of the Renaissance [2] caught the imagination of the Germans. Beauty, passion, "aesthetic immoralism," the will to power: these seemed the great and exciting Renaissance values. Many a poet, from Goethe to the present, has been equally devoted to Greece and to Italy. The Renaissance ideal seems however to have had a particular fascination for those who found the "orthodox" classicism of a Winckelmann a bit cold and stiff. Here Wilhelm Heinse is a representative and somewhat neglected figure. His utopian novel *Ardinghello or the Happy Isles* ends in the Greek archipelago, but is set mainly in Italy; luxuriant color, rather than the whiteness of Hellenic statues, sets its tone.

The appeal of classical Rome was primarily moral and political, not aesthetic. Republican virtue and Stoic fortitude never lacked their admirers, but in German literature at least, ancient Rome is a dullish place compared to Athens.

In the later eighteenth century the islands of the South Seas, Tahiti [3] above all, became an authentic if minor paradise. After accompanying Captain Cook on his second circumnavigation of the globe, Georg Forster described the Pacific islanders much as Melville would a century later. The Tahitians, to Forster, rivaled Winckelmann's Greeks in noble simplicity. Islands, as Bernhard Blume has shown,[4] have a magic of their own. Heine, half wistfully, half skeptically, would set his utopia in the West Indies; he evokes the fountain of youth on Bimini, in "the remote Bermudas."

Just as it used to be fashionable to speak of the "anticapitalist yearnings" of the Germans, one can speak of "anti-Christian yearnings" expressed in their literature. Two other "revolts against Christianity" — not always conscious revolts — should briefly be mentioned. The German Enlightenment, initiated in the late seventeenth century, chipped persistently away at the structure of orthodox belief. To be sure, the *Aufklärer* were more cautious — or less destructive — than their French and British colleagues. Leibniz could still employ his vast learning and ingenuity in the attempt to reconcile science and belief; and even Lessing, two generations later, had to use "Aesopian language" to veil his more advanced theological views. When he edited the *Fragments* of H. S. Reimarus, perhaps the most extreme of contemporary German attacks on the validity of the Bible, he found it appropriate to publish them as anonymous, for the sake of Reimarus' survivors. (The author himself, outwardly a professor of unexceptionable conformity, had been dead for some years.) Cautious the *Aufklärer* may have been, but there can be no doubt about the general tendency of their theological criticism; in the nineteenth century it would become obvious to the dullest eye. But their anti-Christianity (or non-Christianity) appealed not to beauty but to truth — the Protestant conscience turned against Protestantism, to paraphrase Nietzsche — so it does not directly concern us here. Intellectual movements, of course, are not insulated against each other, and many a man of the Enlightenment was a Hellenist too, particularly attracted by the notion of Athenian freedom.

Curiously, the glorification of Northern mythology began almost simultaneously with the eighteenth-century revival of the Greeks. Paul Henri Mallet, a Swiss long resident in Copenhagen, initiated the vogue with his *Introduction à l'histoire*

de Dannemarc (1755); Germans like Gerstenberg and Klopstock soon joined in. The Northerners or Septentrionalists
did not distinguish between Celtic and Germanic lore; the
Druids were felt as somehow German, and a flood of "bardic"
poetry streamed from the presses. The vogue of "Ossian"
contributed to the general enthusiasm; his melancholy had a
particular appeal, and some readers ranked him with Homer.

The admirers of Arminius and the enthusiastic readers of
Tacitus' *Germania* could (and did) plausibly maintain that
they were appealing to a tradition far more natural to Germans than the lore of Elis and Olympia. It is important to note,
furthermore, that the bardic movement was by no means consciously anti-Christian. Klopstock was devoutly pious, and
Herder was a noted theologian and preacher; he has been
called an inspired Unitarian. It would be unhistorical to blame
the Northerners for the excesses of later German romanticism
or the abominations of the twentieth century. Yet a certain
savagery after all does inhere in the Germanic material itself.
The soulful author of the *Messias* becomes downright blood-
thirsty when he deals with Arminius' ambush of the Roman
legions. Northern mythology affords no corrective either to
the more barbarous proclivities of the Germans or to their
recurrent tendency to formlessness. Indeed, many of the most
significant German works, from *Faust* to *The Magic Mountain*, imply that only the classical heritage can furnish such
a balance: the German needs the "otherness" of the Mediterranean element. In any case, the cult of the Germanic past
is not characteristically an aesthetic one. Despite evocations
of the beauty of Siegfried, or attempts like Stefan George's
to associate the Norse gods with the Greek, the movement
typically invokes pagan ideals of a very different type:
strength, patriotism, the rugged manly virtues. Its political
impact has been vast; its artistic achievement — aside from
Wagner's *Ring* — relatively slight.

Appropriately enough, the aesthetic revolt against Christianity had the most impressive aesthetic results. Here the appeal of Greece — of Athenian culture above all — proved far stronger than that of Rome, or of the South Seas, or even of the Renaissance. From Winckelmann to Rilke, from Goethe to George, the majority of the greatest German writers have been "Hellenists" to some significant degree. It is as if Goethe's successors had taken very seriously his admonition that everyone should be a Greek in his own way: "Jeder sei auf seine Art ein Grieche, aber er sei's." [5] Thus a work devoted to aesthetic paganism will necessarily be deeply concerned with the cult of Greece, though the two movements are by no means identical. It is no accident that the founder of German Hellenism, Johann Joachim Winckelmann, was the first thoroughgoing aesthete of modern German letters, [6] and like Goethe a "decided non-Christian" as well. A consideration of his ideas is the necessary foundation of any treatment of our theme.

Few men have had a greater impact on the culture of their native country than did Winckelmann. The "Greek revival" which he initiated profoundly altered the course of German literature: many of its greatest writers from Lessing to our own times would have written differently without his precept and example. His style as well as his ideas were regarded as classic, in more than one sense of that word. His cult of Greek simplicity and grandeur affected music (in Gluck's operas [7]) as well as literature; and of course sculpture, painting, and architecture. Indeed, it influenced the whole history of Western taste, not only in Europe: Thomas Jefferson [8] knew of his ideas. Not only is he regarded as the founder of modern classical archaeology; he had, through Herder, a profound influence on the writing of history. In his view of a culture developing "organically" through an irreversible series of periods he was halfway to the historicism of the nineteenth century. After he settled in Rome in 1755 his fame became a European, almost as much as a German, phenomenon;

through translations, articles in journals, and the enthusiastic
reports of travelers returned from Rome, it rapidly radiated
over Western Europe. Perhaps the most remarkable thing
about his influence was its duration; the first, uncritical vogue
of Winckelmann died down rather soon, but the impact of
his central concepts has persisted — with modifications, of
course — into our own time.

Born in obscure poverty in the little Prussian town of
Stendal, in 1717, he remained unknown for most of his life.
Until 1755, when his first published work, *Thoughts on the
Imitation of the Greek Works of Painting and Sculpture*,
appeared, he led an arduous life as penniless student, village
schoolmaster, and later as the librarian and assistant of Count
Bünau, at Nöthnitz near Dresden. By an extraordinary and
prolonged effort of the will, he made himself, during those
years, a master of classical literature. In later years he described how he used to spend his days "teaching scabby-
headed children their ABC's" and his nights studying and
"praying in similes taken from Homer." [9] At the same time he
managed somehow to acquire a very respectable knowledge
of other fields, particularly of the literature and philosophy
of the European Enlightenment: Shaftesbury, Pope, Mon-
tesquieu, Bayle, and so on, were among the writers he valued
most highly. Above all he was obsessed by the desire to study
Greek art at its source — which to him, as to most of his
contemporaries, meant Rome. He compared himself to Aeneas,
persevering in his quest *per tot discrimina rerum*.[10]

Winckelmann was nearing middle age when his chance
came. His learning and calligraphy had gained him a certain provincial reputation in Saxony [11] some years before he
published anything. The papal nuncio to the court in Dresden, Archinto, was eager to gain a convert of such promise;
the King's confessor, Father Rauch of the Jesuit order, supported his endeavors. Winckelmann was offered the chance
to live and work in Rome, on the condition that he profess

Catholicism. While nominally a Protestant, he was anything but a devout Christian; his recorded opinions [12] waver between skepticism [13] and a kind of eighteenth-century "reasonable religion," [14] and many of his remarks indicate a naturally pagan disposition. Goethe wrote of him as an "antique nature" [15] and devoted a chapter to the pagan elements of his personality. Yet there can be no doubt that a strain of religiosity, Protestant in origin, persisted in his mind. Thus the decision was not an easy one: Winckelmann hesitated for three years and seems to have been plagued by psychosomatic ills [16] before he made the *sacrificium intellectus*. He was apologetic about the step, which is indeed somewhat reminiscent of a Faustian pact; but once in Rome, he appears never to have really regretted it. He who wills the end must will the means.

A year after his conversion, he had captured the imagination of the German literary world by publishing his revolutionary brochure *Thoughts on the Imitation of the Greek Works*, containing his cardinal theses: the absolute validity of Greek art; its essential qualities of "noble simplicity and tranquil grandeur"; and the necessity of imitating the ancients. "The only way for us to become great, aye, if it is possible, inimitable, is the imitation of the Greeks," [17] he proclaimed. "Imitation" (*Nachahmung*) is a somewhat ambiguous term; Winckelmann usually means something like "creation in the Greek spirit" rather than "copying," though much slavish neoclassic work in the fine arts has been laid at his door. After Young and Hamann, only four years later, coined the slogan of original genius, the very word "imitation" became an abomination to the literary vanguard; but the attraction of Winckelmann's Hellenism remained strong nevertheless.

Today the thesis of the statuesque calm of Greek art is regarded as at best a rather tired half-truth. It struck its own time with the force of a revelation. Winckelmann became a national figure almost overnight; with the publication of his

History of Ancient Art (1764), a European one. Except for
Frederick II of Prussia, he was the most renowned German
between Leibniz and Goethe. To the "enlightened" public
of the first half of the eighteenth century, Greek mythology
was a bundle of superstitions, useful at best for the adorn-
ment of pseudo-Anacreontic poetry; [18] to the Pietists, knowledge of pagan antiquity was suspect by definition. The general
hostility to the classic gods and heroes was in part a residue
of the seventeenth-century "quarrel between the ancients and
the moderns." Greek literature was generally considered inferior to Latin; in German schools and universities Greek was
studied primarily as the language of the New Testament.

To be sure, a modest revival of interest, mainly centered
in the universities, had begun well before Winckelmann's appearance on the scene. [19] In Berlin, Göttingen, and Leipzig
scholars like Damm, Gesner, Ernesti, and Christ stressed again
the spirit and the cultural value of ancient literature; enthusiasm for the Greek ideal, dormant since the sixteenth century,
was beginning to stir once more. The vogue of collecting
antique gems prepared the way for an interest in the major
arts of Greece and Rome. Similarly, the excavations at Her-
culaneum and Pompeii, which began in 1738 and 1748 respectively, stirred the imagination of the public; and the
antiquarian publications of Count Caylus attracted considerable attention. Finally, the study of the beautiful was beginning to become respectable in the universities. Alexander
Baumgarten initiated the academic study of aesthetics in Germany. His *Aesthetica* appeared in 1750–58, in the decade when
Winckelmann's first works were published.

Thus Winckelmann might appear only to have reinforced
a trend which had already set in. His ardent, indeed fanatic,
devotion to his cause, his propagandistic skill, and his powerful and eloquent style were of course his own contribution.
More significantly, he desired not primarily the restoration of
humanistic studies [20] but the rebirth of the idea of Greece

itself. None of his predecessors or contemporaries was possessed by so broad, so sweeping an ambition.

Winckelmann's early successes involve a series of paradoxes, or apparent paradoxes. In itself, of course, the call to imitate classical models is one of the oldest of critical imperatives: *

> Vos exemplaria Graeca
> nocturna versate manu, versate diurna.[21]

Furthermore, Winckelmann's knowledge of Greek art, in his Dresden days, was sketchy in the extreme, based on inferior engravings, antique gems, and what must have been a very unsatisfactory view of some copies of ancient statues packed away in a shed at Dresden.[22] Even in Rome he was never able to see the great original works of the fifth century.[23] Late works, like the Laocoön and the Apollo Belvedere, were the source of his highest inspiration; and it is difficult indeed to discern today "noble simplicity and tranquil grandeur" in the Laocoön, that painfully effective product of Hellenistic baroque.

The amazing fact remains: Winckelmann did describe one important aspect of Greek art persuasively and perhaps definitively. There is no lack of speculation about the reasons which made this achievement possible. Obviously, he was reacting against baroque taste; clearly, as Goethe noted, he found in classical culture ideals corresponding to some inner need.[24] More specifically, he may have formed his taste on the ancient gems so much in the mode in the eighteenth century. Above all, I believe, his interpretation of Greek art was based primarily upon his intimate knowledge of Greek literature. To put it crudely, he read into the Laocoön and other renowned statues ideals derived from Sophocles, Homer,[25] and Plato, his favorite authors. Yet his literary taste was far from catholic. Sig-

---

* Translations of all passages quoted in a foreign language will be found in the notes.

nificantly, he had serious reservations about Aeschylus;[26] and although he was very fond of Aristophanes, he ignored the colorful, vulgar, and obscene aspects of Greek culture. If he had any sense of what was later to be called the Dionysiac element, he completely suppressed it.

Winckelmann's vision of Greece, in a word, was a partial and distorted one; but it was based on real knowledge, however limited, and on love. There is to be sure something pale and unreal about his whole concept, and Santayana's irony is not unjust: "How dignified everything was in those heroic days! How noble, serene, and abstracted! How pure the blind eyes of statues, how chaste the white folds of the marble drapery! Greece was a remote, fascinating vision, the most romantic thing in the history of mankind."[27] Yet his evocations of Greek statues are anything but cold; they are full of verve, of romantic empathy and power, and his contemporaries — and a long line of their successors, down to our own time — have reacted accordingly.

A certain freshness and enthusiasm were among Winckelmann's most engaging characteristics. He quoted Plato's statement that a sense of wonder is the foundation of the love of wisdom, and his own sense of wonder proved infectious. In Rome he devoted much of his time to instructing German and Swiss visitors — mainly men and youths of good birth and attractive appearance — in the true faith of Hellenism; he became the aesthetic *praeceptor Germaniae*. Looking back on his career from the height of his Italian accomplishments, he wrote to an old friend: "Behold the life and the miracles of Johann Winckelmann . . . born in Stendal in the Old March [of Prussia]."[28]

Beyond the rather obvious reasons already adduced for Winckelmann's success, there are others which may take us closer to the heart of the matter. At the time when interest in the nonrational factors in life was beginning to rise in Germany, he took the myth seriously — not so much the details of classic mythology, as the great symbolic figures of heroes and gods. In a parallel sense, he took beauty seriously, as the center and crown of life, not as a mere ornament. Finally, a pagan element in his view of the world, soon to be discussed, had an appeal which went far deeper than did the details of his doctrine. To this last point and its implications, this book will be primarily devoted.

As Herder pointed out, the essentials of Winckelmann's doctrine are already clearly expressed in the *Thoughts on Imitation*.[29] Later he refined various points, revising his opinions about matters of detail, some of them important, and assigning greater weight to the factor of history. Broadly speaking, one may say however that while he perfected his style [30] and greatly expanded his historical knowledge during the thirteen years of his Italian career, Winckelmann did not alter the fundamental content of his dogma.

Its central point is as well expressed in the renowned description of the Laocoön as elsewhere. The qualities of that statue are seen as the quintessence of Greek art, and hence, to Winckelmann, of beauty itself:

> The most significant characteristic of the Greek masterpieces, finally, is a noble simplicity and a tranquil grandeur [*eine edle Einfalt und eine stille Grösse*]. As the depths of the sea always remain calm, no matter how the surface may rage, just so does the expression of the Greek figures indicate among all passions a great and resolute soul.
>
> Such a soul is portrayed in the face of the Laocoön, despite [*bey*] the most violent suffering. The pain which appears in all the muscles and sinews of the body . . . nevertheless is not made manifest by any expression of fury . . . Unlike Vergil's Laocoön, he raises no horrible cry . . . Laocoön suffers, but he suffers like Sophocles' Philoctetes: his misery . . . touches our very souls, but we would wish to be able to bear misery like this great man.[31]

The image of the sea, calm in its depths "no matter how the surface may rage," recurs again and again in his writings. Rarely is a "raging surface" mentioned in these images, but the sea is not presented as absolutely calm: Winckelmann's classicism aims at the control not the extirpation of emotion.

Raphael's Sistine Madonna is portrayed in very similar terms: "See the *Madonna*, with a face expressive of innocence and yet with a more than feminine grandeur, in an attitude of blissful repose, with that tranquillity [*Stille*] which prevailed in the ancients' representations of their divinities. How grand and noble is the entire contour of this figure!" [32] Raphael, the prime exemplar of successful imitation — not copying — of the Greeks, has succeeded because he created in the Hellenic spirit. (It is curious that Winckelmann's modern instance accords far better than his classical one with his concept of Greece.)

Characteristically, Winckelmann writes with special fervor in praise of restraint; it is tranquillity which evokes his keenest feeling. On the matter of Greek "calm" [33] the tradition was to divide: one line of Hellenists, including the Goethe of *Iphigenia*, Platen, and George, would uphold serenity as one of the highest of values. Others, from the Storm and Stress to the present, would reject or modify it. Winckelmann's ideal would later, via Schopenhauer, become Nietzsche's "Apollonian" element and be reduced to the status of a dream. [34] The "other side" of Greek life — the Hellas of Bacchanalian orgies — Nietzsche would label "Dionysiac." Heinse, the Goethe of the Prometheus fragment, and the Kleist of *Penthesilea* were all Dionysiac interpreters of Greece before Nietzsche, and in a sense more pagan than the members of the orthodox Apollonian tradition.

Particularly in Winckelmann's evocation of the Laocoön, it will be noted, ethical and aesthetic judgments are inextricably interwoven. Laocoön is here the archetype of Stoic virtue; the Madonna expresses classic serenity rather than Christian compassion.

In Winckelmann's concept there is an Epicurean strain along with the Stoic one; it appears most clearly in his delineation of Greek life. The Greeks were the most joyful of peoples. Blessed by a sunny, moderate climate, uninhibited by bourgeois conventions, free of the scourge of the more unpleasant modern diseases, they could devote themselves to art, to athletics, to leisure. Their whole civilization had a youthful character. They were free in politics as well as in mores; it was perhaps the latter freedom which impressed Winckelmann more. For it was not only admirable and healthy in itself that Athenian youths and Spartan maidens exercised naked or only lightly clad; it afforded Greek artists an unequaled opportunity to study the nude. To Winckelmann and his school the representation of the nude human body was the highest aim of art,[35] above all, of course, of sculpture.

The Greeks were not only youthful, happy, and athletic, he believed; they were also, during their time of political freedom, remarkably humane: they scorned bloody gladiatorial displays.[36] Above all, they were *the* aesthetic people. They held contests in beauty, and parents tried consciously to produce beautiful children. Not content with the empirical beauty by which they were so abundantly surrounded, Hellenic artists rose to ideal or abstracted forms of human perfection.

The cult of beauty lies at the very center of Winckelmann's being. Beauty he considered the highest aim of art; the picturesque and the characteristic lack intrinsic value. He was an aesthetic man if there ever was one; his appeal to Goethe in his Italian period and after, to Heinse, Platen, Walter Pater, and later writers, is symptomatic. An early letter expresses his belief that nature wished to make a painter of him, but that his parents inhibited his innate talent.[37] One need not take this too seriously, but when he adds "everything I have read becomes as it were a painting," one's psychological curiosity is piqued. Like many another learned man, he was intrapunitive enough to feel that scholars are less to be respected than artists.[38]

Winckelmann's repeated efforts to define or describe beauty recall the mystic's attempt to express the ineffable experience of God. Typically, he scorned abstract deductions about the beautiful, though at times he repeated the currently accepted phrases equating beauty with unity in multiplicity or relating it to perfection. At times he was eclectic; at times he expressed his belief in such constructs as Hogarth's line of beauty: the gentleness of unbroken contours was his ideal. Like Goethe, he felt that the natural was never violent. Just as he thought that calm was more beautiful than a storm, Winckelmann considered the broadest generality or typicality superior to particular expression. Beauty has an ennobling effect rather than a specific moral purpose.

In romantic or preromantic fashion, Winckelmann at times abandoned the attempt to define beauty and concentrated on the reactions of the observer of the work of art. The ideal amateur must be possessed of noble character, innate aesthetic sensitivity, and leisure. Above all he must have within himself the tranquillity inherent in the work he is contemplating.[39] There is to be sure a significant rational element in aesthetic appreciation: "Beauty is felt through the senses but understood by the mind." [40] Increasingly, however, Winckelmann aimed at empathetic identification with the work observed. To keep empathy under control, as it were, he stressed intense, concentrated contemplation; like Rilke, he insisted on the importance of really "seeing." At one point he invoked almost literally the "cold shivers down my spine" criterion of beauty, though he limited this reaction to untutored youths.[41]

In Winckelmann's most exalted moments he rose to Platonic heights. From his rapt exclamation "The highest beauty is in God!" [42] it is no great step to the statement that the highest beauty *is* God. This he never quite said, but he is obviously one of the founders of the "religion of art." In Germany, the aesthetic orientation of Weimar "classicists" and Jena "romanticists" continued the Winckelmannian tradition.

Heine was later to speak rather sarcastically of the "art period" (*Kunstperiode*), and it has been remarked that to German intellectuals of that era a poem meant more than a battle, an aesthetic theory more than the whole state. Of particular interest is Winckelmann's absolute subordination of religious to aesthetic matters. His attitude appeared very Greek in the eighteenth and nineteenth centuries, though it would doubtless have shocked Pericles or Sophocles. In a letter from Rome, where he lived in the character of an abbé, he wrote that he could not be bothered with theology: he had more pleasant, not to say more important, things to think about.[43] It has been suggested that he regarded even history under the aspect of aesthetics.[44]

It was sculpture which really appealed to him; the paintings that most attracted him were generally those aiming at sculptural effects, like many of the works of his friend Mengs. His cult of whiteness is of course relevant here; color meant very little to him. With a few notable exceptions, his most eloquent evocations are devoted to statues of the male nude: Laocoön, the Belvedere Torso, and the Apollo Belvedere are the most renowned. The homosexual tendency latent in his work is clearly revealed by his letters. For whatever reasons, a similar tendency occurs frequently among his successors: Johannes von Müller, August von Platen, and Stefan George spring to mind. Few writers have dealt frankly with the matter, but Heine, as Miss Butler notes, openly discussed it.[45]

To decide just how pagan Winckelmann's ethical ideas were is not simple. His view of the world consisted largely of an eclectic mixture of Stoic and Epicurean elements, with a certain admixture of Platonism. To a large extent the study of classical authors seems to have formed his mind; once, during the time of his servitude as a schoolmaster, he was caught reading Homer in church.[46] The influence of his contemporary reading should not be neglected; the great writers of the French and English Enlightenment seem to have inclined him toward skepticism. As Justi put it, he was not only a late-born "relative" of Phidias and Plato but a son of his own time.[47]

Clearly, he had a sense of destiny which recalls the antique. "Superavi te, fortuna" (I have conquered you, fortune), he declared in a letter from Rome.[48] His cult of freedom for the leisured, cultivated few is relevant here. Rejecting Christian humility, he openly expressed the just pride of the Aristotelian "great-souled man." [49]

A definitely anti-Christian note is often heard in his letters. Like Spinoza and Lessing, he believed that the highest morality consists in performing actions for their own sake; he held that Christianity, with its system of rewards and punishments, had discouraged that highest of values, heroic friendship between men.[50] He wrote to his friend Berendis: "One of the causes of the rare occurrence of this virtue, which in my opinion is the greatest of human qualities, is the religion in which we are trained. Temporal and eternal rewards are attached to everything which it commands or praises; friendship between individuals [*Privatfreundschaft*] is not even mentioned in the whole New Testament." [51] Precisely the man endowed with "a great and resolute soul," like Laocoön's, is capable of such friendship.

In his works, Winckelmann's attacks on Christianity are generally veiled. He was an abbé, after all, and he more than once expressed his fear of the Inquisition. But occasionally, like Goethe, he reveals his aversion to the treatment of Christian themes in art, as in his slighting reference to the statues of "sanctified monks" in Rome.[52] Like other pagans of various types, he seems to have been repelled by the radical dualism of the Christian distinction between the divine and the human. In Greece man was not thus alienated. Schiller put the matter explicitly in "The Gods of Greece": "In the days when the gods were more human, humans were more divine." The myth of the deification of Hercules implies that the cleft between gods and men is not absolute; this is perhaps one reason that it attracted many German Hellenists. Above all, it is in Winckelmann's implied acceptance of Greek sensuality and "this-worldliness" that the pagan strain figures most decisively. His fondness for Italy seems to have been based partly on similar considerations.[53]

Doubtless no man born into a Christian culture is a complete pagan, and Winckelmann, who studied theology for a time, could not utterly reject that side of his heritage. In Rome he read the Bible and sang a Protestant hymn of Paul Gerhardt's every morning.[54] In his last will, written when death was imminent, he declared himself a good Catholic. It seems impossible to evaluate this deathbed conversion justly.[55]

The most crucial question is that of the impact of his paganism. Goethe and the other "Weimar Friends of Art" considered him virtually a reincarnated Greek. Schiller's "Gods of Greece," a poem made all the more effective as propaganda by its simplistic rhetoric, championed and indeed exaggerated Winckelmann's dogmas. Other examples of aesthetic anti-Christianity are frequent in the German tradition; they run through the nineteenth century and well into the twentieth.

For all of his enthusiasm for Greece, Winckelmann regarded all mythology as a "web of allegories of things unseen," [56] and he advised contemporary artists to draw on them for motifs suitable for didactic interpretation.[57] Of course he was far from any consistent belief in the literal reality of the ancient gods; only in a few set pieces, like the description of the Apollo Belvedere, do the gods seem actually to exist. His attitude was largely an aesthetic one:[58] the Olympian divinities lived in the world of semblance, of *Schein*, in Schiller's sense.[59] Yet in his renowned prose poems about such statues as the Apollo or the Belvedere Torso he writes with such force and eloquence that the heroes and gods assume a life of their own.

In his set pieces he laid the foundation, perhaps unintentionally, of a new mythology which would fuse Hellenic ideals with eighteenth-century *Humanität*. In such passages as his evocation of the Belvedere Torso he combined description, empathy, and mythological references to produce a kind of poem. Thinking that the mutilated fragment was a torso of Hercules, he felt free to weave the myths and homilies associated with the demigod into his interpretation. Using the first person, like a teacher of art addressing a class, he speaks directly to the reader: "Now I shall conduct you to the much-lauded, never sufficiently praised Torso." [60] He warns us that the statue has been shattered, like some ancient oak; that at first glance we may descry merely a misshapen stone. Soon however we are made to "see" the flank of the Torso; again the image of the ocean is employed: "As, when the sea begins to stir, the surface, quiet before, now misty and disturbed, rises with waves playing — one is devoured by the next, and again rolled forth by it: just as gently here one muscle swells up and flows into the second; and a third, which rises between them and seems to strengthen their movement, loses itself in them; and our glance, as it were, is consumed with it." [61] He turns, as he so often did, to the ethical implications of the work of art: "In the calm and tranquillity of the body is revealed the great, resolute spirit, the man who exposed himself to the greatest dangers from love of justice, who achieved safety for the lands and for their inhabitants, calm." [62] At the end of the essay the mutilated stone becomes a god, just as Hercules himself became one of the Olympians: "a loftier spirit seems to have entered his mortal parts and to have taken their place. It is no longer the body which must yet face the struggle against monsters and breakers of the peace; it is that body which was purged of the dross of humanity on the mountain of Oeta." [63] Here he anticipates the twentieth-century paganism of Stefan George; the body is made divine, the divine made flesh: "den Leib vergottet und den Gott verleibt."

Throughout the brief essay, he uses a wealth of metaphors and of literary and moralizing allusions. His style is carefully calculated to produce a sense of monumental repose; based on nouns rather than verbs, it is deliberate in pace, with a very careful distribution of sentence stresses.[64]

A modern critic might well object that Winckelmann's method here is disturbingly "literary." Indeed it is; though Winckelmann repeatedly stressed the importance of close, concentrated observation, his interpretative enthusiasm swept him with it, here as elsewhere. His inner vision proved decisive; we have less a picture of the Torso than a poem occasioned by it. Winckelmann's problem here was the same as that of Rilke when he chose to describe another mutilated classical statue.

> ### Archäischer Torso Apollos
>
> Wir kannten nicht sein unerhörtes Haupt,
> darin die Augenäpfel reiften. Aber
> sein Torso glüht noch wie ein Kandelaber,
> in dem sein Schauen, nur zurückgeschraubt,
>
> sich hält und glänzt. Sonst könnte nicht der Bug
> der Brust dich blenden, und im leisen Drehen
> der Lenden könnte nicht ein Lächeln gehen
> zu jener Mitte, die die Zeugung trug.
>
> Sonst stünde dieser Stein entstellt und kurz
> unter der Schultern durchsichtigem Sturz
> und flimmerte nicht so wie Raubtierfelle;
>
> und bräche nicht aus allen seinen Rändern
> aus wie ein Stern: denn da ist keine Stelle,
> die dich nicht sieht. Du musst dein Leben ändern.[65]

Rilke too combined description, symbolic interpretation, and direct exhortation, making a cleaner division among the elements of his work than Winckelmann had. If one allows for the differences between poetry and prose, between the eighteenth century and the twentieth, the close interrelationship of the two evocations becomes all the more striking. Winckelmann's essay can almost be considered as a *Dinggedicht*, a "thing poem." The link is one of affinity, or the sharing in a common heritage, rather than of conscious influence.

The unexpected climax of Rilke's poem — "You must change your life" — speaks with a naked explicitness unequaled in Winckelmann. The words express the ethical intention of the tradition of German Hellenism more succinctly and forcefully than he could have done: the message of a heroic past to a cramped and mediocre present. They are as it were the categorical imperative distilled from Winckelmann's belief. Homer and ancient art had indeed changed Winckelmann's life, and he devoted his highest energies to changing the life of his age. He wrote to the Danish sculptor Wiedewelt, after the latter had left Rome: "May the noble majesty of the Apollo, the lofty ideal of the Torso, and the delightful, angelic beauty of the Borghese Genius and the Niobe remain deeply stamped upon you." [66] The aesthetic and moral ideal he sensed in mythology and art was the center of his existence.

The gods and heroes who figure most importantly in Winckelmann's writings play a great part in German literature of the later eighteenth century. Schiller planned to devote a heroic idyl to the deification of Hercules.[67] The statue of Laocoön inspired an ode of Herder as well as the critical discussion which Lessing initiated; Goethe and Herder wrote eloquent descriptions of it. The Apollo Belvedere, the subject of the most famous descriptive passage in the *History of Ancient Art*, appears in Goethe's "Wanderer's Storm Song" [68] much as the archaeologist had pictured him:

> Wandeln wird er wie mit Blumenfüssen
> Über Deukalions Flutschlamm,
> Python tötend, leicht, gross,
> Pythius Apollo.[69]

Another set piece in Winckelmann's *History* was devoted to Niobe and her daughters,[70] and Niobe's sufferings became the theme of a verse drama by the Storm and Stress writer Friedrich ("Maler") Müller. However variously Winckelmann's heroes were interpreted, they were always represented as beautiful, majestic, and morally noble. In that lay their consistency and their appeal to the age. Through his evocations of gods and heroes he had created a potent myth of his own, reviving and transforming the ancient pantheon.

Much of the charm of Winckelmann's "myth" lay no doubt in its utopian quality. It would be cheap and unfair to imply that he manufactured his concept of Greece out of whole cloth. He was in some degree a "deceived deceiver," but there cannot be the slightest doubt of his sincerity. Like many other utopias, Winckelmann's contains a large element of polemic directed against his own age. Thus he contrasts a youthful Spartan, "begotten by a hero, of a heroine," [71] with "a young Sybarite of our time." When he compares Homer's heroes to "the swift-footed Red Indian" [72] one recalls that Diderot linked Winckelmann, as a "charming fanatic," with Rousseau.[73] Indeed, as Goethe pointed out, Rousseauism and the cult of Greece reinforced each other throughout the century; the Greeks were "natural." [74] (Gilbert Bagnani has well described Winckelmann's doctrine as an "odd combination of Hellenism and Romanticism." [75]) In his praise of the political freedom of the Greeks, there seems also to be an implied protest against current German conditions; references to Prussian tyranny often appear in his letters.[76]

Naturally enough, Winckelmann was most utopian in his early essays, especially in the *Thoughts on Imitation*. The Epicurean element proved at least as attractive to his contemporaries as the Stoic, and the youthful, happy nature attributed to Greek culture exerted a special fascination. Herder personified Greece as "the beautiful youth"; Heinse was led to construct a utopian Greece of his own, far more hedonistic than Winckelmann's. Like many writers after him, he eagerly exploited the theme of sexual freedom latent in Winckelmann's notion of Greek nakedness.[77] This particular form of paganism did not interest the archaeologist; it had of course a vast appeal to his successors.

On the other hand, the belief in Greek humaneness also merged easily with Christian ideals and eighteenth-century ideas of *Menschlichkeit*. Thus Goethe could endow his Iphigenia with the noble simplicity of the ancients, the *caritas* of Raphael's St. Agatha,[78] and the quiet inwardness of the Pietists. Later he confessed that he could never have written the drama — one of the noblest of his poems — had he not been then relatively ignorant of the historical Greeks.[79] Possibly it was Hölderlin who was the most deeply moved by Winckelmann's vision. His mythic figures are possessed of greatness of soul, physical and intellectual beauty, patriotism, the love of freedom — indeed of almost every virtue imaginable. They are not pagan in the earthier sense — Hölderlin's own nature was almost saintly — but attempt to fuse antique and Christian virtues.

In later years Winckelmann became more reserved in his portrayal of Greek life, less sanguine about the hope of reviving its glories, and somewhat more "objective" in his analysis of ancient works of art. Thus, in the *History of Ancient Art*, he sharply revised his interpretation of the Laocoön.[80] Along with the growth in his archaeological knowledge, his concept of history had greatly developed. Greek art and culture are regarded in the *History* as living organisms.[81] The fine arts began with the necessary, rose to beauty, and then having reached the stage of the superfluous, began to decline.[82] When all original ideas have been exhausted, art must inevitably languish; this occurred in Greece after the death of Alexander the Great. Other branches of culture ripen and decay in a similar way.[83] Winckelmann wrote at times with an almost Spenglerian fatalism, but he never renounced the doctrine of imitation, nor did he face the fatal contradiction between the notion of historicism on the one hand and of the emulation of the ancients on the other. Yet the following passage, taken from the final paragraph of the *History of Ancient Art*, suggests that his historical sense was gaining the upper hand: "just as a woman on the shore of the sea follows her departing lover with tear-filled eyes, without the hope of ever seeing him again, and thinks to see in the distant sail the image of the beloved. Like such a woman, we have, as it were, only a silhouette of the object of our desires; but this awakens all the greater longing for that which we have lost." [84] The mood of resignation and skepticism suggests Goethe's twenty-first *Venetian Epigram*:

> Emsig wallet der Pilger! Und wird er den Heiligen finden?
> 　　Hören und sehen den Mann, welcher die Wunder getan?
> Nein, es führte die Zeit ihn hinweg: du findest nur Reste,
> 　　Seinen Schädel, ein paar seiner Gebeine verwahrt.
> Pilgrime sind wir alle, die wir Italien suchen;
> 　　Nur ein zerstreutes Gebein ehren wir gläubig und froh. [85]

A letter of Winckelmann's, written in the last year of his life, is signed "Johann Winckelmann, Pilgrim." [86] Inevitably, the highest hopes of founding a "second Hellas" end on a note of melancholy. Yet Winckelmann's impact on German culture remained enormous. His ideas were of course modified and sometimes distorted. Worst of all, his name became, in many instances, a symbol of neoclassic dullness in the fine arts, of dusty plaster casts in seminar rooms, of the official classicism of the Prusso-German Gymnasium. His more sensitive readers, however, have always realized that his intention was something very different: his aim was not academicism but a nobler and freer life. [87]

Chapter II

The Ancient Image of Death: Lessing and His Impact

The great critic Gotthold Ephraim Lessing was the first major writer who was stimulated to creative activity by the new ideal of Greece. Keenly rational as he was, he did not accept Winckelmann's dogmas unreservedly; his was not the type of mind to be swept away by enthusiasm. Unlike the archaeologist, he was not an aesthetic man; his genius appeared in sharp definition and distinction, not in empathy. While his most important work of criticism drew its title from the Laocoön, the statue afforded him an apt example for the demonstration of a thesis; it was not, as for so many others, the concretion of an ideal. His rejection, in *Laokoon*, of entire schools of painting, like the Dutch, and of all descriptive poetry hardly indicates particular aesthetic sensitivity. When Lessing visited Rome, nine years after the appearance of *Laokoon* in 1766, he did not devote a line to the famous statue; it is not clear that he even saw it.[1] Antiquity played the role of a corrective for the follies and sentimentalities of his own time: thus he wrote (forgetting Haemon in the *Antigone*) that no Greek or Roman youth would have taken his own life for love, as Goethe's poor Werther had done.[2] Nor could he share in the belief that modern men, by emulating the Greeks, might bring forth another Hellas. In his view of the drama, especially of the tragedy of course, he stood firmly for Sophocles and Aristotle (and Shakespeare) against French neoclassicism; but not for Winckelmannian reasons.

If Lessing was by no means an orthodox Christian,[3] he was still less a pagan.[4] Profoundly rational though he was, he preferred a consistently fundamentalist Christianity to a shallow or inconsequent rationalism. The question of his own religious belief is a vexed one, and it is not completely clear, for instance, just what his motives were in editing the *Fragments* of the radical deist H. S. Reimarus. He owed much to Spinoza, still more to Leibniz. Basically he seems to have believed in a "Christianity of reason," a religion to which the element of the miraculous is irrelevant and in which all thought of rewards or punishments has been discarded. In *Nathan the Wise* (1779) the concept of active, committed loving-kindness is central; in *The Education of Mankind* (1780), that of a third religion, superior to Judaism and Christianity, which teaches man to do good for its own sake, without fears of hell or hopes of paradise. That Lessing believed literally in the education of man by a personal god is doubtful; he liked to express himself in parables and fables.

Yet Lessing, neither aesthete nor pagan, gave aesthetic paganism one of its most effective beliefs: in the conclusion of his essay "How the Ancients Represented Death" (1769) [5] he stated that the Greek symbol of death as a beautiful youth was preferable by far to the repulsive skeleton of medieval art. Here he appears as the heir and continuer of Winckelmann: the classical symbol is regarded as nobler, more dignified, and more comely than the Christian.

Before examining Lessing's treatment of this theme, we should first briefly consider one or two of his other works. Although the doctrine of noble simplicity [6] plays a minor part in his earlier criticism, he did not really come to grips with Winckelmann until he began his studies for *Laokoon*. For several years he planned a work which was to establish the boundaries between the spatial arts (sculpture and painting) and poetry, which operates in time. After the project was well under way, he decided to use the statue of Laocoön for his prime example and his title. The choice was an excellent one, for Winckelmann's description had drawn the attention of the public to the work of art, which in any case had been renowned since the Renaissance. Winckelmann had argued that the dignified calm of the statue, in contrast to the unrestrained expressiveness of Vergil's description, was an example of the canonical superiority of the Greeks to the Romans. Lessing retorted that the reason for the differing treatment lay in the very nature of the arts involved, not in any intrinsic Hellenic supremacy. The sculptor was bound by the "law of beauty," which ancient artists always observed: "Neither rage nor despair disfigures any of their works." [7] The poet was not thus constrained, and was free to express realistically the tortures of the dying priest.

Lessing's central arguments are familiar, and are in any case only tangential to our theme. (Winckelmann had himself corrected his early interpretation of the Laocoön two years before Lessing's book appeared, thus anticipating its major thesis, though he did not systematically define the boundaries between the arts.[8]) In his treatment of sculpture and painting, Lessing followed the archaeologist faithfully: the fine arts must depict the beautiful; their highest subject is the human form. Like Winckelmann, he believed that there was in Greece a reciprocal relation [9] between human beauty and the beauty of art. For Lessing too the Greeks are a highly cultured, ethically superior people. His Hellenes however are not stoically calm; they are human as well as humane; they express their emotions naturally and openly. "Only the cultivated Greeks can weep and be brave at the same time," [10] he maintained. Similarly, the king in Lessing's brief tragedy *Philotas* (1759) stated: "I am a human being; I like to laugh and weep." [11] This sentiment is very much in line with Lessing's own beliefs; indeed, he held that Stoic tragedy was a contradiction in terms. His Greeks are as humane as the characters of Goethe's *Iphigenia* or as Mozart's Egyptian priests. They are more obviously typical of the eighteenth century than are Winckelmann's.

For a few years, perhaps in conscious rivalry with Winckelmann, Lessing devoted much of his great energy to the study of ancient art and archaeology. They never, however, were remotely as important to him as to the historian of art. He described them to a friend as "one more hobby, to shorten life's journey." [12] In the course of these studies Lessing became involved in a bitter controversy with a productive and fertile popularizer, the once-renowned Christian Adolf Klotz, which centered on the question of how ancient artists had portrayed potentially terrifying or repulsive subjects, like the Furies and death.[13] Its one lasting result was Lessing's essay on the latter theme.

As so often in the history of German Hellenism, the original spark of the new idea had been struck by Winckelmann. In his "Explanation of the Thoughts on the Imitation of Greek Works" he had written that the Greeks avoided all terrifying subjects in major works of art, but he did mention a gem on which death was shown dancing to the music of a flute.[14] Later, in his treatise on allegory, he described a gravestone portraying the figure of sleep as a young Genius with torch reversed, with his brother death.[15] Generally, he maintained, allegorical figures should be attractive.

For his part, Lessing held that when skeletons appeared in ancient art, they did not represent death. Klotz, with typical heedlessness, "refuted" Lessing by listing instances of the mere occurrence of skeletons; this of course did not bear on the debate. It is not surprising that mistakes were made by both parties,[16] and the archaeological correctness of their arguments is no longer a matter of much weight. What does concern us, and greatly concerned the poets and writers of the time, is the conclusion set forth by Lessing in his last three paragraphs:

it is a fact that the religion which first revealed to man that even natural death is the fruit and wages of sin necessarily magnified the terrors of death infinitely. There have been sages who thought life a punishment; but to think death a punishment could, without Revelation, occur to no person who used his reason alone.

From this point of view, then, it was presumably our religion which expelled the old serene image of death from the precincts of art! But since that same religion did not intend to reveal that dreadful truth for our despair, since it too assures us that the death of the pious can only be gentle and consoling, I do not see what should prevent our artists from abandoning the hideous skeleton and again availing themselves of that better image. Scripture itself speaks of an angel of death; and what artist ought not rather to aim at portraying an angel than a skeleton?

Only misunderstood religion can lead us away from the beautiful; and it is evidence of true religion rightly understood if in all cases it guides us back to the beautiful.[17]

Death, to enlightened men, must appear dignified, even beautiful. Like Herder after him, Lessing implies a sharp distinction between a barbarous, "superstitious" aspect of Christianity ("misunderstood religion") and the "Christianity of reason." The sarcasm directed at a revelation which leads men to consider death an evil is hardly veiled. Only a religion which can be fused with classical beauty is worthy of an enlightened age.

II

While Lessing did not and could not write with the fervor of a Winckelmann, his demand that religion guide mankind back to the beautiful was widely heard. Goethe testified to the impact on his own generation:

we thought that we had been delivered from all evil and believed that we had the right to look down with some pity on the sixteenth century, splendid though it was in other respects, when German artists and poets knew how to represent life only in the form of a fool decked out with bells, death in the monstrous form of a rattling skeleton . . .

Most of all we were delighted by the beauty of the thought that the Ancients acknowledged death as the brother of sleep and formed both of them alike to the point of confusing them, as is proper with twin brothers. In this theme we could now really celebrate the triumph of beauty in lofty terms, and banish ugliness of every kind — since after all it cannot be driven out of the world — to the low level of the ridiculous in the realm of art.[18]

Only properly attuned spirits, Goethe continued, could grasp the splendor of such ideas, but on them the effect was "infinite."[19] One of these spirits was Herder, who devoted an essay to Lessing's theme, even using his title.[20] While he doubted that the Greek attitude to death was as serene as Lessing and Winckelmann believed — he rightly cited the importance of euphemism — he gladly accepted the image which they proposed. "Thus our last friend is no horrifying specter, but an ender of life, the lovely youth who puts out the torch and imposes calm on the billowing sea."[21] Dying may well appear dreadful, even in Greek art; rest in the grave, symbolized by the two beautiful youths, is not.[22] Rather startlingly, he maintained that the classical image was not heathen and could be used in Christian churches, for it was Christ who had really transformed death into sleep.[23] With the growth of superstition and the increasing influence of the gloomy Northern way of thinking, the "plebeian" concepts of death as a skeleton, of time with his scythe and hourglass, and so on, had gained power over men's imaginations.[24] Again, medieval Christianity is contrasted to a serene, reasonable faith.

When Herder wove references to the myth of Amor and Psyche into his essay,[25] he anticipated, in a tentative way, the romantic equation of love and death. Sleep kissing the soul is an image of dying. It was natural for his interpretation to take this turn; the winged figures on ancient monuments and gravestones often suggested cupids rather than sleep or death. In his paramyth (Herder's term for a didactic variation on an original myth) "Death: A Conversation at Lessing's

Grave," the figure of love states that he is called death by
mortals.[26] His duty is gently to free the soul from the body
and guide it upwards "to the true enjoyment of nuptial delights." The myth is Christianized, but one dimly hears the
Liebestod motif as well.[27] Novalis and Friedrich Schlegel,[28]
to say nothing of Wagner, were to develop it in a way which
Herder could not have foreseen.

The boldest statement of the theme of death as a beautiful
youth is found in Schiller's "The Gods of Greece." That
poem, an outspokenly polemical declaration of the new paganism, will be discussed more fully later; but one strophe, with
its harsh juxtaposition of hideous skeleton and gentle Genius,
should be quoted here:

> Damals trat kein grässliches Gerippe
> Vor das Bett des Sterbenden. Ein Kuss
> Nahm das letzte Leben von der Lippe,
> Seine Fackel senkt' ein Genius.
> Selbst des Orkus strenge Richterwage
> Hielt der Enkel einer Sterblichen,
> Und des Thrakers seelenvolle Klage
> Rührte die Erinnyen.[29]

Schiller of course knew that things were not really so simple,
and so pretty, in ancient life. His epigram in the *Xenia* tellingly contrasts reality and the aesthetic myth:

> Lieblich sieht er zwar aus mit seiner erloschenen Fackel;
>   Aber, ihr Herren, der Tod ist so ästhetisch doch nicht.[30]

The former medical student, who had written that hunger
and love, not philosophy, make the world go round,[31] could
not completely repress his knowledge of the facts of life —
and the facts of death. Yet in the same collection another
distich rejects the skeleton as a symbol of death: it is ugly.[32]
There is no real inconsistency: life and art are separate realms,
governed by very different laws.

While Schiller sharply opposed the classical to the Christian
view of death, Goethe, in *Hermann and Dorothea*, tried to

reconcile them. The pastor in that very domestic epic argues
that both the wise and the pious can face the thought of death
without dread:

> Des Todes rührendes Bild steht
> Nicht als Schrecken dem Weisen, und nicht als
> Ende dem Frommen.
> Jenen drängt es ins Leben zurück and lehret ihn handeln;
> Diesem stärkt es, zu künftigem Heil, im Trübsal die Hoffnung:
> Beiden wird zum Leben der Tod.[33]

Here Goethe wrote in the spirit of Herder's "Christian
humanism." In other moods he could be even more polemical
than Schiller.

Inevitably, Schiller's poem provoked protests and versified
refutations. The first really telling retort was made by Novalis
in the fifth of his "Hymns to Night" (1800).[34] Novalis begins
the poem with a brilliant picture of Hellenic culture at its
height. Life was an "eternally bright festival" celebrated by
gods and men. The wine tasted sweeter, for there was "a god
in the grapes," and love itself was an ecstatic tribute to the
most beautiful of goddesses. Everyone revered the delicate,
various flame of life as the supreme gift.

But one dreaded figure threatened the Greek idyl: shifting
suddenly into verse, the poet invokes a force against which
even the gods are helpless:

> Es war der Tod, der dieses Lustgelag
> Mit Angst und Schmerz und Tränen unterbrach.[35]

He praises the gallantry of the ancients in representing death
as beautiful and gentle:

> Ein sanfter Jüngling löscht das Licht und ruht —
> Sanft wird das Ende, wie ein Wehn der Harfe.[36]

Yet this gallantry is in vain; it does not render death less sad
or enigmatic. The Olympian world disappears; nature becomes lifeless; faith and poetry depart.

Novalis has challenged the Olympian religion at its weakest

point; portraying death as beautiful is indeed a dusty answer
to the anxious questions of man. As a Christian, Novalis could
reply by weaving into his myth the birth and resurrection
of Christ, born, as the fifth Hymn puts it, in "the poetic hut
of poverty," among a despised people. The ending of his
poem is devoted to the ascension of Christ, of the Virgin,
and of all mankind. Sorrow and death are forever banished;
the hymn closes triumphantly, with a fusing of erotic and
cosmic imagery:

> Nur *eine* Nacht der Wonne —
> *Ein* ewiges Gedicht —
> Und unser aller Sonne
> Ist Gottes Angesicht.[87]

In a few pages Novalis has expressed his whole philosophy
of history. As if to pay a final tribute to the vanquished
world of the Greeks, he included the myth of a poet, "born
under the serene sky of Hellas," who went to Palestine to
glorify the infant Christ, and then traveled joyously to India,
where he continued to sing ecstatically of the new gospel.

Despite Novalis' eloquence, the image of the beautiful
youth did not vanish from German literature or art. Death
appears in that form, appropriately, on Winckelmann's memorial in Trieste.[88] In the nineteenth century the Genius
figures in Lenau's "Ziska," [89] and, in Christianized form, in
Eichendorff's "Twilight of the Gods." [40] Characteristically,
Heine gave a realistic twist to the tradition: in his poem
"Morphine" the brother who represents sleep is also the pro-
vider of opiates, but only the other gives lasting rest. The
last lines are marked by Sophoclean pessimism:

> Gut ist der Schlaf, der Tod ist besser — freilich
> Das beste wäre, nie geboren sein.[41]

In the twentieth century the classical youth recurs, slightly
disguised, as the boy Tadzio in Thomas Mann's *Death in
Venice.*

Chapter III

Antiquity and Reason: Wieland

One of the most popular German authors of the eighteenth century, Christoph Martin Wieland (1733–1813) plays a part in the rise of aesthetic paganism which is important but not easy to define. A complex and sensitive nature, easily swayed by his enthusiasms, Wieland oscillated in his younger days between Pietistic Christianity and an Epicurean view of the world, between a seraphic cult of disembodied spirits and the fascination of the senses. Yet these seeming opposites, the religious and the erotic, both represented a departure from the heavily didactic mode of earlier rationalism. His sensibility was "modern" and had a rococo tinge: he did not advocate a return to nature — or to Hellas. He was fascinated by Greek culture and knew a great deal about it, but he was never an uncritical believer in Winckelmann's ideal.[1] Latin literature, as Goethe suggested, was more germane to his nature than Greek.[2] After a complicated, more or less dialectical development, which we must briefly trace, he reached a flexible but rather consistent position, in which elements of Horatian urbanity, Shaftesburian aestheticism, and "natural Christianity" were blended. Anything but a "Greek reborn," very much the *Aufklärer*, though by no means only that, he believed that happiness might be attained on this earth, in this life, by combining moderation, rational enjoyment, and a decent regard for the rights of others. To look down on Wieland's "shallow" eudaemonism was long fashionable. After the latest collapse of German irrationality, his countrymen have come to regard him more kindly,[3] though he is probably respected more widely than he is read.

While still a very young man, Wieland wrote religious verse in the manner of Klopstock and Bodmer. With his Pietist background and education, his orientation seems natural enough, but Wieland's early cult of virtue was so extreme that it took no great powers of divination for Lessing to sense the element of affectation in it.[4] Significantly enough, one of his earliest works was *Anti-Ovid or The Art of Love,*[5] which appeared in 1752, when he was only nineteen. (One recalls that Frederick II of Prussia wrote an "Anti-Machiavelli" shortly before he inherited the throne; then he rapidly put Machiavellian policies into effect.) Before too long, the young poet would shift from a "Platonic" to a very earthy point of view; the interest in erotic matters runs through his work as a whole. In the early 1760's Wieland changed from one of the most edifying to one of the most voluptuous of contemporary writers; his vein becomes that of the younger Crébillon rather than of Klopstock. He did not long continue, however, to write in the vein of his saucy, and at times rather luscious, *Comic Tales* (1765); he was searching for a middle ground of his own. The story of that search is told symbolically in his novel *Agathon* (1766), his first important work. Typically, Wieland found it necessary twice to revise the book [6] before expressing his final convictions in his later philosophical novel, *Agathodämon* (1799).

At this point, Wieland should be defended against two charges which have been all too often raised against him. That his moral and philosophic convictions shift radically, in the various versions of *Agathon* as elsewhere, is no sign of insincerity, but of the reverse. He was the child of an age of transition; emotional and rationalistic impulses were both strong within him. Typically, copies of Voltaire and Bayle were smuggled into the pious seminary, Klosterbergen, where he received most of his education.[7] Like Goethe after him, he admitted that he could be influenced by his surroundings, like a chameleon;[8] but it would be simple-minded to take this image too literally. Wieland's life was largely taken up with the attempt, at least partially successful, to reconcile opposing forces in his own psyche.

Second, it is perfectly clear that Wieland devotes much attention and skill to depicting erotic matters. His characteristic love scene is a seduction, attempted or successful. What is *not* clear is the old charge that Wieland dwelt on amorous matters because he was a low fellow who enjoyed pandering to the "Frenchified" tastes of salacious readers. It would seem a fairer inference that he found sex, especially sexual temptations, an important part of life — particularly of the life of young people. He represents it as such in a long series of narrative poems, and in his novels. (It is at least conceivable, also, that he deliberately employed erotic scenes to make his philosophical novels more readable.)

Characteristically his descriptions have the voluptuous charm of a Boucher;[9] often there is an arch, teasing quality which seems very rococo. Wieland's characters are keenly aware of their senses, but they are rarely morbidly so. Once he had seen the impossibility of a completely "ethereal" love, he vindicated the importance of the physical kind; but Wieland rarely let his readers forget that both the spirit and the body are essential. In a famous line Schiller was to limit man's choice to the harsh alternatives of sensual pleasure and spiritual peace — *Sinnenglück und Seelenfrieden*. Wieland recognizes the tension between the two but tries to unite them in a viable relationship. In his most charming works, *Musarion* and *Oberon*, he succeeds in convincingly showing such a synthesis. During the Storm and Stress period he was attacked for not depicting sexual matters with "antique directness."[10] But neither antique directness nor Storm and Stress coarseness was his forte.

Once he reached maturity, Wieland appears as one of the most sensible of men, so rational that he recognized the importance of an irrational "x," a *je ne sais quoi*, in life. Here, one suspects, is a reason for his lifelong preoccupation with sexual matters. In the reasonable world of the eighteenth century they represented a dynamic, exciting, unpredictable element; to Wieland perhaps the most fascinating aspect of the poetic. (He was not a complete aesthete in Winckelmann's sense, though he had a considerable sensitivity to art; and while he describes landscapes with great charm and skill, he did not share in the Rousseauistic raptures about nature.) After his marriage he had a very stable, possibly even a staid existence, but this did not decrease in his eyes the importance of the erotic. Love in his works is an ordeal linked with danger; it cannot be evaded. Even the exemplary hero and heroine of his *Oberon* are tempted, fall, and undergo punishment before the romance can reach the happy ending toward which it obviously and inevitably moves.

It is suggestive that hetaerae play a central part in several of Wieland's major works.[11] He was clearly fascinated by the notion of women who were cultivated and intelligent as well as beautiful and untrammeled by convention. It is true however that Danaë and Laïs, the two most notable courtesans who appear in his work, do not achieve complete happiness: Laïs even comes to a bad end.[12] In the abstract — and when he was writing prose, so to speak — Wieland felt that woman's proper role was that of faithful wife and dutiful mother.[13] Yet the most attractive of his heroines, Musarion, is no bourgeois; she combines freedom and culture, and is far from conventional though essentially virtuous.[14] She is an ideal in whom the traits the poet most valued are wishfully combined.

Like many other works of Wieland, *Agathon* is set in ancient Greece: in this case, in the fourth century B.C. Here as elsewhere the Hellenic element is largely one of costume and mask. To a great extent, Agathon represents Wieland himself, torn between sentimentality and metaphysical enthusiasm on the one hand and hedonistic materialism on the other. (These elements appear in the novel as Platonism and the Epicureanism of the sophist Hippias, respectively.) Agathon, a very soulful young man, undergoes a process of development or *Bildung*; he is in fact a forerunner of Goethe's Wilhelm Meister. Agathon's psychology is what seems to interest Wieland most: he is self-conscious and indulges in many long speeches of self-analysis. Yet it would be wrong to write off the Greek aspect completely. *Agathon* is no historical novel, but Wieland may well have sensed an affinity between late Hellenic culture and his own time.[15] As Emil Staiger says, he probably knew more than Goethe or Hölderlin about classical antiquity.[16] In intention at least the novel presents two worlds: Agathon's own, and beyond that, for the perceptive reader, the eighteenth century. In this, as in its irony and its playing with antitheses, it anticipates to some extent a work like Thomas Mann's *Joseph and His Brothers*.

Essentially it is a book about religious attitudes or at least about the proper *Weltanschauung* for a sensitive and intelligent young man. Agathon gradually liberates himself from a sentimental and ascetic philosophy which is essentially a metaphor for Pietist Christianity; to that extent the book has a pagan aspect. Yet he finds that hedonism and materialism are still less satisfactory. The thrust of the book is toward a third position, a golden mean, a fusion of ethical and aesthetic elements. Agathon's emotional development is parallel; he first loves, spiritually, the appropriately named Psyche, who turns out to be his sister; later the golden-hearted hetaera Danaë becomes his mistress. Their love is by no means merely sensual; Danaë has reformed under its impact; and it seems quite likely that Wieland once planned to have the two marry, though the matter is left open. (In the later versions, Danaë finds it necessary that they renounce such hopes and maintain a purely "Platonic" relation.)

Rather boldly Wieland presented the ex-courtesan Danaë as a "beautiful soul," intellectually and aesthetically gifted, as well as in the art of living. From his reading of Shaftesbury he had drawn a new ideal, neither seraphic nor frivolous.[17] He found in it a salutary stress on self-knowledge and moderation and a warning against empty speculation. The harmony of moral, intellectual, and physical beauty in the notion of the virtuoso who has developed all his powers attracted him equally. As far removed from fanaticism as from cynicism, Shaftesbury championed an enlightened enthusiasm to which Wieland could respond. A true son of the *Aufklärung*, Shaftesbury believed that man could abandon dogma and superstition without sacrificing the cardinal virtues of "natural Christianity," and that he could live a happy, harmonious, and virtuous life.

This would seem the answer to Agathon's problem, but apparently Wieland found it satisfying only in some moods. There is a certain ambiguity in Shaftesbury: how great a role does Christian virtue really play in his philosophy, dominated as it is by ideals of the Enlightenment and the Renaissance? Differently put: happiness may be harmonized with the virtues, but with which virtues? (One might expect Agathon to follow the agreeable Epicurean Aristippus after his moral liberation; rather, he becomes a protégé of Archytas, a man of the most austere morality). In reviewing an earlier work [18] of Wieland's, Lessing noted his frequent praise of Shaftesbury, and remarked: "Shaftesbury is the most dangerous enemy of religion because he is the subtlest. And if he had ever so many other good qualities — Jupiter scorned the rose in the serpent's mouth." [19] That Wieland stressed a severe morality in his last revision of *Agathon* may have derived in

part from his timidity, his fear of offending his public.[20] More
essential was the complexity of his own divided nature. Even
his admired Horace has a Stoic aspect as well as an Epicurean
one.

One should note also that *Agathon* is in part a political
novel: the hero undergoes chastening experiences at the court
of a Sicilian tyrant and elsewhere. Perhaps the philosophy of
the virtuoso suffices at best in the personal realm and one
needs a sterner creed for public life. Wieland himself was
keenly interested in politics and education as well as in the
private sphere; a purely aesthetic (or sentimental) education
did not satisfy his intellectual demands.

For all its breadth and its skill of psychological analysis,
Agathon leaves us with a sense of inconsistency: the author
is clearly none too sure about his central problem, how virtue
and happiness are to be combined.[21] He deals with the question
more successfully in the verse narrative *Musarion* (1768).
To demand profundity from this delightful work would be
breaking a butterfly upon a wheel, but the poem makes excellent sense within its modest limits. The naïve youth Phanias
deserts his love Musarion in order to devote all his energies
to learning wisdom from the conversation of a pair of preten-
tious philosophers, one a Stoic, the other a Pythagorean.
(Wieland has made things easy for himself by representing
both of them as hypocrites and boors.) Musarion follows her
faithless swain, but he scorns her as too earthy and insuffi-
ciently virtuous. Soon however both philosophers are un-
masked; it is a typically rococo note that she manages to
expose the Pythagorean's true nature by "accidentally" allow-
ing him to see her half-bared bosom. Disgusted with his
mentors, Phanias makes impetuous love to Musarion; Wieland
again is able to describe his favorite scene, an attempted
seduction. She resists him until she can be reasonably sure
that this time his love is serious. (Neither the protestations
of ethereal virtue nor sudden bursts of sensuality are to be

trusted.) The couple then retires to a sort of Sabine farm
and "lives happily ever after." Their life exemplifies the
"charming philosophy" which Musarion — and Wieland in
many moods — upheld:

> Die reizende Philosophie,
> Die, was Natur und Schicksal uns gewährt,
> Vergnügt geniesst und gern den Rest entbehrt;
> Die Dinge dieser Welt gern von der schönen Seite
> Betrachtet, dem Geschick sich unterwürfig macht,
> Nicht wissen will, was alles das bedeute,
> Was Zeus aus Huld in rätselhafte Nacht
> Vor uns verbarg . . .
> Nicht stets von Tugend *spricht*, noch von ihr sprechend, *glüht*,
> Doch, ohne Sold und aus Geschmack, sie übet.[22]

Horatian Epicureanism [23] and distrust of hypocrisy could not
satisfy Wieland completely — he was neither simple in character nor simple-minded — but they were forward steps in
the pursuit of happiness.

Vast though it is, most of Wieland's literary work is concerned with relatively few themes: the search for an ideal of
humanity combining morality and sensuous enjoyment; the
ironic treatment of human foolishness and failings of all sorts,
especially the unmasking of hypocrisy; the moral and intellectual development of young people; relations between men
and women. From the point of view of this study, it seems
defensible to leap over the writings of his middle years,[24]
even though that entails neglecting a masterpiece like the
verse romance *Oberon*. We must however pay some attention to the three highly confessional novels of his later years.
Unfortunately they show a decrease of his skill — though not
of his joy — in telling a story. They are didactic and philosophical, revealing rather directly the author's final conclusions about religion, the proper role of enjoyment in this
life, and his old question of virtue versus happiness. In the
first of them, *Peregrinus Proteus* (1791), the erotic element

is again stressed; in *Agathodämon* (1799) and *Aristippus* it has faded into the background.

Wieland had long been concerned with the element of conscious or unconscious hypocrisy in fanatic religious enthusiasm (*Schwärmerei*). In *Peregrinus Proteus*, set in a time of religious ferment, the second century A.D., he deals with a sincere fanatic.[25] The novel was suggested by Lucian's *De morte Peregrini*, which Wieland had himself translated some two years before. Peregrinus, convinced that he is a semidivine spirit or daemon, has Platonic, Gnostic, Christian, and Cynical phases, long believes in magic, and finally ends his own life by leaping into the flames, like Empedocles. As he admits, he has always missed the Aristotelian mean; he is always the dupe of his own temperament. Labile as he is, he is entangled in a number of amorous experiences; one of them is remarkably sordid. Yet he appears as no villain but basically "a good man in his dark urging," though, unlike Goethe's Faust, he is not really "aware of the right path." When, as frequently occurs, he realizes that he has been deceived, he reacts strongly against his deceivers. He is deeply attracted by a family of simple, Johannine Christians. The father of this family speaks to him very movingly of Jesus:

> Who has ever spoken with such a combination of loftiness and simplicity, so profoundly and yet so understandably, in a way so befitting God and yet so human, of heavenly and divine things? It was impossible for an unprejudiced mind to listen to him without feeling the truth of his words, or rather feeling that it was Truth itself which spoke to men in the shape of the Son of Man.[26]

Like Goethe, Wieland expressed reverence for Christ without committing himself to belief in Christian dogma or respect for the hierarchy. In fact, most of the Christians who appear in *Peregrinus Proteus* are schemers who are secretly conspiring to overthrow the Empire and set up a theocracy.[27]

Agathodämon also deals with the religious instinct, and with Christianity in particular. As noted, it is Agathodämon, not the sage Archytas of *Agathon*, who speaks for Wieland himself.[28] In the course of a long life, Agathodämon has become convinced of the dangers of the will to believe, but at the same time he holds that a religious sense, a "striving for the infinite," is inborn. Believing that the end may justify the means, he has joined a religious order which deliberately manipulates popular superstition in order to revive the old belief in the Olympian gods. This, he hopes, will lead in turn to a moral reform. Again Wieland has set his work in the period of declining paganism and rising Christianity. Again he uses the motif of the secret society: the order to which Agathodämon belongs has been responsible for the overthrow of the tyrant Domitian. Clearly, Agathodämon's religion is an instrument, not a value in itself.

His concept of Jesus is in line with the general ideas of the Enlightenment: "one of the best mortals who ever lived." [29] The Resurrection is explained rationalistically. Although Jesus perhaps deceived Himself, He was no hypocrite. He made the Jewish national god humane and universal. Indeed, if the ethics of Christianity were applied, earth would become a heaven.[30] Jesus was not really interested in matters of dogma, and what he called "belief" was "not comprehending, but catching hold of [*nicht Begreifen sondern Ergreifen*] the element which cannot be comprehended." [31] Unfortunately but inevitably, a hierarchy is springing up,[32] superstition and belief in mysteries are growing. Agathodämon prophesies the rise of a very powerful priestly caste and of the cult of saints.[33] The Christian theocracy is certainly not the expected "kingdom of God," but at least it will civilize the barbarians.[34]

For his own part, Agathodämon holds that a man should not follow Jesus "slavishly" but work out his own salvation.[35] His personal belief includes an intuition of infinite oneness, of a "general spirit of nature" or a "universal father." [36] In other words, he reaches beyond the evidence of his senses toward a sort of pantheism.[37] Probably he speaks for Wieland when he states that while he cannot discuss these matters with precision, he does not doubt that there is a certain religious reality.

Wieland's last novel, *Aristippus*, has two main aspects. Primarily it is a philosophical discussion, combining praise of Socrates' life and death, an attack on Plato, especially on the *Republic*, and a sympathetic presentation of the Epicurean Aristippus and his beliefs. Much of this novel in letters is concerned with the career of the hetaera Laïs. Wieland studies her character in very interesting detail, but he is no longer fascinated by her profession and does not exploit the opportunity of presenting voluptuous scenes. In his treatment of Plato, Wieland again rejects metaphysical speculation and religious fanaticism and also the totalitarian aspects of the *Republic*. Two forms of the good life are represented: the moral heroism of Socrates and the enlightened Epicureanism of Aristippus. Aristippus is rewarded with a happy marriage at the end of the book. When Wieland has him name his daughter Arete (virtue), the seal of the author's approval is evident.

To a large extent, Wieland did finally achieve the synthesis for which he had sought so long. The oscillations of the earlier works are not characteristic of the late novels. In an oration delivered after Wieland's death, Goethe well spoke of the union of morality and sensuousness, of intelligence, moderation, and joy in life, which characterized the older writer.[38] It has been pointed out that the classical authors guided him to a "serene and measured affirmation of natural, sensuous existence." [39] To use the possibly ironic phrase of the Declaration of Independence, Wieland believed in the pursuit of happiness; he did not pretend that the chase was easy. Rather harmoniously he united the ethics of (partly Christianized) Horatian enjoyment with the general philosophy of the Enlightenment. Like Lessing, he transcended that philosophy in some of his late works. Of the two ideal figures of his last novel, Socrates represents man in a state of almost unique perfection; Aristippus, the norm for human beings who are not heroes but have taste, good will, and intelligence. Goethe stated that Aristippus spoke for Wieland,[40] and Goethe was in a position to know.

Chapter IV

The Greeks and History: Herder

Johann Gottfried Herder is remembered above all as one of the great initiators of a truly historical attitude toward the past. Each age, he believed, must be judged by its own standards; each national culture has its unique, incomparable value. Life on this planet is a triumphant progress — "the movement of God through history" — toward the highest possible development of man's total powers, his *Humanität*. Thus one would expect Herder to be keenly interested in the attainments of the ancient peoples, but to want no part of a cult of classical superiority, still less of any doctrine of imitation.

Herder's mind, however, was large, complex, and various; consistency was no hobgoblin of his. A series of paradoxes underlies his views of history and of life. He held that each age was in a sense equally valuable — though in Rousseauistic moods he thought his own time shockingly decadent — but he nevertheless espoused the notion of progress. Christian though he was, his stress on *Humanität* inevitably deflected men's eyes from the other world; thus the Catholic poet Eichendorff could write that he contributed to the "artificial paganism" of the nineteenth century.[1] Undoubtedly there was much of the aesthete in Herder, as his admirable translations and his gift of "empathetic" criticism bear witness,[2] but he was never able fully to develop his sensuous side; it appears in his essay on plastic art and, infrequently, in a few other

passages. Indeed, his final break with the classicism of Goethe
and Schiller was based largely on the conviction that his
Weimar colleagues had become too aesthetic, too pagan. He
could denounce the imitation of Greek models with all the
violence of the Storm and Stress, but he never completely
overcame his predilection for Greece, the "beautiful youth"
among the family of nations. To Herder, as to so many
others, the concepts of Greece and of paganism were interrelated, though by no means identical. The story of his relation to paganism is largely that of his reaction to Winckelmann's ideas.

As a young man, Herder read Winckelmann's works with
a particular devoutness and fervor. Like Rousseau's, they
conjured up the vision of a golden age: "I read them with a
feeling like a youth's on a lovely morning, like the letter
of a far-distant bride, from a happy time that is past." [3]
Herder's early days, spent in East Prussia (where he was
born in 1744) and Livonia, were almost as cramped as
Winckelmann's had been; he too heard the message of youth
and beauty in the desolate North. Before he was twenty-one,
he had read the *History of Ancient Art*, a rather bulky work,
seven times.[4] Winckelmann's unique enthusiasm and the
beauty and force of his style helped to make the book one
of Herder's decisive cultural experiences. From his teacher
Hamann, the "magus of the North," he had learned very
different lessons: the importance of the primitive element in
poetry, the viciousness of all "imitation," the value of the
Biblical tradition over against the Greek. Soon he would place
Ossian on the same lofty height as Homer. Doubts of Winckelmann's accuracy as a historian arose very early.[5] Before long
Herder turned the historical method adumbrated in the *History
of Ancient Art* against its author: since Greek culture arose
under special conditions, and had blossomed, decayed, and
died, it was futile to talk of reviving or imitating it.[6] But the
impression made by Winckelmann could never be effaced;

the Greeks remain eternal models of beauty, and later, in Herder's "classical" period, of *Humanität*.

In Herder's first significant book, the *Fragments concerning Recent German Literature* (1766–1767), Greece plays a central role. After a description, still somewhat rococo in tone, of Arcadian life in that "temple and grove of lovely nature,"[7] comes the call for another Winckelmann to write the history of Greek literature and philosophy. In those realms too, he implies, the Hellenes stood first. Logically, then, he proceeds to measure a series of contemporary German writers against comparable Greek poets. Greece is closely allied with nature in his eyes; ancient life was more spacious, ancient mores were more genuine. Thus Theocritus is freer and more natural than Gessner; Herder hints, but does not state, that he is far greater. Throughout, Herder avoids a moralizing approach. The Greeks are the criteria but not the models: an authentic history of Greek thought, based on a careful study of local and national factors, would "make accessible the fountain of good taste and free us from wretched imitators of the Greeks."[8] The last is the characteristic Herderian twist: the study of the past proves that no duplication of its achievements is possible, but we may and should vie with them.

In a later revision, doubts about Greek hegemony begin to appear. Ancient history is obscure; "the Greeks alone shine out from this night."[9] Willy-nilly, we see all of antiquity through Greek eyes; it is inevitable but unjust.[10] Led by these considerations to question the legitimacy of the current revival of Hellenism, Herder exclaims, in his characteristically ejaculatory manner: "God of our Neo-Greeks, art thou the far-seeing Greek Apollo, or a Baal?"[11]

A famous speculative passage deals with the question of what the Greek tradition would have meant to modern culture if it had reached us directly, without the intermediacy of Latin and the later Romance tongues.[12] Implied value

judgments begin to emerge: Greece, allied to nature — and
later to Shakespeare, Ossian, and the folk song — is good; the
Latin-French-neoclassic tradition is relatively bad.[13] Three
years later he would contrast Homeric simplicity and directness in sexual matters with the Augustan decorum of Vergil:
the Roman, dealing in ambiguities and sly hints ("They enter
the same cave") is actually less moral.[14]

In one of the *Fragments* Herder takes up the theme of
mythology,[15] to which he was to return again and again
throughout his career. He challenges the views of Christian
Adolf Klotz, who maintained that all the classical myths were
based on error and superstition. Herder concedes this; he
agrees that the Greek and Latin tales must not be endued, in
our time, with religious meaning.[16] Yet they have a double
value: they are beautiful in themselves and their study may
enable modern man to invent myths of his own.[17]

Herder's insight into the nature of myth was sharpened by
the experiences of his long sea journey of 1769 from the
Baltic to the northern coast of France. He heard the songs
and tales of the sailors, noted their beliefs and above all their
dependence on the unpredictable whims of wind and ocean.
Identifying himself with a Greek voyager, he felt that primitive sailors must have sensed in every incident the intervention
of higher powers.[18] Later in his *Journal of My Voyage*, in
sketching out his elaborate plans for the reform of education
in Livonia, he returns to the theme of myth. Greek mythology
is only one among hundreds, he conceded, but because of its
intrinsic interest it must be included in the plan of study. Not
that the pupils, in an enlightened age, should be led to belief
in the ancient tales: "one can't do too much to destroy the
merely fabulous element in mythology . . . it's unbearable.
But as poetry, as art, as national manner of thought, as phenomenon of the human spirit . . . it's great, divine, instructive! " [19]

A second volume of essays, the *Critical Forests*, continues and broadens Herder's discussion of the myth and its uses. In a consideration of various issues raised in Lessing's *Laokoon*, Herder treats the "law" laid down by Winckelmann and followed by Lessing, that the representation of beauty is the proper aim of the artist. It was, says Herder, the major but by no means the only aim of the Greeks. The dominant figure in a Greek work of art must be beautiful, but subordinate ones may be frightful and even repulsive.[20] Similarly, the "mythic circle" is centered on beauty; in art, the Olympian gods are stylized in the direction of harmony and repose. Yet, Herder is quick to add, "blessed peace" in itself does not suffice to form a myth; there must be action, *élan*.[21]

By a rather indirect route, Herder has reached the position of regarding all of Greek mythology as a unified, integrated work of art.[22] He notes also that, because of its beauty, it is the most suitable for depicting the "sensuous part of religion." [23] Above all, a truly mythical figure is no mere allegory; it is concrete and real. The Greek experienced a statue of Bacchus *as the god*, intuitively, not as a figure with various physical attributes whose meanings had to be puzzled out.[24] When artists use the myth, they become poets; its figures bring a dynamic element into works of sculpture and painting.

Another essay in the *Critical Forests* continues Herder's attack on Klotz. That mythophobic critic had sanctioned the use of a few elegant classical references in poetry — like the substitution of Ceres for bread — "for these words have already lost their mythological power." [25] Of course this is precisely the type of mythical reference which Herder objects to. He points out that the whole question of a later writer's use of Greco-Latin tales is a highly complex one; Milton's procedure he warmly defends. In every case, aesthetic criteria must decide, not religious or philosophical considerations. On the vexed question of the use of Christian myths, Herder notes that the Bible was not intended for illustration by artists: "the most perfect has no image." [26]

Unsuited for representation in the plastic arts, the Judeo-Christian tradition has a compensating advantage in literature. In the evocation of "wisdom, power, majesty, everything lofty and so to speak incomprehensible in the godhead," Oriental poets, especially the authors of the Old Testament, far surpassed the classical writers.[27]

Klotz's suggestion that Christ be represented in the manner of the Apollo Belvedere is ironically noted.[28] Herder tried the reverse method in his ode "Laocoön's Head!" (1768); he employed the *interpretatio Christiana* and had the priest, a symbol of suffering humanity, welcomed by angels upon his ascension to heaven.[29] The poem is not a success; Herder's practice, as so often, proved inferior to his theory.

Increasingly, in Herder's later work, his concept of Greek myth becomes more suggestive. It is humane, as well as beautiful, beyond all others, presenting "the content of humanism in the form of beauty," as Fritz Strich well puts it.[30] Man can experience the spirit only through physical forms: hence the vast importance of the myth, which reconciles spirit and body.[31] Perhaps the absence of plastic art in Hebrew culture was a factor which made Herder, fascinated though he was by the poetry of the Bible, turn back to the Greeks again and again. Without physical beauty there can be no full *Humanität*. Whereas a "national" or Nordic myth corresponded better with Herder's theories of history, Greek mythology (and the myth of Greece) attracted him as no others could.

Thus Herder formed a vivid and useful concept of what Greek myth had meant; he realized however that it no longer could sustain religious belief. He was no Hölderlin or Stefan George, who could expect the return of Dionysus or Apollo. He maintained furthermore that Christianity was on the whole too abstract, too exalted, to furnish proper "mythic" material.[32] Perhaps as a Roman Catholic he might have held differently, but he was a Protestant of the Protestants, as his

reactions to Rome were to show. He is one of the most perceptive of the many Germans, from Winckelmann to the
present, who have sensed the unique usefulness of myth.
While he recommends, in a late essay, the employment of
Nordic myths [33] and wrote didactic "paramyths" himself, his
"quest for myth," to use Richard Chase's helpful phrase, was
not characterized by the urgency of a Friedrich Schlegel or a
Nietzsche. Perhaps he was too much the son of the Enlightenment for that. By no means a pagan himself, Herder prepared
the way for the paganism of his successors by describing persuasively what the impact of the myth, especially of the Greek
myth, had been and might be again. He forged a weapon
which others put to uses he neither foresaw nor approved.
This indeed was the general and melancholy fate of Herder's
most influential ideas. One of the great founders of modern
nationalism, he would have loathed the forms which nationalism took in the nineteenth and twentieth centuries. [34] Similarly,
though he was one of the first to think historically, he would
have abhorred a "historicism" which refrains from all moral
judgments.

This is not the place to deal at length with Herder's reactions to the myth of Greece during his career; a considerable
literature already exists on the subject. [35] A few key ideas
recur like leitmotivs: Greece is the "beautiful youth" in the
development of mankind; Greece represents one of the highest
points in all of human history; Greek culture must always
be emulated, never copied; the Greek statues are a symbol,
perhaps the most beautiful symbol, of fully achieved *Humanität*. Several of Herder's later works bear, however, on
the matter of aesthetic paganism, and should be treated in
some detail.

From this point of view Herder's essay "On Plastic Art"
is highly revealing. Not published until 1778, it was mainly
written in the creative years which brought forth the *Fragments* and the *Critical Forests*. It owes much to Herder's

examination of Greek statues at Versailles and in the Mannheim Hall of Antiquities, and still more to Winckelmann.[36]
Avowedly, Herder's main aim was to distinguish the principles governing painting on the one hand and sculpture on the
other; but the implications of his essay go much further.

As the title implies, the center of Herder's treatise concerns
sculpture, which means, in this context, Greek sculpture.
This art, being three-dimensional, appeals primarily to the
sense of touch, he argues, whereas painting depends on sight.
Being essentially tactile, statues are extraordinarily real, while
a painting is "a dream of a dream." [37] The sculptor himself
must have the sense of intimate corporeal contact with his
subject: "woe to the sculptor . . . of Hercules . . . who
never felt the breast, the back of Hercules at least in his
dreams." [38] Dealing with "forms . . . as uniform and eternal
as simple, pure, human nature," sculpture transcends time and
is beyond history.[39] In this sense the Greeks are canonical.
Their statues represent archetypes and norms of human
beauty. He anticipates his later thesis that Hellenic statues
are concretions, as it were, of the spirit of *Humanität*. Here
Herder accepts one of the central beliefs of the myth of
Greece; his debt to Winckelmann is obvious. As Winckelmann had done before him, he gives an account of the characteristic beauties of the various parts of the body.[40] He describes
various features and organs with fervid eloquence, expressing
his regret that he cannot speak as frankly as the archaeologist
did. Yet he cannot accept the doctrine of classical repose
without strong reservations; the human body must express
striving, not the stasis of perfection.[41]

Nowhere else does Herder appear as pagan, or nearly
pagan, as in this work; a sensuous element in his personality
appears, which he generally repressed in his other works.
There is of course an inherent sensuality in his emphasis on
feeling or touch, and Herder implies an almost physical bond
between sculptor and statue, statue and viewer. "The *slender*

body, the rounded knee, the tender hip, the grape of the youthful breast" [42] are the very essence of the sculptor's art. Herder is quick to add that naked statues do not stir lust, as paintings of the nude may well do; in a most unpagan sentence, he objects to "Last Judgments full of flesh, like hay." [43] Rubens was not for him.

Like many another admirer of the ancients, Herder combines his praise of Greek life with a polemic against his own time. The noble nudity of classical statues is contrasted to the corsets and stays of the eighteenth century. Yet he is emphatic in his statement that Greece is dead; it cannot be revived. The Greeks could love youths and boys innocently and joyfully; today such relationships are impossible. [44] Greek youths could consider gods and heroes "their ancestors, their equals." [45] Today, not even the edict of an absolute despot could reinstitute Hellenic *paideia*: "Set up Greek statues so that every dog pisses on them and still you won't give the slave who passes them every day, the ass who drags his burden, any sense that they are there, or that they should come to resemble them." [46] With remarkable social realism, Herder has indicated the limits of what Schiller was to call aesthetic education. A Greek statue may indeed bid the individual to "change his life"; its impact on the overburdened masses, as Herder indicated, is likely to be zero. He adds an apt sarcasm about Greek statues set up around a parade ground, [47] with apparent reference to Potsdam under Frederick II. Elsewhere Herder expressed hope for a revival of the Greek spirit; the tension between his historical sense and his longing for renascence was never really resolved.

On the whole, the strength of Herder's paganism is less than overwhelming. He could praise Greek nakedness with Winckelmannian verve, but was careful to add that he did not advocate nudism in contemporary Europe. [48] Similarly, he remarked in the *Journal of My Journey* that too much chastity was as vicious as too much unchastity, [49] but the

general tone of that diary is Christian. While he interpreted
the Song of Solomon as a glorification of marital love,[50] he
nevertheless objected to too sexual a reading.[51] Often he uses
nuns or cloisters as examples of bigotry and undue asceticism.[52] He seems in effect, though not explicitly, to distinguish
between two Christianities: a religion of the vulgar, marked
by superstitions and the fear of the flesh; and a higher,
"reasonable," humane Christianity or Christian humanism.
Paganism at its best is superior to the first, but clearly inferior
to the second. (Of course some might deny the latter belief
the name of Christian.) Herder was after all the son of the
Enlightenment as well as a progenitor of romanticism.[53] Recent
German criticism, with its cult of irrationality, has done much
to obscure his provenience.

Two other essays of the year 1778 deal incisively, and rather
skeptically, with the question of Greece. A note of cultural
criticism is implied in the title of the prize essay "On the
Effect of Poetry on the Mores of the Peoples, in Ancient and
Modern Times," and Herder writes with almost Platonic
severity about the dubious role played by all poets except
the Hebrew prophets.[54] He is sharply critical of the aesthetic
life, which is typified by the Greeks. Their gods appeared
"naked, like beautiful human beings in form and also . . .
human, often too human, in action."[55] They were themselves
enormously gifted, natural and "light"[56] — an adjective expressing some praise and more blame. The "youthfulness"
which Herder had often admired now appears as a dubious
boon: that the Athenians starved during the Peloponnesian
Wars rather than giving up daily visits to the theater shows
how childish they could be.[57] The Greek addiction to ped-
erasty is briefly noted.[58] If one wishes to enter the lists for
any mythology, he concedes, then let it be the Greek.[59] But
the myths, "mere popular legend," reflect a low morality;
their effect on the religion and ethics of the people was unfortunate. For the moment, Herder has assumed the position

he deplored in Klotz's "debunking" essays. Yet he ends his discussion of the Greek culture with a brief tribute [60] worthy of Winckelmann himself. That tension between the ethical "Nazarene" and the aesthetic "Hellenic" strains which was central in Heine's view of the world is here clearly apparent in Herder's.

His "Monument to Johann Winckelmann," while highly laudatory in tone, also revolves about critical questions. What has been the effect of the recent mode of antiquity? Do we live like the ancients, or like sophists and pedants? [61] In a few studios, something of the classical spirit remains, but the rest of modern life is of a radically different nature. With heroic subjectivity, Winckelmann read his own ideas of glory, beauty, and love into "dead marble." [62] Herder shows the dubious validity of Winckelmann's ideal by having an imaginary Egyptian criticize the *lack* of repose in Greek statues. [63] At the end of the essay, he again turns to his hope of a rebirth of the Greek spirit in Germany. [64] Perhaps the spirit of Winckelmann will enter into an artist who will transform his theories into actuality and "create Greek men and Greek art for us." Only such a genius could, like Medea, magically awake the dead. In the final sentences, Herder admits his doubts of the possibility of such a revival. His eulogy is weakened, if not vitiated, by a historical skepticism he cannot repress.

Nine years later, in the section of his *Ideas toward a Philosophy of the History of Mankind* devoted to the Greeks, the historical spirit has been completely victorious. Greece is indeed the *locus classicus* of his historicism: even the loveliest flower fades. [65] Herder, doubtless in the spirit of conscious self-discipline, begins his discussion of Greek culture with an appeal to "impartial truth." [66] Greece appears as a very high point in human history, but not as an absolute, nor as a Winckelmannian myth. To be sure, the Greeks stood first in the arts, but their aesthetic achievement was part of an indivisible cultural totality; one cannot revive one aspect of their culture without the others. No Hellenic sculpture can be produced without the "superstition" which inspired it.[67] On the whole, Herder seems to deny that Greek life can or should be revived: "We wish to learn to value them properly without becoming Greeks ourselves." [68] He remains however somewhat ambivalent on this matter. Modern man appears sadder and wiser than the joyous, youthful Greeks; he should therefore read their literature while still young himself.[69] But one tremendous achievement remains: the Greeks "became what they could become." [70] By realizing their full potential they made themselves the greatest example of national self-fulfillment. To the Herder of the *Ideas*, this is the highest praise which any people can earn.

Herder's Italian journey of 1788 and 1789 provides, like Lessing's, a melancholy contrast to Goethe's. He had looked forward eagerly to it, and he may in fact have had the latent capacity to experience Rome and the South in somewhat the way Goethe did. Indeed, his report of a visit to a temple of Diana near Spoleto has a pagan ring. The inner temple had been consecrated, but, he wrote to his wife Caroline: "I climbed as though mad onto the altar, to the niche where the holy goddess had stood; she wasn't there, though; an inferior image of the Crucified stood on the altar." [71] Like the most enthusiastic of tourists, he sent Caroline a twig from the temple, a leaf picked in his first olive grove, and a sprig of laurel. He planned to make the revision of his treatise on plastic art his first Roman labor.[72] Arrived in Rome, he wrote home that he was living among statues, oblivious of the passage of time, like a man in love.[73]

But the conditions of the trip were about as unfavorable as can be imagined.[74] He was plagued by financial worries, as Goethe never was; he was annoyed at the sudden decision of his companion, F. H. von Dalberg, to include his mistress in the party, and irritated by the lady's numerous whims. His Protestant distrust of Catholic Rome soon asserted itself. He felt the city enervating and preferred Naples, but even there was a prey to homesickness and Northern melancholy.[75] During the latter part of the journey, he was distracted by the possibility of a "call" to Göttingen. Repelled by Italian mores, he lived an "ethereal" life; [76] "where everything is sensual, one becomes unsensual," [77] he reported. One senses a deliberate Northern protest and the revolt of the Nazarene against the Hellene. To some extent his attitude seems to have been influenced by resentment of the free, pagan life which his friend Goethe, according to current gossip, had lived among the artists.[78] Possibly too he felt obscurely guilty because of a "Platonic" relation between himself and the painter Angelika Kauffmann. Whatever the reasons, Herder reached a state of mind in which he violently rejected Rome, Italy, classical art, and the whole aesthetic way of life.

In a long poem, "Stanzas," he poured out his feelings. A spirit, speaking from the grove of cypress trees, tells him that he is being punished for youthful sins. The whole poem is an amazing document of gloom, resentment, and masochism. The classical South is represented by Medusas. Herder expresses his bitter thanks at their revelation that the world of ancient art is dead — and deadly:

> Dank also Euch, Ihr göttlichen Medusen,
> Die mich gelehrt, dass Ihr Medusen seid.
> Dank Euch, Ihr todten Künste, kalte Musen,
> Zerfallne Mauern, Grab der Eitelkeit.
> Wenn je dem falschen, je dem Marmorbusen,
> Statt wahren Herzen, Weihrauch ich gestreut,
> So nehmt von mir den letzten Zoll hienieden,
> Der Reue Zoll, und lasst mich ziehn in Frieden.[79]

Art, he goes on, is vain unless it is related to life; aestheticism is contrasted to true *Humanität*. Rome, both classical and contemporary, is denounced in its turn:

> Daneben sah ich, darf ich Dich auch nennen,
> Du inhumanes, alt- und neues Rom!

Doch wer wird Dich im Namen nicht schon kennen,
   Du Capitol, und Du St. Peters Dom?
Du Pfuhl, aus dem, die Erde zu verbrennen,
   Ausging ein alter und ein neuer Strom,
Von Kriegern einst bewohnt und Senatoren,
   Von Pfaffen jetzt bewohnt und Monsignoren.[80]

One involuntarily recalls Luther in Rome, or the reactions of various German romantic poets to Napoleonic Paris. This *furor Teutonicus* (*et Protestanticus*) is of course not typical of Herder, but the verses are worth discussing as representative of a recurrent German resistance to classicism which should not be underestimated. Fortunately, Herder's last comments on Greece and the classical tradition are far saner and more balanced.

The main goal of the *Humanitätsbriefe* (1793–1795) was to describe fully that ideal of complete human realization which Herder had adumbrated in the *Ideen* and elsewhere. To do that, for Herder, involved the reconciliation of the ethical with the aesthetic, and the humane with the humanistic. Again, of course, the Greeks are directly involved. All men, he argues, have an inclination toward *Humanität*; it is potentially the "character of our race." [81] To realize his potentialities, modern man needs exemplars: the Greeks remain eternal, though not perfect models.[82] Homer's standards were humane: he deplored war, and even his Achilles behaved kindly to the aged Priam.[83] Possibly the Greeks of a later day were too much devoted to aesthetic concerns; this would explain their instability in dealing with political affairs.[84]

In a later section of these *Letters*, Herder adopts the dialectical method to discuss the complex relation of the modern world to the classical tradition.[85] The first speaker takes a firmly humanistic line: all European culture is founded on the achievements of the ancients; they alone set the standards which save us from excess of all sorts. They have established the archetypal gestalten for all mankind. Then various objections are raised.[86] The Greek poets, after all, wrote without classical inspiration. Very few men have the kind of knowledge of antiquity which might make a genuine renascence possible. We tend rather to mirror ourselves, Narcissus-like, in the past.[87] (Goethe's Faust made the same point.[88]) The final synthesis is about what one would expect: the ancients should inspire, not tyrannize.[89] The innermost value of classical studies is that they lead us to "the good, the true, and the beautiful." [90] Herder reaffirms his belief in a Christian humanism somewhat reminiscent of Shaftesbury's.

Attempting further to reconcile Christianity and the classical world, Herder contrasts the original, "humane" religion of Christ to its medieval form which, after the decay of the Dark Ages, sank to the belief in radical evil.[91] (Here he appears as the ally of Goethe and Schiller against Kant, who had recently posited an absolutely evil element in human nature. This was too much for the men of Weimar: in Goethe's forceful if inelegant phrase, Kant seemed to them to have "beslobbered his philosopher's cloak.") [92] "Decayed" Christianity, to Herder, was "plebian"; it could not form part of the great synthesis.

At the same time, he was at pains to distinguish his synthesis from the humanistic ideal which Goethe and Schiller were attempting to establish in the middle and late 1790's.[93] Aside from personal and political reasons for the divergence, he felt that the two great poets placed too strong an emphasis on the aesthetic factor. He reacted coolly to Schiller's *Letters on the Aesthetic Education of Man*.[94] Broad-minded though he was, he found the sensuality of Goethe's *Roman Elegies* and *Venetian Epigrams* unpleasant.[95] In addition, he seems to have been ambivalent about the new classicism of works like Goethe's *The Natural Daughter*, and he rejected such "pagan" ballads as "The Bride of Corinth." [96] When he died in 1803, he was estranged from the two poets, indeed somewhat embittered.

Herder's relation to the aesthetic movement was thus a complex one. Something of an aesthetic man himself, he was still more an ethical one. Sensitive to some, at least, of the charms of paganism, he clung to the position of enlightened Christianity. Repeatedly, as we have seen, he was torn between a sense of historical necessity and a hope for the rebirth of the noblest of Greek values. His main contribution to aesthetic paganism, while in a sense involuntary, was a vast one: more than any other man of his generation he called attention to the importance and the appeal of myth. In the majority of cases, the myths exploited by the great German writers who followed him were pagan ones.

Chapter V

Prometheus: Young Goethe

Goethe's range was so vast, his interests and allegiances, particularly during his youth, were so varied and so shifting, that to approach him from any single point of view is necessarily unsatisfactory. One can hope at best for partial insights. Although Greek art and literature undoubtedly formed one of his greatest cultural experiences, it was but one among many. At a given time the impact of Shakespeare, or of Spinoza, or of some observation of the natural world, was the decisive one; and each stimulus was constantly modified by many others. The mind, Goethe wrote in *Faust*, works like a loom:

> Wo Ein Tritt tausend Fäden regt,
> Die Schifflein herüber-hinüberschiessen,
> Die Fäden ungesehen fliessen,
> Ein Schlag tausend Verbindungen schlägt.[1]

Thus it is nearly impossible to isolate a given element of his thought without doing violence to it. In trying to describe Goethe's attitude one almost necessarily adopts a chronological approach, but while this reduces the difficulties, it by no means eliminates them. In his works of the early 1770's, which are generally labeled "Storm and Stress," Christian and pagan, altruistic and highly individualistic strains intermingle. The result is not chaos but an outlook of extraordinary complexity.

In Goethe's very early lyrics, Greek mythology is used

for ornamentation, in the usual manner of the rococo; the myths are taken very lightly. The pagan note sounded in his "Wedding Night," for instance, is of no particular ideological significance, for the poem remains within the tradition of the epithalamium. More Goethean is the sense of a close, almost erotic, bond between the poet and nature in his "Inconstancy," but the brief poem ends with a rococo cynicism.

Yet in the very years when Goethe was writing these verses, as a student in Leipzig, his drawing-master Adam Friedrich Oeser was initiating him into Winckelmann's dogmas. Apparently their influence, while not immediately evident, went deep. A letter of 1770 expresses the poet's sense of gratitude to Oeser: "His instruction will affect my whole life. He taught me that the ideal of beauty was simplicity and tranquillity." [2] Two visits to the Hall of Antiquities in Mannheim, in 1769 and 1771, [3] reinforced the lesson. Goethe found a "forest of statues" [4] there; the Apollo Belvedere impressed him the most deeply, along with the Laocoön, the Dying Gaul, and the Dioscuri. In a letter of the period (to Herder), occurs the following exclamation or eruption, bursting through the context: "Apollo Belvedere, why dost thou show thyself to us in thy nakedness, so that we must be ashamed of ours? Spanish costume and rouge!" [5] The impact of the Mannheim statues must have been tremendous, though Goethe tried to expunge it from his mind:

for the immediate future the effects were small . . . Hardly had the door of the magnificent hall closed behind me when I wished to find myself again; yes, I tried rather to free my imagination from those forms, finding them burdensome, and only by a very circuitous path was I to be led back again into this sphere. Nevertheless, the quiet fruitfulness of such impressions is invaluable. [6]

The ideal of simplicity and tranquillity was not to assert itself until much later. For the moment, under the guidance of Herder, Goethe was devoted to other ideals: original genius and "characteristic" force rather than beautiful form.

Hellenism seemed remote, its champions pedantic. Perhaps a passage from *The Sorrows of Young Werther* gives a clue to Goethe's attitude. Werther is describing an encounter with a studious young man: "he turned to me and unloaded a lot of learning, from Batteux to Wood, from de Piles to Winckelmann, and assured me that he had read all of the first part of Sulzer's *Theory* and owned a manuscript of Heyne on the study of ancient times. I let the matter drop."[7] Yet Werther was devoted to one great figure of antiquity: the healthy "closeness to nature," the patriarchal quality of Homer moved and attracted him.

Poor Werther, to be sure, could perceive only those aspects of Homer's poetry which helped to assuage his own *Weltschmerz*; Goethe's own view of Homer was broader and less sentimental. His "Artist's Morning Song" represents a reverent artist before the altar, reading his liturgy from the works of "holy Homer";[8] the close analogy to Winckelmann's "praying in metaphors from Homer" has been noted.[9] Most striking of all is Goethe's description of a bust of Homer, which appeared in Lavater's *Physiognomic Fragments* (1775–1778). This brief evocation is almost a prose hymn, but it is not marked by Werther's subjectivity: Goethe views the bust with emotion and even with awe, but finds Winckelmannian calm and classic self-containment in the face and head of the poet:

It is Homer!
This is the skull in which the enormous gods and heroes have as much space as in the broad heaven and the boundless earth . . .
Purposeless, passionless, this man passes calmly through life; he exists for his own sake, and the world he contains within him is his occupation and reward.[10]

At this time, as later, Homer was one of the great teachers who guided Goethe through the "school of the Greeks." He saw in the epic poet not only "nature," but sincerity, vigor, and wholeness.

The paganism of the Goethe of the Storm and Stress was very different from Winckelmann's; it appears not only in his use of Greek mythology but in the whole range of his production. In those years he felt himself drawn to figures of superhuman stature: Prometheus, Faust, Caesar, Mohammed, Shakespeare, and Pindar. The idea of genius was the great watchword of the literary revolution, and in the Titans Greek mythology furnished the paradigm of genius in revolt. Looking back on the early 1770's, Goethe wrote in *Poetry and Truth* of his pity for the Titans, noting that even "the bolder members of that race, Tantalus, Ixion, Sisyphus," were among his "saints," [11] as were the more conciliatory figures who resisted the Olympians passively. He well pointed out that the tragic suffering of the Tantalids, that "tremendous opposition" which appears in the background of his *Iphigenia in Tauris*, was responsible for part of the effectiveness of the drama. While the classical world may also appear patriarchal, as Homer did to Werther, or idyllic, as in the poem "The Wanderer," the Titanic note is dominant.

Even when Goethe glorified the founder of a monotheistic religion as a hero of altruistic love, he drew on non-Christian sources for material to fashion his magnificent "Mohammed's Song." Similarly, the idea of a benevolent god, an "all-loving father," is expressed in an image taken from Greek mythology. Possibly the fact that the Christian religion was an institution of contemporary society made it seem inadequate to the expression of Storm and Stress emotion. In the fragmentary epic "The Wandering Jew" Christ appears at the opposite pole to the church; if He returned, He would be crucified again.

Goethe's fragmentary drama "Prometheus," like the great ode of the same title, presents the Titan as the revolutionary genius who is also the supreme artist. He has created man and instructed him in the arts. Above him he acknowledges only fate; he rejects the Olympian gods and all they represent, including any conventional system of morality. In their cruelty the gods do not feel the slightest concern for the sufferings of other beings. Prometheus speaks for the young men of Goethe's generation. He proclaims — with an anachronistic side glance at Rousseau — that his creatures are not degenerate, nor are they to be judged by rationalistic standards of good and evil:

> Seyd arbeitsam und faul
> Und grausam mild
> Freigebig geitzig!
> Gleichet all euern Schicksaals Brüdern
> Gleichet den Tieren und den Göttern.[12]

When Pandora, his daughter, observes a couple making love and cannot understand their actions, Prometheus' explanation implies clearly that sexual love, as part of the world he has made, does not fall under the control of the Olympians.[13] It is presented as the supreme experience; not beyond good and evil but good in itself. His reference to the sexual climax as "death" stands in a long tradition leading down through and beyond Wagner's *Tristan and Isolde.*

Goethe has pictured a human world free of divine sanctions. His Prometheus is primarily universal, not Greek; he is the mythological figure whom young Goethe most ardently invoked. Shaftesbury had described the artist as "a second maker; a just Prometheus under Jove," and Goethe characteristically associates the highest creativity with the name of the Titan. His name is linked with Shakespeare's,[14] and occurs also at the climax of Goethe's eloquent essay on Gothic architecture.[15] It is the more remarkable — and at the same time typically Goethean — that the poet does not completely identify himself with the Promethean attitude. In the drama he was able to project his close sympathy with Prometheus, and yet to transcend his point of view; the Olympians are not really the malevolent beings the Titan thinks them. As Minerva tells him:

Den Göttern fiel zum Loose, Dauer
Und Macht, und Weisheit und Liebe.[16]

Eventually, had the work been finished, Prometheus would doubtless have been reconciled with the gods; Goethe's own "acceptance of the universe" is here foreshadowed. It is profoundly characteristic of him to acknowledge the justification both of convention and of revolt — each as a Hegelian "moment," as it were — and to attempt to establish a harmony between them.

In his attempt to see both the positive and the negative aspects of a character or doctrine, Goethe could not always achieve a true resolution of conflicting insights; ambiguity occasionally prevails. This is the situation in one of his more drastic dramatic skits, "Satyros." Again, the strong man in revolt appears in a Greek world. The Satyr is a Rousseauist primitive, who voices half-mystical beliefs reminiscent of Herder, and a faith in nature like Goethe's own.[17] He is a champion of the "golden age" of sexual freedom, nudism, and vegetarian fare. He is crude and often ridiculous, but charismatic, especially to women; he sways the mob and not only the mob. Having carried natural behavior too far, he is discovered attempting rape and has to flee, but he is not totally defeated; Psyche, a local maiden whose name may well be symbolical, will presumably accompany him.[18] Goethe himself felt the appeal of a Rousseaustically colored paganism; his mockery here is self-mockery in some degree.

Another brief drama, "Gods, Heroes, and Wieland," illuminates the relation between Goethe's pagan strain and his concept of the Greeks. To the young Goethe the Hellenic heroes were enormously powerful, indeed colossal figures; they were, so to speak, classical forebears of the rough Storm and Stress hero or *Kerl*. One of the gravest sins of French neoclassicism, in his eyes, was that it had reduced the godlike Greeks to the level of gallant courtiers. In his address on Shakespeare he had sarcastically maintained that Greek armor was too great and too heavy for the "little Frenchman," [19] and derived from this assumption the thesis that all French tragedies were parodies of themselves. The most gifted representative of "French" taste in German letters was Wieland,[20] whom Goethe had once greatly admired and would admire again but who was anathema to the young Hotspurs of the Storm and Stress. When Wieland wrote a *Singspiel* "Alcestis" (1773) [21] and accompanied his mediocre text with an essay implying that it was superior to Euripides' *Alkestis*,[22] he became fair game. The reaction was swift: Goethe wrote his farce, perhaps the most amusing of his literary polemics, in the same year.

The action of the little satire recalls Aristophanes' *Frogs*. Mercury summons the unfortunate Wieland from his sleep to Hades, where Euripides, Admetus, and Alcestis indignantly confront him: they have heard of his insipid play and his slurring remarks about themselves. He does not recognize the real Greeks: "my imagination never produced such images." [23] They reproach him for the impossibly "noble" morality of his *Singspiel* and try to explain the actual emotions of Alcestis and Admetus; Wieland cannot understand them:

You speak like persons of another world, a language whose words I hear, whose meaning I cannot grasp.
Admetus: We're speaking Greek. Is that so incomprehensible? . . .
Euripides: You're forgetting that he belongs to a sect which tries to persuade every victim of the dropsy and consumption, every . . . hopelessly wounded person: once they were dead their hearts would be fuller, their minds more powerful, their bones stronger. He believes that.
Admetus: He only pretends to.[24]

"He only pretends to" is a very palpable hit at Wieland's oscillations between Pietism and freethinking. He seems about to escape scot-free when Hercules appears. Again, Wieland does not recognize an actual Greek: this creature is a colossus, whereas his own Hercules was a "well-formed man *of medium height*" [25] — the last a sarcastic reference to the rationalist

notion that everything about the Greeks was moderate by
definition. Hercules speaks as very much of a *Kerl* — enormously strong, magnanimous, fond of drink and women.[26]
Prodicus' Hercules at the crossroads was Wieland's man, he
points out. The virtue he prates of is a phantasm; true virtue
means valor, pride, sexual prowess, unstinting generosity. To
Wieland's objection that most of these qualities are now
considered vices Hercules replies with the central point of
the debate: modern man wavers between two abstract ex-
tremes labeled "virtue" and "vice." [27] Rather, he should consider the middle way the right one, as indeed peasants and
other simple folk still do. Something might have come of
Wieland, the demigod concludes, if he had not sighed too
long under the yoke of his religion and its moral dogma.[28]

It would be foolish to take every word of this lighthearted
piece [29] as a literal statement of Goethe's convictions, but still
more foolish to ignore its general tendency. The conviction
that the morality of the ancients was on the whole saner and
more enlightened than Christian ethics persists throughout
Goethe's work. He departed from it occasionally, as in
Iphigenia in Tauris, Wilhelm Meister's Wanderjahre, and
perhaps in *The Elective Affinities*; but the pagan point of
view is the norm. This is particularly the case in the realm
of sexual ethics.[30] Thus Clara, in *Egmont*, becomes the hero's
mistress without any sense of sin or guilt; she scornfully rejects her mother's charge that she is a "fallen woman." [31]
She is by no means a demonic superwoman à la Storm and
Stress but essentially a simple girl: middle-class ethics are subverted from within. As if to emphasize her importance,
Goethe identifies her, at the end of the tragedy, with the
goddess of freedom. The hero of his *Stella*, torn between two
women, is rewarded with both of them. More serious than
this youthful vindication of bigamy — Goethe later gave the
drama a tragic ending — is the role played by Philina in
Wilhelm Meister's Apprenticeship. She is a promiscuous if

charming little baggage, but Goethe clearly finds something very admirable in her, and gives her one of the great lines of the novel: "If I love you, what business is it of yours?"[32] As the poet himself pointed out, this is a free variation on Spinoza's sublime statement: "He who loves God cannot ask that God love him in return."[33]

Thus Goethe's paganism appears in his "Germanic" works as strongly as in his Hellenizing ones; it informs dramas as sublime as *Faust* and as deliberately ridiculous as "Pater Gruel," which is, like the skit about Wieland, a protest against too ethereal a morality.[34] Whenever man departs too far from the real, the actual, indeed the fleshly — he implies — absurdity and hypocrisy result. "This-worldliness" (*Diesseitigkeit*) is the necessary precondition of sanity. This conviction, later elaborated in his attacks on the German "Nazarene" painters of the early nineteenth century and on romanticism generally, is already latent in the Goethe of the Storm and Stress.

His position was neither amoral nor cynical, and should not be confused with the "aesthetic immoralism" of a Heinse or a Nietzsche. Even his Hercules is fundamentally good-hearted and generous; the "culture heroes" Prometheus and Mohammed are basically altruistic. For all his youthful admiration of exuberance and strength, Goethe had a remarkably keen sense of the perils of *hubris*. On the rare occasions when he uses the word "superman" (*Übermensch*), the term has ironic force.[35] Essentially, I believe, Goethe found the morality he associated with the Greeks — and with other figures whom he revered — freer and broader than the Christian, with a sounder balance between individualism and altruism. Similarly, he was far from having an "irreligious" habit of mind. The sense of union with the divine has rarely been more powerfully expressed than in his "Ganymede," with its image of the loving youth borne upwards, "embracing, embraced," toward the "all-loving Father."[36] Rather, the spe-

cifically Christian form of religion did not normally appeal
to him, for reasons partly intellectual, partly aesthetic, which
he was later to formulate in detail.[37] That Pietistic mysticism
attracted him in the months when he was lying ill after the
breakdown which ended his student career at Leipzig does
not weaken the force of this generalization;[38] if anything,
it strengthens it.

Yet there is evidence too of a genuine bond to the figure
of Jesus and to the Bible, if not to Christianity itself, in two
brochures of 1773, "Letter of the Pastor of *** to the New
Pastor of ***" and "Two Important Biblical Problems not
Previously Discussed." Employing in the "Letter" the point
of view of a completely convinced but unorthodox Protestant
minister, he champions a religion of love, rejects the dogmas
of eternal punishment[39] and the damnation of the heathen,[40]
and calls for loving acceptance, not merely tolerance, of other
sects. In "Two Important Biblical Problems," he argues that
the "Tables of the Covenant" were not identical with the
Ten Commandments of the catechism, and gives a sympathetic interpretation of the phenomenon known as "speaking
in tongues." Both rigid orthodoxy and cold, "modern" exe-
gesis of the Bible are rejected. The religious empathy and
keen interest in theological questions shown here by the
author of the apostrophe to the Belvedere Apollo may surprise us, but they are undeniably real. This religious dualism
is particularly marked in Goethe's later years.

While Goethe does not mention Winckelmann by name
until his Italian journey, we can infer a good deal about his
relation to Winckelmann's myth. In his Storm and Stress
days he poured scorn on Grecizing moderns; contemporary
use of Greek materials struck him as mainly Frenchified, and
French culture, except for Rousseau, Diderot, and Mercier,
seemed a bad thing to the *Genies*. Clearly, it was the Greek
vogue, not the Greeks themselves, that Goethe rejected.[41]
Any treatment of Greek themes must be authentic, somehow

"original," and free of rococo prettiness. Reviewing a collection of Salomon Gessner's idyls, he expressed the wish that Gessner had confined himself to native materials and avoided describing the "little feet of ivory nymphs." [42] His drastic defense of Rubens' paintings points in the same direction: "You find Rubens' women too fleshy! I tell you, they were *his* women"; [43] in other words flesh and blood, and "characteristic," not idealized. Goethe tended to oppose literary vogues as such and, at the time, any dogma of imitation. This did not of course make him insensitive to the beauty and nobility of ancient art. He did not deny the validity of Winckelmann's vision, but for the time being he avoided involvement in it. His Greek heroes and gods have many of the Winckelmannian qualities, though only his Apollo is tranquil; they are, however, more dynamic.

Perhaps an equally important component of Goethe's image of Hellas was Pindar's poetry, as interpreted by the Storm and Stress. [44] Unaware of the elaborate, highly formalized metrical scheme of his odes, Goethe and his contemporaries thought of them as free verse, as "natural" outpourings of emotion. Thus Goethe's "Wanderer's Storm Song," a dithyrambic, powerful, at times rather incoherent poem, is Pindaric in intention, not in effect. He was also inspired by the celebration of heroic, keenly competitive young athletes in the odes. But above all, Pindar's poetry appealed to him through the sense of mastery it imparted, as a famous letter to Herder makes clear: "When you stand boldly in the chariot, and four young horses rear against your reins in wild disorder, and you guide their strength, and whip the one that strays back into line — another rears up, and you whip him down — . . . until all sixteen feet carry you to your goal in the same rhythm. That is mastery, *epikratein*, virtuosity." [45] The image expresses control as well as power. While the passage conveys a sense of movement and action which one would seek in vain in Winckelmann's prose, the notion of mastery involves self-mastery, and anticipates the direction which Goethe was to follow. Self-control was precisely the quality the Storm and Stress lacked.

If one considers Goethe's Storm and Stress works as a whole, one finds that he was more "classical" — at least in matters of form — than he presumably realized himself. Above all, an intuitive sense of artistic discipline distinguished him from the other *Genies*, men like Lenz, Wagner, and Klinger, with whom the public associated him. If *Götz von Berlichingen*, especially in its first version, is shapeless and undisciplined, *Werther* is a masterpiece of symmetrical construction. Even in Goethe's most revolutionary theoretical essays a sense of the validity of aesthetic norms at times appears. Thus while his essay "On German Architecture" (1772) praises the richness and power of the Gothic style and mocks contemporary imitators of the Greeks, it has its classical aspect.[46] Describing the impact made on him by the Strasbourg Cathedral, he wrote: "An impression of wholeness and greatness filled my soul." [47] Other Storm and Stress critics rejected almost all aesthetic criteria; [48] Goethe characteristically made standards flexible but did not discard them. He implied that the despised Gothic fulfilled the ultimate requirements of classical art, if these were broadly interpreted. It was an act of reconciliation, though very likely an unconscious one. One is reminded of Lessing's thesis that Shakespeare was essentially Aristotelian.

But literary classicism, we must remind ourselves, is by no means identical with paganism. Classical themes and forms may of course be put to Christian uses, as in Racine's tragedies and Goethe's *Iphigenia in Tauris*. As a young man, Goethe did not reach any neat, final decision between paganism and Christianity, nor did he in his old age. In some of the greatest poetry of his Storm and Stress period, like "Ganymede" and "Prometheus," both strains are mingled, as they are in the second part of *Faust*.

Chapter VI

Islands and Idyls:
Heinse, Müller, and Forster

♩ ♩

Perhaps the most "pagan" of the German writers of the eighteenth century, Wilhelm Heinse (1749–1803) was an ardent admirer both of Renaissance color and Greek form. As a young writer he generally followed the rococo tradition, but before long he came under the spell of Winckelmann. Soon to be sure he rejected the archaeologist's ethical beliefs: "quiet grandeur" could not long satisfy this least restrained of Hellenists, but in aesthetic matters he could never completely free himself from Winckelmann's ideal. Essentially, however, his Hellenes were flesh while Winckelmann's were marble; he admired them (and certain other peoples) as beautiful and uninhibited, "natural," and vigorous. The most famous Greeks, like the most brilliant Italians of the Renaissance, were marked, he thought, by extraordinary vitality and sensuality and an equally extraordinary indifference to moral judgments. He admiringly mentioned Alcibiades and Phryne as representatives of the Greek spirit. Attacks on Christianity, direct as well as oblique, are frequent in his writings.

Like most of his contemporaries, Heinse owed a heavy debt to Rousseau.[1] Much of Jean-Jacques' creed he found soft and sentimental, but he could not resist the appeal of the natural. One can consider him a "tough" Rousseauist,[2] in the sense that Crane Brinton has spoken of tough Nietzsche-ans. A believer in freedom (for the happy few) he was one of the very unusual persons in the eighteenth century who defended Machiavelli. In his view of the struggle for survival he anticipated Darwin, and many of his aphorisms read like Nietzsche's.

Heinse was also very much the aesthete of the more vigorous sort; he suggests Hemingway rather than Oscar Wilde. His tastes were remarkably inclusive. Attracted almost equally by sculpture and painting, he wrote eloquently about the fine arts, and also devoted most of his novel *Hildegard von Hohenthal* to music. Yet nature appealed to him even more than did art; he has left glowing descriptions of the "romantic" Alps and of Italian landscapes. The highest beauty, to him, was that of the human form, above all, of the female nude. Expressions of his basically sexual approach to art and life are everywhere in his fiction and verse, and appear still more freely in his diaries. His insistence on the subject can become tiresome and even unpleasant — Wieland referred to one of his early works as "priapism of the soul" [3] — and it does not fall far short of an obsession. Some of his erotic passages are highly effective, written with verve and color; others give the sense of too calculated a lasciviousness.

However we evaluate Heinse as a writer, his historical contribution is clear. More than any of his contemporaries, he established that psychological connection between Greek beauty and the "emancipation of the flesh" which was to form so important an aspect of the later concept of Hellas. For better or worse, he sexualized the myth: sexual freedom was one of the fundamental tenets of his utopia. His influence radiated in various directions.[4] His cult of free love impressed Friedrich Schlegel, Brentano, Richard Wagner, and the "Young Germans" of the 1830's and 1840's; the picture drawn in his *Ardinghello* of the "Bacchantic" life of the Renaissance influenced Tieck and others. Heinse's technique of describing works of art also helped to establish a tradition in German prose.[5] Even Hölderlin, so different a personality, was deeply indebted to his vision of life in the Greek archipelago, as his novel *Hyperion* bears witness.

Heinse's early writings do not greatly concern us. Some of them, like the erotic tale *Laidion* (1774) are pagan enough, but one cannot feel that the author really believes in the antiquity he presents to us. Like a more daring Wieland, he mingles tales of Greek amours with arch comments on the philosophy of his own time. Hedonism appears as the crown of life, Laïs and Aspasia as models of human behavior. Yet one cannot take any of this seriously; here is no believed myth, but a poem which deliberately titillates its readers with erotic frivolities.

Heinse was too intelligent and energetic to content himself with producing tinsel like *Laidion*. Various "cultural experiences," to use Gundolf's term, did much to form his mind: the study of classical and neoclassical aesthetics, of Italian literature, and of Renaissance art, and above all his exposure to the contagious excitement of the Storm and Stress. He came to believe in the unique importance of a specific national or folk tradition, to distrust all abstractions, to insist on the specific experience.[6] (This belief, of course, clashed with residues of neoclassic dogma; he was no systematic thinker and was often inconsistent.) His heathen strain continued strong, but he began to envision a Northern, modern paganism. The most striking result of his new orientation was the series of essays *Letters from the Düsseldorf Gallery of Paintings* (1776–1777), especially the letters devoted to Rubens and to some of his works.

Heinse has by no means abandoned either the Greeks or the older, normative aesthetics completely. He starts with a fiery evocation of Greek life, but admits that he no longer knows as much of Greece as he once had; "lost is lost." [7] The Greeks were the most beautiful of peoples, but their beauty does not really communicate itself to us; a nation can respond to only that beauty which has grown organically within its own culture. Thus the moderns cannot properly appreciate the nude.[8] From the Renaissance on, artists have degraded the ancient archetypes:

> The antique statues are a troupe of comedians, with whom they [the artists] wander about in the world; they dress them up for the roles they are supposed to play. Zeus plays God the Father; Apollo, the Son; Niobe or her daughter, the mother; and the slaves, the thieves on the Cross; Mercury, the Angel Gabriel; Hercules, Samson; Venus, Eve; Pan, Moses; and Laocoön, some prophet or other.[9]

The gods and heroes seem in almost as pathetic a state as in Heine's "The Gods in Exile." Heinse's attitude toward them is generally less negative than this, however; Niobe remains the ideal of feminine courage: "the woman who still stands in all her strength and perfection among the most cruel sufferings, who seems to breathe the words: 'You conquer! but I remain who I was, great, noble, and beautiful above all human beings.' "[10]

It is not that the Greeks have lost anything in Heinse's eyes; rather, it is his new awareness of temporal and national factors which makes him turn to the moderns; they are more accessible. His admiration of Rubens, moreover, is based less on theory than on direct aesthetic experience: the color, force, individuality, and sensuosity of Rubens' paintings almost overwhelmed Heinse. Far from objecting to the fleshiness of Rubens' females, he seems to have sensed in it a symbol of strength and vigor — of Northern paganism, as it were. Rubens is the "Hercules of painting."[11]

Heinse presented him first as an individual before turning to his painting. The artist appears as the universal talent, indeed as a superman: "a painter of emotional power and broad scope: 'great man and statesman . . . tender and faithful in his personal relations, a patriot, and lordly and splendid like the King Eagle in the heavens.' "[12] Although a courtier, he was close to living reality, inspired by "holy Nature." Rubens could not of course "create Greek beauty out of nothing"; but he possessed the same qualities of "abundance and fire" as the ancients did; he created "Flemish beauty for Flemings." [13] He assumes the same role here that Shakespeare played in the literary criticism of Herder and the young Goethe: he is the Northern genius who does not imitate the ancients because he is their equal, their "brother."

In treating individual paintings, Heinse characteristically pushes theory into the background: he forgets his remark about the nude and glories in Rubens' use of it. The Amazons, in flight from the Greeks, like the Daughters of Leucippus abducted by Castor and Pollux, appear as concretions of Storm and Stress verve, of martial and erotic powess.

In 1780 Heinse was finally able to fulfill his wish of many years and visit Italy. He stayed there for three years, reveling in classical and Italian art, scenic beauty, and accounts of Renaissance life. Mediterranean art vanquished that of the North; Titian, Raphael, and the Belvedere statues displaced Dutch painting in his esteem. Even Rubens is obscured by the glories of the South. [14]

His diaries of these years read at times like a series of hymns to sensuality. The view of Naples suggests the naked body of Venus to him. [15] Venice provokes similar associations; like Hemingway, he was struck by the erotic possibilities of the gondola. [16] His reactions to painting and sculpture, even to religious pictures, are of the same sort. [17] After he had become acquainted with (relatively) authentic classical statues, he formed — retrospectively — an unfavorable judgment of the reproductions in the famous Hall of Antiquities at Mannheim, [18] that shrine of German Hellenism where Herder, Goethe, and Schiller had worshiped. Winckelmann he now called "a fantastic dreamer," [19] but he still could not break away completely from his dogma. At times, as in a comment on the Venus de Medici, Heinse managed to reach a compromise between the cult of vitality and that of tranquillity: "No other nation expresses life as vividly, and yet tranquilly, as do the Greeks, but fully animated." [20]

In his description of the Milan cathedral Heinse's rejection of Christianity is the most clearly revealed:

> The cathedral is the most admirable symbol of the Christian religion that I have yet seen, gigantic and like the work of an apprentice in plan and execution . . . The adornments fit in right well, and are really something for old women and stupid peasant boys. The toothpicks, attached outside . . . make the building prickly as a hedgehog . . . From its front doors in antique taste to the curlicued Gothic ones it really represents the Christian religion down to our times and the ingenious artifices that Calvin and the Berliners and other modern Pharisees have added to it . . . Certainly one must confess that such a building conforms far better to the Christian faith than does St. Peter's . . . in Rome, where one sees at once that the people who built it . . . didn't have a jot of belief in their religion. But this [church,] in its gloomy choir, sharp, angular arches, enormous columns without living form, and the pile of nonsensical ornamentation, displays nothing except hell, death, and damnation, a terrible God who punishes every human error with eternal torments, and a mad mob of simpletons, visionaries, and deceivers.[21]

One element in Heinse's paganism, as later in Nietzsche's, is the belief that life is its own aim. The Neapolitans, he noted, "bathe and sing and jest and simply feel their happiness." [22] Naples gave him a sense of what life in the Greek islands must be like,[23] a theme he developed later in his most important novel, *Ardinghello*. On occasion his view of life can be very earthy indeed: "Why talk of honor! The real man (*Kerl*) is the fellow who carries out his plans and lives happily. What do we care about the future? A pretty girl on the bed . . . and three bottles of wine on the table are more than all honor." [24] Normally however he was less Falstaffian. The *virtù* of the Renaissance man became his ideal of human conduct; will to power appeared as the driving force of all living beings.[25] One perfect entity is superior to a mass of mediocrities. Increasingly he tended to the aestheticism of the strong (or would-be strong) man; the members of the elite are to rule and to enjoy all the pleasures; only they are capable of perceiving beauty.

In *Ardinghello or the Happy Isles* (1787) he expressed this "aesthetic immoralism" [26] most fully. The novel is not only the most impressive statement of Heinse's view of the world, but his most nearly realized work of prose fiction. The hero Ardinghello combines the qualities Heinse most admired: he is the Storm and Stress *Kerl*, the great-souled man of Aristotle, and the universal man of the Renaissance. After a colorful career in sixteenth-century Italy, he is attracted to the Greek islands and sets up his ideal state there; to Heinse, both Italy and Greece are essentially symbols of the aesthetic form of life. (On occasion he used Tahiti, Circassia, and Georgia as minor symbols of similar content.) [27]

Of the plot of the novel little need be said: erotic scenes, orgies, duels, and a battle at sea alternate with descriptions of paintings, statues, and landscapes, and with dialogues about the nature of art. On first reading it seems formless indeed; but there are integrating factors. The most intense passages are devoted to love-making and to evocations of art; these, Heinse implies, are the activities of man most highly charged with *élan vital*, and thus they are closely interrelated. Furthermore, his orgies are presented as pictures — *ut pictura poesis* — while his renderings of paintings and statues are usually erotic; the two strains are drawn together. Heinse appears in this novel as a master of German prose; the style is vividly clear; descriptions glow, particularly in the amorous passages. At times he achieves almost Joycean effects by piling up adjectives unseparated by punctuation; thus he writes of the "tender naked warm sweet firm form" of a woman's breast. [28]

Ardinghello is a painter, an amateur of various other arts, and an enthusiastic admirer of the Greeks; above all he is a man of action and a lover. The noblest instinct of the human spirit, he believes, is to unite itself with beauty wherever it is found; he quotes Plato for his own purposes.[29] Like Goethe's Hercules, his mentor Demetri objects to a view which would split man's nature into "two absolutely opposed, distinct halves";[30] we must accept the world as it is. Middle-class morality, by denying freedom in love, would destroy man, but Ardinghello successfully defies it. After a series of amorous conquests he finally encounters, in Fiordimona, his equal in intellect and will power. She could be his friend as well as his beloved. A "virtuoso" in love, she scorns marriage and is as unfettered by convention as he. Like him, she has been unabashedly promiscuous; as a superwoman, she will now presumably be true to her superman, but not because of any regard for society. She is one of the first in the long line of emancipated heroines in German literature which includes Schlegel's Lucinde, Tieck's Vittoria Accorombona, and, on a far different plane, Goethe's Helen. With various other free spirits, many of whom have been friends or mistresses of Ardinghello, she joins his utopian colony on the Happy Isles.

Throughout the novel, the aesthetic life is contrasted to the Christian; differently put, a bacchantic existence is set off against that of the burgher or the crowd. A cult of beauty is celebrated. Only vital and joyous persons or peoples can produce beauty: "without Pericles and Aspasia, Alcibiades, Phryne and the like . . . no Phidias, Praxiteles, and Apelles."[31] Thus it would be folly to try to imitate Greek works of art without first reinstating the naked exercises of the gymnasia, Greek games and mores.[32] Even if we did, we should lack the Hellenic religion. Consistently, Ardinghello does introduce the Greek way of life, as he understands it, when he founds his island republic. The artist is the man of superior energy. "Gothic" morality will produce only Gothic art.[33] Christianity can be respected only to the extent that Christian artists have been productive, and the highest praise of a Christ of Michelangelo is that he resembles "a suffering Alexander, Hannibal, Caesar." [34] Once the utopian state had been established, the priests were re-educated: they "made their living in a more decent manner." [35]

Classical sculpture has again become, to Heinse, the highest manifestation of art, but his view of it is far different from Winckelmann's. Laocoön's whole body, he writes, "trembles and quivers and burns, swollen by the torturing, killing poison." [36] Here his eye was doubtless more exact than Winckelmann's, but when he writes that the Belvedere Torso perhaps once "rocked a sweet creature of pleasure in his arms," [37] his own characteristic subjectivity is obvious.

The bacchantic note recurs throughout: Ardinghello likes to disguise himself as Bacchus, and the first volume of the work ends with a tremendous naked orgy in Rome — orgies were "holy" to Heinse. He clearly recognized — and accepted — the Dionysiac aspect of Greek life. His Dionysus, however, is not Nietzsche's god of tragedy but the incarnation of sexuality.

The utopia which concludes the book contains a rather surprising emphasis on political matters. To be sure, the inhabitants of Ardinghello's islands lead free, naked, and joyful though culturally productive lives, but the aesthetic element is no longer primary. Questions of the state, of common property, of the abolition of the family, and even of votes for women engage their attention. Only the strong deserve freedom; happiness is based on power; conflict is necessary if stagnation is to be avoided. The rococo paradise of *Laidion* has vanished; even in the Archipelago, stern facts must be faced. Machiavelli is studied by the islanders, [38] as are Plato and Aristotle; his influence has modified Winckelmann's and Rousseau's. Deeply involved in *Realpolitik*, Ardinghello secretly plots to overthrow the power of the Turks. "But after an era of happiness this aim was frustrated by implacable fate," [39] as the last sentence of the novel puts it.

In his erotic prowess, Ardinghello recalls Simsone Grisaldo, the hero of Friedrich Maximilian Klinger's drama of that name (1776). This mighty warrior, a latter-day Samson, is the incarnation of a sexual fantasy: he is the benevolent and beneficent seducer: beneath the cloak of a Don Giovanni beats a heart of gold. The women whom he loves and leaves are grateful for their experiences.[40] When a critic remarks that Grisaldo "enjoys his existence with radiant serenity and peace of soul, like an Olympian god,"[41] one smiles; he is no Winckelmannian hero, but a representative of the "tough" side of the Storm and Stress.

To return to Heinse: he appears most irreverent, from a Winckelmannian point of view, in his treatment of the Greek gods. He even denied that Greek statues of Venus, Zeus, and so on, really represented divine beings; rather, they portrayed human beings of unusual beauty. Freedom from all conventions and a Rousseauistic naturalness were ultimately as important to him as beauty. "The great principle of the Greeks, not only of their artists, was to create nothing that is not nature, and to despise everything middle-class, everything merely conventional; from this, beauty later arises of itself."[42] On one point, however, he is close to the high classicism of a Winckelmann. "The beautiful human being in sheer consciousness of his existence, in passionless repose, is the most suitable object for the imitation of the artist,"[43] he wrote in *Ardinghello*. The words "sheer consciousness of his existence" have connotations which transcend the aesthetic: the belief that a fulfilled life contains its aim in itself. It is one of the ideas which Goethe most strongly emphasized in his essay on Winckelmann.

II

In its island setting, Heinse's utopia has some affinity to the idyl, but the character of life there is vigorous and active rather than pastoral. Inevitably, the lighter side of the myth of Greece found expression in authentic idyls as well as in Heinse's novel. When Heinse's contemporary Friedrich Müller took over the genre from the enormously popular Salomon Gessner, he made a radical change in its spirit and tone. Gessner's persons have the rococo charm and fragile prettiness of Dresden figurines; they are in no sense pagan. In sharp contrast, "Müller the Painter," as he is generally called, stressed the natural; his satyrs and shepherds, it has often been observed, tend to behave like the peasants of the Palatinate.[44] As a member of the Storm and Stress generation, inspired by Shakespeare, Milton, and Klopstock, Müller brought the idyl down to earth.[45] Of his own idyls, which are set in classical, Biblical, and German landscapes, only the first group concerns us here.

These "Greek" idyls — like "The Satyr Mopsus," "Bacchidon and Milon" (both 1775) and "The Faun Molon" (not published until 1912) — are realistically rustic, at times crudely so. Müller's centaurs and fauns are strong, tough fellows, at times larger than life, full of rough humor, occasionally brutal; but their brutality is preferred to human hypocrisy.[46] Drawing absolute moral distinctions is silly, we are told here as in Goethe's "Satyros." Satyr Bacchidon has been compared to Falstaff. Another satyr, Mopsus, has the tastes of a German peasant: he promises his beloved that he will feed her until she is as fat as a healthy piglet.[47]

Stimulated by the erotic drive in all of nature, Müller's shepherds and fauns express themselves with "antique" directness, not with the *délicatesse* of Gessner's. Without the slightest jealousy, two brothers share the favors of a nymph [48] — a typical example of Storm and Stress permissiveness in sexual matters. On the other hand, stern or comic reality may intervene: the faun Molon worries about poverty and his wife's illness; an amorous satyr, trying to leap into a nymph's arms, lands in a thorn bush.

Müller has a sense of Dionysian frenzy: he writes of staggering in inspiration, "full of the god"; the sun dances, the forests, even the stars, reel.[49] Generally, though, his figures value eating and drinking above all other delights — an indication of how Northern he was, even in his pagan mood. Enormous amounts of wine are consumed; the stress is clearly on quantity.

Vigor and crudity, qualities utterly foreign to the conventional idyl, mark Müller's language. Satyr Mopsus exclaims ecstatically, to his love: "Oh, I can't stand it any more when I think how nice it would be if you'd hang on my back, at each tit a shaggy boy with wide-open mouth and young, swelling little horns."[50] The idyls of German peasant life reveal an even more colloquial aspect of the author.

In the landscapes described in these works, Müller sensed the same vitality and fertility that he celebrated in his fauns and shepherds.[51] While Heinse wrote as an intellectual, with a certain forced sensuality, Müller seems to have experienced the world with uncomplicated directness. Thus, as Richard Alewyn has remarked, his descriptions seem more natural, more original, and in that sense more pagan;[52] but his paganism is rarely aesthetic, and most of his work is only tangential to our theme.

III

Besides its many geniuses of the first rank, the latter eighteenth century produced a great number of brilliant lesser figures. Few of them had more remarkable careers than (Johann) Georg Forster. His father, Johann Reinhold Forster, was noted as a traveler, translator, and student of nature; Georg Forster was even more versatile. Having accompanied his father on Captain Cook's second circumnavigation of the globe (1772–1775), the younger Forster published his monumental account, *A Voyage round the World*, in English, in 1777. In his *Views of the Lower Rhine* (1791–1794), he appears as one of the early champions of medieval art and

Gothic architecture, standing between the normative aesthetics of the older generation and the empathetic appreciation of the romantics.[53]

Even more striking than Forster's range and versatility is the excellence of his prose. Friedrich Schlegel, noting the clarity, naturalness, and freshness of his style, rightly described it as classic.[54] Quite possibly his involvement in the actual world, his wide travels, and not least his intimate knowledge of English, kept his writings free of professional heaviness.

Unlike most German intellectuals, Forster was keenly interested in practical problems of politics and economics. Ardently sympathetic with the ideals of the French Revolution, he was one of the leaders of the ill-fated revolutionary government of Mainz. Later he moved to Paris, where he died in 1794, during the Reign of Terror, concerned at the course which events were taking and somewhat disillusioned, but still a staunch believer in human freedom. Goethe's moving lines in *Hermann and Dorothea*, depicting the fate of a young idealist who perished in Paris during the Revolution, may well have been written with Forster in mind.[55]

It may be that Forster's descriptions of the South Sea Islands, and especially of Tahiti, were the most influential of the many achievements of his brief life. Besides his own observations, he drew on the works of earlier explorers, Rousseau's belief in the noble savage, a pantheistic faith in nature, the old dream of Arcadia, and not least on Winckelmann's vision of Greece.

In Forster's account the Tahitians appear hospitable, generous, innocent, and "contented with their simple way of life." [56] For one villain in the South Sea Islands, one finds fifty in any "civilized" country, he believed, and he expresses the hope that contact between the natives and Europe may be broken off "before the corruption of manners which unhappily characterizes civilized regions" reaches them.[57] He admits how-

ever that instances of petty theft and promiscuity occur; [58] he
is disappointed to find radical social inequality even in the
"state of nature." [59]

While the morals of the Tahitians are generally admirable,
their beauty is even more so. Many of them, to be sure, are
far from handsome, but the norm is high; [60] clearly, it is
Winckelmann's norm: "They are all well-proportioned, and
some would have been selected by Phidias or Praxiteles, as
models of masculine beauty. Their features are sweet, and
unruffled by violent passions. Their large eyes, their arched
eyebrows, and high forehead, give a noble air to their heads." [61]
If their dress does not completely possess "that perfect form,
so justly admired in the draperies of the ancient Greek
statues," [62] it is still far more advantageously adapted to the
human figure than any modern fashion known to the explorer.
While one does not doubt that the islanders were actually
beautiful and graceful, it is clear that Forster's way of seeing
had been formed by Winckelmann. Object and subject are
in harmony.

The landscape is as beautiful as the people themselves are.
The country lived up to Bougainville's term "Elysium,"
Forster recorded; it could also boast "romantick scenery." [63]
When he wrote that "shady trees, covered with a dark-green
foliage, bore golden apples," [64] he doubtless recalled the Hes-
perides; we think of Henri Rousseau's paintings, and perhaps
of Mignon's Italy.

Forster was by no means a complete pagan like Heinse:
while he noted the sexual freedom of unmarried Tahitian girls
with tolerant objectivity, he remarked that the voluptuousness of the natives was their worst trait. [65] Vindicating the
reputation of the island women, he wrote that only one group
of them, drawn from the lowest class, was made up of prostitutes. [66] Nor did he describe Tahiti as a utopia: the ethical
and aesthetic shortcomings of its people are set down as we
have seen. Yet Forster did picture the Tahitians as nobler and

more beautiful than contemporary European Christians, did portray them as the Hellenes of the South Seas, in physique if not in intellect. His account is an important part of the tradition of German paganism.

In two important essays, Forster appears as an admirer, though hardly a disciple, of German Hellenism. The first, "On Schiller's 'The Gods of Greece,'" is a defense of that poem against Count Friedrich Leopold Stolberg's outspoken polemic. Greek mythology, Stolberg maintained, combined "the crudest worship of idols with the dreariest atheism." [67] Forster, both courteous and skillful, makes a strong plea for freedom of expression, before turning to the poem itself. Schiller attacked, he maintains, the "philosophic," not the Christian, concept of God. [68] People no longer have any literal belief in the anthropomorphic Olympians, but is not the Christian God conceived anthropomorphically also? [69] "Greece was more than a mother and nurse to our spirit"; [70] shall we reject her completely? And at the least, one can admire the poem without worshiping "fabled" divinities.

The second brief article, "Art and the Age," which appeared in Schiller's journal *Thalia* in 1789, reads in part almost like a prose paraphrase of "The Gods of Greece." "Is there even one endurable statue of the later periods for which Greek mythology did not have to provide the thought, the shape, and proportions, Greek costume the garments?" [71] runs his rhetorical question. Modern art is "immeasurably" inferior; he lists various causes, drawn from Winckelmann and Schiller, for its low state. [72] Forster contrasts Greek culture to medieval barbarity and the coldness of the contemporary world and notes that the creative youth of mankind will never return. [73]

To return to the theme of the South Sea Islands: the discovery of Tahiti, and especially Forster's descriptions of it, made considerable impact on German literature. In a fascinating study, Winfried Volk distinguishes between "utopian-philosophic" and "aesthetic-erotic" treatments of the theme; [74]

sometimes, of course, both strands are found in a single work. Thus in Friedrich Wilhelm Zachariae's "Tahiti or the Happy Island"[75] (1777) the virtuous but amorous natives seem to have the best of both worlds. The innocent girls resemble "shepherdesses in Arcadia."[76] They are beautiful almost beyond European imagination, and "naked, except that a light garment flowed about their loins, which latter they had colored dark blue."[77] But the short poem ends with an anti-European twist characteristic of the age: soon white men will destroy this paradise; freedom, just and simple mores, and holding goods in common will all be abolished.[78]

One of the most notable appearances of the theme, which can be traced down to and beyond Stevenson and Gauguin, is in Lord Byron's *The Island* (1823). While the poem tells, in heroic couplets, of the "mutiny on the Bounty," it makes the usual points about life in the South Seas: natural beauty, community of goods, unspoiled and courteous islanders, the ruinous impact of European civilization; above all, there is a dusky maiden, described with real Byronic verve, and possessing "A form like Aphrodite's in her shell."[79]

Perhaps the most interesting aspect of this tradition, at least for Americans, is the line running from Winckelmann and Forster to Herman Melville. The following passage would not be out of place in *Typee*. "The calm contented state of the natives; their simple way of life; the beauty of the landscape; the excellence of the climate; the abundance, salubrity, and delicious taste of its fruits, were altogether enchanting, and filled the heart with rapture."[80] Actually it is in Forster's *Voyage*. Conversely, when Melville writes, describing the Marquesan islanders: "nearly every individual of their number might have been taken for a sculptor's model," and "Many of their faces present a profile classically beautiful,"[81] he seems to echo Forster. He too fears the advent of civilization and Christianity.[82] The connection between aesthetic paganism and the novelist may be indirect, but it is real.[83]

Chapter VII

Iphigenia and Italy: Goethe

♩♩♩♩♩♩♩♩♩♩♩♩♩♩♩♩♩♩♩♩♩♩♩♩♩♩♩

The years from Goethe's journey to Weimar in 1775 to the surreptitiously prepared flight to Italy in 1786 were a time of responsibility, of largely altruistic labor for the state and for his friends, and of a conscious struggle for self-control; they were not a period in which "pagan" tendencies were likely to flourish. Probably they made up a salutary stage in the poet's development, but there were losses as well as gains. Something was clearly wrong; the headlong, almost panic nature of Goethe's escape to Italy would be evidence enough. Perhaps one may venture the opinion that he was living too much for others, too little for his own genius; differently put, that the domination of Charlotte von Stein, and perhaps also the responsibility Goethe assumed toward the young duke, estranged him from himself. The poet's testimony that he dared not, for years, look at any Latin work is eloquent.[1] Longing for the South, for the Mediterranean, is the most poignant element in *Wilhelm Meister* as it is in *Iphigenia in Tauris*. In both works the classic South, the Italy his father had loved, fused into one image with Winckelmann's Greece, for which Goethe longed:

> Kennst du das Haus? Auf Säulen ruht sein Dach,
> Es glänzt der Saal, es schimmert das Gemach,
> Und Marmorbilder stehn . . .[2]

The *Drang nach Süden* was suppressed and more or less subterranean for years; when it prevailed, the result was a psychological and poetic revolution. And though Goethe's "Greeks," under Charlotte's influence, might appear more Christian than pagan, they would assume a very different aspect once the tie to her was broken.

As Barker Fairley has brilliantly shown, Frau von Stein stood in Goethe's mind not only for purity, order, *caritas*, and healing love; she was also associated with ideas of Christian dualism, self-abnegation, and otherworldliness, with the belief that man stands completely apart from the rest of nature.[3] The cluster of forces working in this direction, including Spinoza's ethics and the concept of duty to society, was opposed by another cluster in which the development of the individual, the integral wholeness of nature, and the appeal of the ancient world were joined. Charlotte and her ideals inspired some of Goethe's most beautiful poems; they were unable, in the long run, to satisfy his intellectual and personal demands.

Inevitably, the poet of these years speaks in two voices; a psychological tug of war is going on. Numerous poems invoke "the gods"; "Wanderer's Night Song," a prayer for inner peace, is directed to a single, all-merciful God. (It is not a matter of a virtuoso operating with different mythologies; the problem goes far deeper.) Some poems celebrate self-reliance and self-confidence;[4] another warns of the "Limitations of Mankind." There is a strong sense of the power of fate, often recalling Greek myth. In his "Hartz Journey," as in *Iphigenia*, there is an attempt to reconcile the classic and the Christian; the image of fate's shears occurs, but also the appeal to the father of love.

> Ist auf deinem Psalter,
> Vater der Liebe, ein Ton
> Seinem Ohre vernehmlich,
> So erquicke sein Herz![5]

Within the general situation determined by fate, Christian love may still play a role. The sense of harsh destiny and the trust in a benevolent god are equally felt. Perhaps the intellectual dissonance makes the poem the more poignant. In "The Divine" Goethe distinguishes absolutely between the rest of creation and man:

> Nur allein der Mensch
> Vermag das Unmögliche:
> Er unterscheidet,
> Wählet und richtet.[6]

It is perhaps his most "Charlottean" poem, yet it contains a sly hit at man's theological notions and perhaps at the gods themselves: we revere the immortals *as if* they were human, *as if* they always acted with the motives of the best of men. The Platonic exaltation of "Dedication" contrasts with the celebration of physical love in "The Chalice." Making all allowances for the changes in man's situation and moods and the particularly rich variety of Goethe's mind, one does sense here that conflict between two souls within one breast of which Faust complained.

The epic fragment "The Mysteries" (1784) attempts a synthesis of the two strains. Generally the tendency of the poem is toward a blending of eighteenth-century humanism and Christianity, toward self-mastery and discipline, as its setting in Montserrat and its cast of knightly monks suggest:

> Von der Gewalt, die alle Wesen bindet,
> Befreit der Mensch sich, der sich überwindet [7]

are its most memorable lines. Twice the symbol of a cross wreathed in roses appears:

> Es steht das Kreuz mit Rosen dicht umschlungen.
> Wer hat dem Kreuze Rosen zugesellt? [8]

In line with the whole syncretic nature of the poem, we have here as its climax the idea of uniting sadness and joy, suffering and love, in one fused ideal. The roses represent "ancient thought, turned toward life" as Mme. Bianquis well puts it.[9]

Like Ibsen and Stefan George after him, Goethe joined here
in the tradition of the Third Kingdom, with its dream of a
new religion higher and nobler than Christianity. One thinks
of George's line about "the Christian dancing" and Lawrence's "The Man Who Died." To reconcile renunciation
with a philosophy of enjoyment is not easy: it is not surprising that the poem remained a fragment. But when, in old age,
Goethe's whole intention becomes conciliatory, we find him
making such comments as the "very serious jest" that he could
revere both Christ and the sun.[10] He has returned to the
theme of "The Mysteries."

In *Iphigenia in Tauris* (1787), the moral, more or less
Christian note predominates. Paradoxically, this variation on
a Greek myth is one of Goethe's least pagan works. It is
extraordinary how Christian an interpretation emerges in
Iphigenia, a work separated by only a few brief years from
the Storm and Stress robustness of the recent past and the
aesthetic eroticism soon to emerge in works like the *Roman
Elegies*. To be sure, there is an authentically pagan element
in Iphigenia, particularly in the "Song of the Fates," but
precisely this element is vanquished. At times almost Pietistic
in its inwardness, the drama has a negative importance in the
story of German paganism, though a very great positive
significance in the history of Enlightenment thought. As
poetry, to quote Schiller, it is beyond praise.[11]

Iphigenia is a drama of inner crisis; its true stage is the
human soul. Both Orestes and his sister, the priestess Iphigenia,
are subjected to moral and psychological ordeals; both are
purified by them. Iphigenia's crisis is less acute than her
brother's: even to save him, his friend, and herself, she finds
herself unable to lie to the barbarian king; he in turn, essentially noble, allows the Greeks to depart in peace. Iphigenia's
scruples would be excessive if not absurd in another; in her,
whose purity Goethe found mirrored in Raphael's St. Agatha,[12]
they do not strain our credulity. At the same time, the fact that

she does at first attempt to lie and loses for a while her usual serenity saves her character from being marked by too inhuman a perfection.

Iphigenia is extraordinarily inward, soulful, full of sentiment. Her first famous line — "Das Land der Griechen mit der Seele suchend" — [13] is characteristic. (Mignon expresses longing for a southern homeland far more concretely.) The priestess does not calculate, she feels; the words which her heart speaks express the ultimate truth in her eyes and in the play's.

Her subjectivity reaches its apex in her appeal, or rather ultimatum, to the gods at the moment of crisis. Thus far she has considered them good; by their action they must now save her and her image of them:

> Rettet mich,
> Und rettet euer Bild in meiner Seele! [14]

Man is the judge of the gods — an essentially impious position, though Iphigenia is of course unaware of any heresy.

Iphigenia is an expression of that fusion of Storm and Stress feeling and Enlightenment ideas which produced, as Korff put it, the Weimar synthesis.[15] Its tolerance — thus the Taurian figures are anything but barbarous — recalls Lessing's *Nathan the Wise*. In its "happy ending," in its vindication of the gods' goodness, and not least in its diction, the optimism so often attributed to the eighteenth century prevails. Even Iphigenia's fetters are "solemn, holy"; the Immortals love the "good" races of men, she is convinced, though her own family's experiences have not borne out this assumption.

Generally, the diction reflects the two influences which largely shaped the play: Pietistically tinged Christianity and the Greece of Winckelmann. The key adjectives of the drama — quiet, calm, pure, noble, holy (*still, ruhig, rein, edel, heilig*) — are mainly drawn from the Pietist vocabulary; most of them, as we have seen, are at the same time central in Winckelmann's prose.[16] Thus form mirrors content very neatly: the language itself has a double heritage. In the statuesqueness of the bearing, grouping, and gestures of its characters, and in the relative lack of color, *Iphigenia* also derives from the archaeologist. When Orestes addresses his sister as "great soul," we are reminded of Laocoön and Niobe.

At the height of her moral anguish, Iphigenia almost reverts to a view of the gods which Hesiod or Aeschylus would have found familiar, and sings the "Song of the Fates" which her nurse had taught her years before:

> Es fürchte die Götter
> Das Menschengeschlecht!
> Sie halten die Herrschaft
> In ewigen Händen,
> Und können sie brauchen
> Wie's ihnen gefällt!
>
> Der fürchte sie doppelt
> Den je sie erhoben!
> Auf Klippen und Wolken
> Sind Stühle bereitet
> Um goldene Tische.[17]

The erstwhile favorite of the gods is cast into outer darkness; they continue their serene existence:

> Sie aber, sie bleiben
> In ewigen Festen
> An goldenen Tischen.[18]

In the archaic view (which Hölderlin also expressed in "Hyperion's Song of Fate") the gods are cruel and jealous; man's life is dominated by fear and "bronze" necessity; whole families, like the Tantalids, may be cursed eternally. By boldly imposing her vision upon the gods, Iphigenia renders the old theology and the old ethics obsolete.

As is well known, Goethe came to feel that *Iphigenia* was too full of sentiment to be truly antique.[19] It has been argued that *Tasso* and *Egmont*, in which tragic fate is stronger than "pure humaneness," [20] are closer to his own essential view of the world.[21]

A mild sort of neopaganism figures briefly but significantly in *Torquato Tasso* (1790) when the protagonist evokes the Renaissance version of a Golden Age in which everything pleasing — to the man of cultivated taste — is permitted.[22] The Princess (whom he loves) corrects him primly: only the truly proper is permitted. No doubt the excessive decorum reflected in *Tasso* was a major force in forming Goethe's decision to escape to Rome.

That escape, he believed, was necessary to ensure self-preservation, even survival. However noble his life in Weimar, however exalted at times, it had become bitterly unhappy. His existence in the last years had been worse than death, he wrote back from Rome.[23] Obedient to his daimon, he fled from Germany without telling his closest friends or even Charlotte, who of course could never really forgive him. The "daimon" — which one might translate as the voice of the subconscious — seems to have known that radical measures were needed. Perhaps Goethe feared that he would be "talked out" of his journey, perhaps he was aware of an ambivalence; at any rate he confronted his friends with a fait accompli.

By anticipation, he seemed to know that there were certain classic, Southern qualities which he could experience in Italy and somehow incorporate into himself. These qualities are foils to the gloomy characteristics of the North. By becoming a Southerner, or half a Southerner, he hoped to regain spiritual health. Thus he felt that a man who really used his eyes in Rome would gain "solidity";[24] he does not need to say explicitly that the German character is flaccid or abstract. Similarly, the Italians are whole human beings, or at least they have the chance to be;[25] they do not suffer from the dreadful fragmentation of which Hölderlin and Nietzsche were to complain. In classic life and art, as in nature, Goethe found greatness, simplicity, freedom from curlicues and from pettiness of every sort. Like Heinse, he had come to loathe the Gothic, writing of its "tobacco-pipe columns, little pointed towers and crenelations." [26] How can a man who has seen the Juno Ludovisi bear to look at gargoyles? Gothic architecture, which he had so eloquently defended in youth, became symbolic of a whole world of Northern superstition and ugliness — not merely of the barbarism which the term had long connoted. In Rome, living in the sun, he would find it "salutary . . . to live in the midst of a completely sensuous people" [27] — however great its faults. Finally he would be able to see things and persons as they are, clearly, purely. [28]

At the climax of Thomas Mann's *The Magic Mountain*, Hans Castorp has a vision of the beautiful, serene existence lived by the "people of the sun" in a Hellenic landscape; it is a symbol of life, opposed to the romantic allure of death. Goethe had foreseen that in Italy he would live with such a people. Arrived in Rome, he found his anticipation more than fulfilled and felt like Pygmalion after the lovely statue had come to life: when the girl "finally came up to him and said 'It is I!' how different was the living woman from the sculptured stone." [29]

To an amazing extent the poet managed to combine the zest of a vacation with a really Faustian energy and drive. He was not in Rome only to enjoy himself, he wrote, but to learn; [30] actually he did both, besides writing and revising a great deal and producing well over a thousand paintings and drawings. Rome was a school (later, he spoke of the "school of the Greeks") and he had to begin his studies in an elementary class. He was touched by reading Winckelmann's letters about his early experiences in Rome, where he had come a generation earlier: "a still poorer fool than I . . . he too was so German and serious about a thorough, solid knowledge of antiquities and art. How valiantly and well he worked his way through." [31]

If Goethe largely identified himself with the archaeologist as "the pupil of the Greeks," [32] he still maintained his own individuality. The *Italian Journey* reveals a battery of interests ranging from meteorology to painting. It, and still more the letters Goethe wrote at the time, testify to spontaneity and verve. For all his "German seriousness," the man who lived under the name of Miller or Möller, trying hard to preserve his incognito, and who traveled through Sicily on muleback, seems to have enjoyed himself vastly. A certain self-consciousness there inevitably was, but Goethe after all stood near the beginning of a tradition. [33] A gulf separates him from the nineteenth-century visitors who so systematically sought after light from the South. Heine's bitter phrase "travelers in culture" is characteristically accurate.

The *Italian Journey* also reminds us of that unexpected practicality in Goethe's nature — the burgher side — which saved him from the fate of Werther or of Hölderlin. Details of city life in Naples or crop-growing in Sicily interested him keenly. Yet it is his interest in natural science which forms one of the great themes of the account. To discover the archetypal plant he finds as great an achievement as to learn the secret of Greek sculpture. Indeed, the realms of nature and art are harmonious; their laws, he came to believe, are the same.

Goethe does not tire of maintaining that he has become a different and better person. [34] His view of his own metamorphosis is in line with his concept of nature and his whole faith in dying to be reborn. In escaping from Northern gloom and the neurosis of the recent past, he gave the main credit to Italy. If only "poor" Albrecht Dürer could have been as fortunate, could have seen more of Italy, he wrote. [35] Essentially, one feels, the Italian adventure was a success because it was only in part an escape; it was also, even more importantly, a turning toward new tasks and a new, freer way of life.

In Goethe's account of his journey, as in his letters, one can observe a gradual hardening of his attitude toward Christianity and Christian art. Despite the suddenness of his flight, there was no violent, abrupt aesthetic revolution. Some of his descriptions of works of art seen on the way to Rome praise treatments of very Christian subject matter, though often with reservations; he writes of the "indescribable inwardness" with which the Virgin regards the risen Christ in a picture of Guercino's.[36] He even commends a Guido Reni in Bologna, in which the Madonna gives suck to the infant Jesus[37] — a subject which he later attempted to banish completely from the realm of art. Possibly, pagan stirrings are already apparent in Goethe's remark that the Virgin seems to be nourishing "not a child of love and joy but a substituted heavenly changeling" which she accepts humbly and uncomprehendingly. There is a certain ambivalence, more observable in the unretouched letters and diaries than in the *Journey*, in some of even the early comments. An entry made in Venice, for example, rejoices that "Christian zeal" has not melted down the famous horses of St. Mark's.[38]

During the first months of his stay, Goethe often expresses annoyance at the luxury of the Church and its theatrical ritual; he seems on the whole anti-Catholic rather than anti-Christian. He is too much of a "Diogenes" to be impressed by the "hocus-pocus" of the Mass;[39] and he mentions his Protestant reaction to the sight of the Pope "humming and swaying back and forth" before the altar.[40] Twice he cites Christ's words "Venio iterum crucifigi" (I come to be crucified again) from the legend of the Wandering Jew.[41] He even contrasts the simplicity of early Christianity to the "baroque paganism" of Catholic ritual;[42] this is no avowal of Evangelical faith but a bitter reproach to the Roman church, delivered in true Enlightenment style. As the context makes clear, Goethe's intention was "to observe true nature and noble art," not to vindicate primitive Christianity.[43]

As time goes on, his tone changes: the longer the poet stayed in the South, the further he moved from what Trevelyan has called "Iphigenia" morality.[44] Thus he wrote with reference to Herder's *Ideas*, a work proclaiming man's rise to ever nobler humanity: "I too must say, I think it true that humanity will finally prevail, only I fear that at the same time the world will become one great hospital and each man the humane sick-nurse of the next."[45] Too much nobility, "applied Christianity," and softness will make the earth a depressing institution. If his words were exclamatory or more violent, one might be tempted to attribute them to Nietzsche. An Easter passage, written in Goethe's last months in Rome, needs no comment: "The Lord Christ is just now rising, with a horrible noise."[46] Goethe's really bitter and sweeping rejection of Christianity would not be expressed for another year or two, but it is quite clear in what direction he is moving.

The excursion made to Magna Graecia and Sicily in 1787 served, by removing Goethe from the ambience of Rome for a few weeks, to bring him more directly face to face with the Greek world itself. Twice he visited the Doric temples at Paestum; he was frank to admit that the austerity of authentically Hellenic architecture was at first alien to his taste.[47] Though he soon came to sense its grandeur, there is none of the rapture that marked his reaction to lighter, later works of Hellenistic or Roman art. In Sicily it was not architectural remains but the landscape which seemed genuinely Greek, even archetypal. Reading the *Odyssey* here revived Goethe's desire to write a drama about Nausicaa, the daughter of King Alcinous who had so hospitably welcomed the shipwrecked Odysseus.[48] What if the princess, ignorant of the hero's marriage, should fall in love and finally, having learned the truth, kill herself? A few very beautiful lines were written down, scenes were sketched out, but the plan contains such disparate elements that it could hardly have been carried out; it is clearly the product of a mind in transition. The poet aspired to the robust objectivity of Homer, yet several of the lines recall the "modern" style of *Iphigenia* and *Tasso*, and the motif of suicide because of frustrated love recalls *Werther* rather than the Greeks. Goethe would have been sentimentalizing Homer — the last thing appropriate to his new orientation.[49]

Goethe's emerging paganism was of course no formal creed — he did not think in rigid categories — but its general nature is not hard to grasp. One important element is the poet's attitude toward death. Describing gravestones in Verona, he writes that the wind which comes to our nostrils from the graves of the ancients is laden with fragrance as if it had been blown across a rose-covered hill. He continues:

> Here is no kneeling man in armor who awaits a happy resurrection, here the artist, with more or less skill, has always represented only the sheer presence of men, and thus continued their existence and made it lasting. They do not fold their hands, do not gaze toward heaven; but they are what they were, they stand together, feel sympathy for each other, love each other.[50]

Goethe has varied the classic theme set by Lessing in "How the Ancients Represented Death";[51] it was fast becoming a commonplace.

Equally important, and intimately related to the Hellenists' attitude toward death, is the emphasis on realizing one's existence here and now. (Nowhere is Goethe farther from the otherworldliness of his recent past.) He contrasts the splendor of "great, true existence"[52] with the "fairy tales" told to help people from day to day. The ancients faced reality, he implies; many moderns need to be told comforting lies, "and therefore so many churches were built."[53] It is wrong, indeed morbid, to divide the world between a sinful present and a holy state to come; life on this earth is sacred. After about a year in the South he can write that the moment is all; intelligent men so arrange their lives that they contain a maximum of "sensible, happy moments."[54] One thinks with some amazement of Faust's wager, and recalls with still greater surprise that Goethe wrote one of the most Northern, grotesque scenes of his greatest work in the anti-Faustian atmosphere of Rome.

At this time too the concept of the gestalt becomes central: the figure, either in literature or sculpture, which is self-contained, clearly formed, solid, with simple, flowing contours. In poetry, Goethe's Dorothea is a concrete example of this ideal; in art, above all the statues of the Greek gods. He writes in Sicily of "shapeless" Palestine, and of Rome with its confusing abundance of shapes; only in the direct Hellenic succession does one find a true gestalt.[55] Goethe in the school of the Greeks suggests Rilke the pupil of Rodin, turning away from the facile sentimentalities of his early verse and learning to write about "things." However great the differences between the two poets, they are here in the same tradition.

Shapes, of course, cannot be created or comprehended without the senses, and the vindication of the sensuous is an integral part of Goethe's new faith. The Italians, who live naturally and vividly, in the sun, are counterpointed against the somber Germans beset by their clouds. Of a statue of Leda Goethe wrote, with a nice play on words, that it had a "high sensuous sense" (*von hohem sinnlichen Sinn*).[56] Sexual emancipation in literature and in life — not promiscuity — was an aspect of the classic existence. While the outspokenly erotic poems, like the *Roman Elegies*, are mainly based on later experiences, Goethe's "favorite personal poem,"[57] to Cupid, and his "Amor as Landscape Painter" indicate that the "Platonism" of Weimar has been left behind.

The statues of the Olympian gods, which had already played a considerable part in Goethe's inner life, became dominant in his existence, not only as symbols but as actualities.[58] They are uniquely beautiful: the head of Juno in his room is "like a book of Homer's"[59] and they have magic power as well; [60] the Apollo Belvedere lifts one above ordinary reality. [61] At times the poet's attitude is half-playful: thus on Christmas Day, 1786, he writes about offering his morning prayers to the colossal head of Jupiter; [62] a few days later he repeats a story about the English tourists who kissed the hand of the Minerva Guistiniani. [63] Yet basically he is serious: surrounded by classical statues, one's thoughts turn to man "in his purest state"; this makes the observer himself "alive and purely human." [64] (As Schiller proclaimed, the gods are not divided from man by an unbridgeable gulf: they can serve as norms or archetypes.) As a good classicist, he came like Winckelmann to maintain that the nude human figure is the highest subject of art, in part precisely because it is the closest to the Greek image of the gods. Goethe remarks that in his youth, in Frankfurt, he obtained casts of Laocoön's head, Niobe's daughters, and other figures. "These noble figures were a sort of esoteric antidote whenever the weak, the false, the mannered threatened to get power over me." [65] They also stirred up a painful longing for something then unknown. These comments about the effect on man made by the antique statues stand almost at the end of the *Italian Journey*. It is not unreasonable to read them as the climax, the "moral," of the whole work. Again one thinks of the conclusion of Rilke's "Archaic Torso of Apollo": "You must change your life."

A work by a writer closely associated with Goethe, Karl Philipp Moritz' *Mythology* (*Götterlehre*: Vienna, 1792) helps to illuminate the meaning which the pagan gods had for the poet. Moritz, who was befriended by Goethe in Rome, hails him as the best interpreter of the gods and prints several of his poems in full to illuminate the essential nature of various figures of Greek myth. Mythological poems Moritz calls a language of the imagination; the myths are not mere allegories nor are they to be regarded as history. As true works of art, myths and mythological figures exist for their own sake. [66] Jupiter, for instance, means primarily himself, not "upper air."

Yet in a way each god represents all of nature (we might say an aspect of nature). The gods are by no means moral, any more than nature is; they are forces. Imagination has given them human shape.

This view makes the gods symbols in Goethe's sense: they are real in themselves and stand at the same time for some broader entity. One might say that for Moritz or Goethe Juno or Jupiter was an aesthetic actuality of the highest order. While neither writer could have said, like Hölderlin, "Apollo has smitten me," both believed that a Hellenic statue or a poem, through its very beauty, could affect the life of modern man.

Goethe's new view of art and literature is implicit in what has been said so far. Phidias and Homer are the supreme masters; not Rubens, Ossian, or even Shakespeare. Reading the *Odyssey* in Sicilian surroundings had convinced him that the classic is the natural and the natural the classic.[67] The whole conflict between ancient and modern could be summed up in a few words: "they represented existence, we usually the effect; they described the ghastly, we in a ghastly way; they the agreeable, we agreeably, etc." [68] From this contrast he derived a belief in the absolute superiority of the classic, and did not waver in his conviction for many years.

The central insight of Goethe's Italian period is the intuition that nature and the greatest art — Greek art of course — illustrate certain intrinsic laws or archetypal principles: "These lofty works of art, being at the same time the highest works of nature, were brought forth by men according to true and natural laws. Everything arbitrary, merely imagined, falls away; there is necessity, there is God." [69] Just as the "archetypal plant" gives the essential form of all plants, Greek sculpture has created forever the archetypes of man, and even the "primal horse." Art is not a second nature in the sense of an imitation, but is parallel to nature, which now is not the wildly dynamic force of Goethe's Storm and Stress days, but an ordered macrocosm. Aesthetics prevails over any ethics which is not equally founded on nature. The beautiful is worshiped because it is literally the real and the true.

The *Italian Journey* ends with a triad of motifs of parting and renunciation: a beautiful statue unbought, the "fair Milanese lady" [70] unloved, the citing of lines written by Ovid on his exile. Why, one may wonder, did Goethe never return to Rome? [71] There would seem to be several reasons: partly perhaps the intuitive knowledge that the past cannot be recaptured except in art; partly the sense that he had now absorbed what Rome had to give him. After all, he was to live and write as a "Roman" for some years, back in Weimar. Yet the deepest reason lies in the variety and dualism of his own nature. Still less than Winckelmann, could he repress his Northern side completely. Not only did he write crucial scenes of *Faust*, including the very unclassical "Witch's Kitchen," in Rome; he perfected his most Christian work, *Iphigenia*, at a time when he seemed to be turning more and more to paganism.

Paganism however dominates the themes and attitudes of the *Roman Elegies*, published in 1795, but mainly written several years earlier. In style too this cycle of erotic poems represents Goethe's first major effort to write objectively, like a Greek. As always he uses his own experiences — in this case transposed into a different setting — as raw material, [72] but he has striven to present everything in timeless, typical, plastic form. Thus the beloved of these poems is not primarily a vividly realized individual, but a sort of archetypal woman, simple, sensual but devoted, of truly classical beauty. In the third Elegy the lovers are stylized by being associated with a whole series of mythical predecessors. Drawing motifs from literary tradition, especially from Catullus, Propertius, and Tibullus, also removes the poems further from Goethe's usual confessional mode and gives them more distance. While the lover is unmistakably Goethe — or better his Italian *persona*, "Filippo Miller, Tedesco, pittore" — he too is stylized, as the

"Northern barbarian." Writing with "antique openness," the poet does not suppress the economics of the affair: the lover has supplied fine clothes, a carriage to take his mistress to the opera, and so forth. Of course the historical consciousness of modern man cannot be completely banished, but the problem is treated lightly. The school of the Greeks is still open, Amor tells the poet, even though the antique age is no longer new for us, as it was for the happy artists whom love inspired. If he wishes to revive the past, he too must live happily: "Lebe glücklich, und so lebe die Vorzeit in dir!" [73]

The contrast between the gloomy North and the brightness and warmth of Rome is more explicitly proclaimed than in the *Journey*. Gray, depressing days are associated, in the seventh Elegy, with sterile introspection. Here love is still accepted with the readiness and frankness of the figures of classic myth:

In der heroischen Zeit, da Götter und Göttinnen liebten,
    Folgte Begierde dem Blick, folgte Genuss der Begier. [74]

There is another sort of love, he admits: some of Amor's arrows make the frustrated lover ill for years. Shades of Werther, and of Charlotte!

The course and the minor vicissitudes of a happily realized love supply the raw material of the *Elegies*. The accent is on fulfillment; the beautiful present, the here-and-now, is celebrated. The lover proclaims his complete triumph early in the cycle. Toward the end, he prays that the god will grant everyone "the first and last of all the world's goods" [75] — in other words, sexual happiness, as the context makes clear. In the four Elegies which Goethe withheld from publication,[76] he is still more outspoken; he remarks on . . . "des geschaukelten Betts lieblicher knarrender Ton" [77] but devotes a poem to the dangers of venereal disease; Hermes (Mercury, quicksilver) however brings healing.[78] The two Elegies devoted to Priapus repeat antique themes and are as brutally direct as any Roman poem.

Yet it is the love of a poet and artist of which the cycle tells, of a man determined to steep himself in antiquity. Playfully, and without mentioning Horace, Goethe refers to his famous lines:

> Vos exemplaria graeca
> nocturna versate manu, versate diurna.

He accepts only half of this advice; at night Amor keeps him busy. Yet as a poet and especially as a sculptor, he has learned from love:

> Und belehr ich mich nicht, indem ich des lieblichen Busens
>   Formen spähe, die Hand leite die Hüften hinab?
> Dann versteh ich den Marmor erst recht; ich denk und vergleiche,
>   Sehe mit fühlendem Aug, fühle mit sehender Hand.[79]

From human flesh one comes to comprehend marble; in a statue one senses human emotion: "Blicke der süssen Begier, selbst in dem Marmor noch feucht."[80]

In the *Elegies*, then, Goethe celebrates physical fulfillment; the intellectual element does not dominate but has an important place. One thinks of Rilke's poem inspired by the line of Count Lancorońsky — "Nicht Geist, nicht Inbrunst wollen wir entbehren" —[81] except that Goethe seems less to be proclaiming a program than confirming the existence of a happy state of affairs. In the sphere of love, as in aesthetics and elsewhere, the poet's great aim is now to state, and to glorify, the typical, the norm, the "classic"; here too he sees expressions of the laws which shape nature and art.

That happiness no longer obtains in the *Venetian Epigrams*,[82] which are often discussed in connection with the *Elegies*. The reasons are obvious: both groups are classic in form, pagan in content; both have frequently been found shocking. The change of mood is startling, however: in the *Epigrams* Goethe writes as one bitterly disappointed in Italy, in man generally (the French Revolution had frightened and disgusted him); he is scornful of the mob but finds the upper classes unbearably dull. While the "I" of the *Epigrams* is eager to return to his beloved in the North, he occupies himself *faute de mieux* with prostitutes during his enforced absence. Goethe's letters of the time betray the same bitterness: thus he wrote Herder and his wife that he must get to Venice before Palm Sunday: "To have some gain, as a pagan, from the sufferings of the good man [Christ], I absolutely must hear the singers of the Conservatory and see the doge in solemn procession." [83]

The first few epigrams of the 103 published as a unit in 1795 establish the tone and touch on the major themes. The first leads one to expect faunlike license, bacchantic fury, above all a profusion of uninhibited life:

> Sarkophagen und Urnen verzierte der Heide mit Leben:
> Faunen tanzen umher, mit der Bacchantinnen Chor
> Machen sie bunte Reihe; der ziegengefüssete Pausback
> Zwingt den heiseren Ton wild aus dem schmetternden Horn. [84]

Quickly the other important notes are struck: the primacy of sexual love; bitter annoyance with the alleged dishonesty of the Italians; deceived pilgrims and deceitful priests; a generally harsh view of life — no man can achieve more than to feed himself and the children he begets. [85] The vehemence of his rejection of Christianity is striking; Jesus was Himself deceived, we read. [86] Such views are not representative of Goethe at any other period; [87] he is generally too conciliatory to express himself with extreme violence, and inclines far more to reverence than to polemics. Writing at a time when he finds himself, most uncharacteristically, the victim of boredom, he is quite simply surly; he even complains that he has only one real talent, writing German, and that working in so poor a medium is the ruin of his life and art. [88] Yet obviously the anti-Christian strain cannot be ignored; it expresses an attitude often latent or implied in other works. Perhaps the very fierceness of Goethe's resentment betrays conflict, a subconscious sense that the religion he had inherited still exerted its attraction.

That is sheer speculation; the *Epigrams* themselves say nothing of any such pull. Some were suppressed, for obvious reasons. In one of the most interesting of these the poet states, not without a certain sympathy, that Jesus failed to follow the right path on earth; none of His followers will find the way to a reasonable enjoyment of life any more than He did.[89] (One thinks, as so often in reading German literature of the last two centuries, of D. H. Lawrence.) Another poem seeks the causes of religious hysteria in sexual frustration;[90] it is as specific as a psychoanalytic diagnosis. Homosexuality and other perversions play some part, and the anatomical frankness is complete.

A few years later the malaise of the Venetian days had been largely overcome. It was to take a good while, indeed until the time he wrote *Hermann and Dorothea* (1797), before Goethe could come to regard the French Revolution with objectivity and calm, but in realms aside from politics a variety of forces, especially his friendship with Schiller, helped to banish bitterness and depression.

In the famous letter of August 23, 1794, which led to the alliance between the two poets, Schiller stressed the Greek, objective aspect of Goethe's genius. When Schiller described the difficulties of writing classical poetry in the contemporary world, he showed an amazing intuitive sympathy:

> If you had been born as a Greek, yes even as an Italian, and if a choice nature and an idealizing art had been your surroundings from birth, your path [toward attaining a classical style] would have been infinitely shortened, would perhaps have been rendered quite unnecessary . . . Now, since you were born a German, since your Greek spirit was hurled into this Northern world, you had no other choice than either to become a Northern artist yourself or by substituting in your imagination, through the power of thought, the element of which reality had deprived it; and thus intellectually, as it were, giving birth to a Greece of your own from within.[91]

Goethe had chosen the latter alternative. Through this letter and the conversation which preceded it by a few days, Schiller largely overcame both Goethe's distrust of him and his own envy of the older man. Each poet had a liberating and stimulating effect on the genius of the other. As Hermann Grimm put it, the algebraic formula for their union is not "G+S" but "G(+S)+S(+G)." [92]

Naturally enough, in the works written during the alliance with Schiller the pagan strain continues, though it is not usually dominant. In the *Xenia* (1796), a jointly composed collection of epigrams in distichs written to castigate the follies of their contemporaries, one of the major targets is Christian piety in literature. From Klopstock down, none of the religious poets is spared. A more positive aspect of Goethe's this-worldliness appears in the eighth book of *Wilhelm Meister's Apprenticeship*, which he finished with the benefit of much advice from Schiller. To make the "Hall of the Past," where the true accounts of various characters' lives are stored, a building of dignity and beauty, Goethe modeled it after a classic temple. In such surroundings it was appropriate that the motto "Remember to live" replaced "Memento mori." In their celebration of the nude body, the fictional "Letters from Switzerland" (1796) recall the *Roman Elegies*, but their mood is emotional and Northern, not classic. During the "ballad year"(1797) Goethe wrote two poems in the genre, "The Bride of Corinth" and "The God and the Bayadere," which are pagan with a vengeance, but what one can only call the nastiness of some of the *Venetian Epigrams* has vanished.

"The Bride of Corinth" is essentially a protest against Christian asceticism. As in Schiller's "The Gods of Greece," the one invisible God has vanquished the "bright host" of the Olympians.[93] In her "illness and delusion" the mother of a recently converted family has consigned her daughter to a cloister, although she had been promised to a young Athenian; she has pined away:

Opfer fallen hier,
Weder Lamm noch Stier,
Aber Menschenopfer unerhört.[94]

The bride appears to the young man; he trustingly embraces her but she has become a vampire; he is doomed. Only if the two are burned on a sacrificial pyre can their spirits escape and "hasten toward the old gods." In his maturity Goethe normally shunned any motifs which he found pathological; the cruel, the superstitious, the "night side" of life repelled him. The choice of vampirism would seem to have symbolic implications: an otherworldly religion has sucked the blood of mankind.

In a less uncanny way "The God and the Bayadere" is equally subversive of accepted morality. For once, the wine of paganism is poured into an Indian vessel, not a Greek one. The "bayadere," a Hindu dancer, comes to love the god (without realizing his identity) so intensely that she thinks of him as her husband. Flinging herself into the flames, she is raised to heaven. (Inevitably, the bright young Schlegels took the poem as reflecting the relation between Goethe and his mistress.) The last lines, with their reference to repentant sinners, read almost like a parody of Christian belief:

Es freut sich die Gottheit der reuigen Sünder;
Unsterbliche heben verlorene Kinder
Mit feurigen Armen zum Himmel empor.[95]

Perhaps we should be careful not to interpret Gretchen's apotheosis at the end of *Faust* in too Christian a light.

In some ways Goethe's epic (or idyl) *Hermann and Dorothea* seems at the farthest remove from paganism. Of course it is "classic" in form with its hexameters, Homeric tags, and so on; but surely the worthy pastor, the mother with her quick, instinctive charity, and the other paragons of domestic virtue are German Protestant and bourgeois to the core. Yet the action is not without its epic aspects, and Dorothea, beautiful, of heroic stature, has the gestalt of a pagan goddess.[96] She and Hermann declare their love with the speed, though not the boldness, recommended by the *Roman Elegies*. That it is the pastor who objects to inculcating the fear of death in children is a nice touch.[97] He speaks as an enlightened, humane Christian but also as a man who has read Winckelmann and Lessing — and Spinoza.

> Zeige man doch dem Jüngling des edel reifenden Alters
> Wert . . .[98]

Remember to live! The mother recommends marriage to her son with Homeric directness: "Dass dir werde die Nacht zur schönen Hälfte des Lebens." [99]

This is not to deny the staid, "German" element in the poem. It is rather that a partly epic, partly middle-class content, in *Hermann and Dorothea*, corresponds to a style which is in part classic in its objectivity and monumentalization, but in part ironic, even parodistic. The line "Von der begeisternden Freiheit und von der löblichen Gleichheit!" [100] and the half-line "und tat bedeutend den Mund auf," for instance, have considerable sly humor.[101] Although the poem is a compromise, a hybrid, it nevertheless has a high degree of aesthetic unity: Goethe combined antique and contemporary elements with the greatest dexterity.

Goethe's brief elegy "Hermann and Dorothea" (1796), a poem about a poem, helps in the interpretation of the epic and also suggests indirectly that it too served a cathartic function. The elegy begins abruptly, in the defiant mood of the *Venetian Epigrams*, as if it had a chip on its shoulder. Was it a crime, the poet inquires, that he followed Propertius and Martial, that he imitated the ancients in life as well as in literature, remained unimpressed by names and dogmas and scorned the mask of hypocrisy? [102] Soon bitterness has been purged; he summons his friends to a feast at his home; over the wine he will read his poem. Though he writes only as "the last of the

Homerids," [103] treating a relatively quiet and modest theme, perhaps — he suggests — one can gain insight from his treatment of the sorrowful epoch just past.

Far more ambitious was his attempt to write a truly Homeric epic in German, "Achilleis," which was to recount the love and death of the greatest of the Greek heroes, filling in the narrative gap between the *Iliad* and the *Odyssey*. "I love the man who desires an impossible goal" [104] runs a famous line of *Faust*. In the late 1790's the project must have seemed less extravagant than it appears in retrospect. It was a time in which successful translations of Homer had been achieved; since Klopstock, the hexameter had become well acclimatized in Germany; Goethe, especially after his travels in Sicily, was steeped in Homer; since his alliance with Schiller his creative productivity had again become great. The plan owed a great deal to the revolutionary *Prolegomena ad Homerum* (1795) of Friedrich August Wolf. As a creative writer Goethe could not but resent Wolf's theory that the *Iliad* and the *Odyssey* are the work of many different hands; yet again, precisely as a writer it encouraged him: he would hardly have ventured to vie with Homer himself — had he been but one poet — but could appropriately take his place in the ranks of the Homerids. For two years he worked intermittently at the enterprise but abandoned it after finishing one canto in 1799.

Just why the poet broke off the attempt is not an easy question to answer. No one who has read the first canto with reasonable sensitivity is likely to dismiss the poem curtly as a "failure"; Achilles' situation, faced as he is with the knowledge of certain death, stirs one's sympathy; there are many beautiful lines; and the imitations of Homeric similes, for example, are no mere exercises but fascinating in themselves. Such a line as "Also genossen sie still die Fülle der Seligkeit alle" [105] (evoking a gathering of the gods) conveys the quintessence of Goethe's ideal of paganism. The gods appear as archetypes of superhuman beauty and strength, but as capable of great hardness and cruelty; the presentation is on the whole remarkably objective. There are however passages of very modern, self-conscious sentiment:

> Ach! das schon so frühe das schöne Bildnis der Erde
> Fehlen soll! die breit und weit am Gemeinen sich freuet.
> Dass der schöne Leib, das herrliche Lebensgebäude,
> Fressender Flamme soll dahingegeben zerstieben.[106]

The presence of a modern element is obviously inevitable and need not be felt as aesthetically disturbing, any more than it is in the "Helena Act" of *Faust*. (There Goethe, making a virtue of necessity, emphasizes the non-Greek aspect rather than trying to suppress or conceal it.)

At least part of the reason that so little of the epic was written, it has been suggested, lies in the basic plot.[107] Achilles does not perish as the result of his heroic choice of a short and glorious life but is murdered during the course of a love affair; thus he does not die a Rilkean "death of his own," and the intrinsic unity of the action suffers.

Two years later Goethe wrote the brief dramatic sketch "Helena in the Middle Ages," which he described as a satyr play and an episode in *Faust*. As in "Achilleis" he faithfully reproduces classic metres; in diction he has a debt to the tragedians, just as he borrowed from Homer in the epic fragment. Only a few pages of the "episode" exist; Faust has no chance to appear, and indeed hardly anything has transpired. Yet we feel an extraordinary vitality in the supernatural ugliness and rudeness of Phorkyas; even if we did not sense Mephistopheles in this disguise, we could hardly fail to realize the presence of an element very alien to Greek tragedy and akin to Goethe's devil in its sarcastic negativism. Perhaps it is this link to the sphere of *Faust* which makes the fragment more intensely alive than "Achilleis" is. Goethe was very keenly aware that Greek mythology included grotesque and even repulsive elements. Thus his Phorkyas, one of the Graiae, is described as "gray-born, one-eyed, one-toothed." [108] As a good classicist, he could not feel that such ugliness was central in the pagan world; he exploits it here as comic relief and as contrast to the beauty of Helen.

In a very different setting the contrast between beauty and dark, destructive forces appears in the essay Goethe appended, in 1803, to his translation of Cellini's autobiography. Here the Renaissance has replaced Greece as the symbol of life, and religious fanaticism functions as the negative element, but the basic conflict is the same. After devoting some enthusiastic paragraphs to the life of Lorenzo de' Medici, he adds, with obvious distaste: "A grotesque, absurd monster, the monk Savonarola, opposes himself ungratefully, stubbornly, with frightening effect, to this great, beautiful, serene life; priest that he is, he disturbs, in the hour of death, the serenity hereditary in the House of Medici." [109] (Thomas Mann, like Gobineau, was also to find the contrast between Renaissance prince and Christian monk symbolic, though his Savonarola is far removed from Goethe's "unclean fanatic.") Cellini himself is portrayed as very much the universal man and the hot-blooded Italian. [110] Goethe's admiration for him seems a good bit cooler than his feeling for Lorenzo.

In the 1790's and for the first few years of the new century, Goethe was deeply involved in the attempt to establish the dominance of a strictly classical, Hellenizing taste in Germany. Ironically, he devoted an increasing effort to matters in which he was himself the least gifted: aesthetic theory and the practical problems of painters and sculptors. That he tried to establish himself as *praeceptor Germaniae* in the fine arts was the result of very human self-deception. One hates to think of the poet wasting his time setting pedantic themes from Greek mythology as the subjects of the annual competitions which his "Weimar Friends of Art" sponsored for seven years; the pictures which resulted were mediocre indeed. And it is depressing to recall that Goethe devoted time and energy to such enterprises as writing a biography of a third- or fourth-rate landscape painter like Philipp Hackert. On the whole the story of these efforts is a dreary one and can be passed over rapidly, especially since much of the poet's writing during these years is devoted to rather technical matters. Yet the campaign has its significance in the history of ideas, especially as an attack on the medievalizing tendencies of German romanticism.

Even in this, perhaps the least impressive aspect of his career, there is much with which one can sympathize. In the journal *Propylaea* (1798–1801) and elsewhere Goethe insisted on the importance of approaching a work of art with really aesthetic standards, of respecting the "value and dignity" of the object itself, not the "dark indefinite feeling" it may stir up in the beholder.[111] Repeatedly he points out the dangers of dilettantism, sentimentalism, and subjectivity. His essay of 1798 on the Laocoön group warns against reading too many ideas and ideals into the statues. Though he agrees generally with Winckelmann's interpretation — the tragic element is subordinated to harmony and beauty — he rejects too literary an approach. The group of statues does not tell a story but presents a situation.

It is the exclusive emphasis of Goethe and his associate the Swiss artist and scholar Heinrich Meyer[112] on the classic and neoclassic which vitiates the aesthetic efforts of these years. Again the reader is told that the human body is the proper subject of art. "Let us make gods in our own image."[113] The beauty of Venus is contrasted with the depressive effect of an Ecce Homo;[114] Goethe does not seem to realize that he is himself stressing the content, indeed the propagandistic intention, of works of art. His insistence is almost monomanic: he had eloquently praised Gothic architecture and would do so again, but now holds that no one could be capable of free, active serenity in a medieval church or castle.[115] Worst of all, the repetitious restatements of what can only be called a party

line become boring. It is not strange that the *Propylaea* failed
after some two years and that the Weimar competitions did
not affect the development of painting or sculpture. Goethe
applied similar standards in his direction of the Weimar
theater. It is amusing to read in a contemporary account of a
performance of *Macbeth*: "The witches were young girls
with lovely figures and right nicely dressed." [116]

Yet at the height of his hyperclassical period Goethe wrote
to Schiller: "we stand against modern art like Julian against
Christianity, except that we are a little clearer than he." [117] This
seems to be a more or less conscious admission of defeat, and
more definite statements were to follow. Before moderating
his stand, however, Goethe was to make a ringing declaration
of classicism and paganism, his eulogy of Winckelmann. [118]

In this essay of 1805, the archaeologist appears as a Greek
reborn, as a pagan, above all as a fulfilled and triumphant
figure. He was one of those harmonious and successful persons whose existence is the crown of the whole creative process. "For of what use is the expenditure of suns and planets
and moons, of stars and milky ways, of comets and nebulae, of
developed and developing worlds, unless at last a happy man
rejoices unconsciously in his own existence?" [119] Herder and
Lessing had their doubts about the role Winckelmann played
in Rome; Goethe has no reservations. [120] Arranging his discussion topically, under headings like "The Antique,"
"Friendship," and "Beauty," Goethe monumentalizes his
predecessor. As an "antique nature" Winckelmann possessed
the whole cluster of pagan virtues: "this-worldliness, universality, health, integrity," and so on. He perceived the moral
element in Greek art, the transforming effect of beauty. In
the Olympian Zeus, the "god had become a man to raise man
to a god." [121]

Many had felt that Winckelmann's conversion to Catholicism left a stain on his character. Goethe explained that, since
the historian of art naturally thought as a pagan, the distinc-

tion between the two confessions had no significance in his eyes.[122] Furthermore, divorcées and renegades have a charm of their own, a certain *haut gout*, like old game.[123] Winckelmann's change of confession makes his life and character appear more "romantic." (Very neatly, Goethe managed to insult his ideological opponents triply: conversions were becoming the mode, Friedrich Schlegel had recently married a divorcée — the couple would soon be converted also — and the equation "romanticism equals decay" could hardly be more clearly implied.) Schlegel, like other romantics, was infuriated;[124] one cannot blame him.

Winckelmann has another aspect in the eulogy. While he was as Greek as any modern man can be, there was an element of restlessness in him, and above all a driving dynamism which reminds one of Faust,[125] though Goethe does not mention so Germanic a figure: "We find him always active, busied with the moment, seizing and holding it firmly as if the moment could be complete and satisfying, and just in this way he let the following moment teach him." [126] This is not meant as a reproach; nowhere in the essay is there a word of blame. Even Winckelmann's sudden and early death has preserved him in our minds as vigorous and strong.[127] Thus at the end of the tribute the author reminds us of another hero, Achilles.

Writing to Schiller after the spring of illness in which he had completed "Winckelmann," Goethe cited the tag "in doloribus pinxit" (He painted this in the midst of sorrows).[128] He hoped that no one would sense his ill health in the work, nor is that likely. It would seem still less likely that Goethe would write in the same year that Greek models alone cannot suffice "us Northerners," [129] but such is the case. Without the romantic tendencies of "uncultured centuries" we would have neither *Hamlet* and *Lear* nor the dramas of Calderón, he continues. Since we probably shall never equal the ancients, we must at least maintain the high level of such "barbarian" achievements.

The passage is suffused with irony, and in any event the contradiction is not complete. If Sophocles is beyond reach, emulate the "barbarian" Shakespeare! Clearly the practicality if not the justification of an exclusive classicism, at least in literature, is now denied. As will appear, Goethe's taste, even in art, was soon to become increasingly catholic though the Greeks would remain his special favorites, as they were Humboldt's. Like so many other of his works, "Winckelmann" seems to have had a cathartic effect, but it is not Goethe's last word about the antique in its relation to modern man. That last word would be spoken only in the second part of *Faust*.

Chapter VIII

The Semblance of Paganism: Schiller

ↄↄↄↄↄↄↄↄↄↄↄↄↄↄↄↄↄↄↄↄↄↄↄↄↄↄↄↄↄↄↄↄↄↄ

In dealing with Schiller's relation to the myth of Greece one is faced by a whole complex of problems. What was the degree of his affinity with "the Greeks" as Winckelmann saw them? Did Schiller always remain too much a man of the Enlightenment to become a Hellenist like Heinse, Hölderlin, or Goethe in his Roman days? Was Schiller not basically too much the idealist and the man of abstractions to share whole-heartedly in the enthusiasm for Greek art?

Paradoxically, the champion of aesthetic education was less of an aesthetic man than Winckelmann was, and it is difficult to state with certainty whether beauty is more of a means than an end to Schiller, even in his *Letters on the Aesthetic Education of Mankind*. A related question is that of his paganism: some have maintained that he wished to turn to a "religion of Greece," but it would be simple-minded to take his poem "The Gods of Greece," for example, as a literal statement of his religious beliefs. Certainly Schiller was no Christian in any orthodox sense; but with his basically dualistic view of life and his intensely moral orientation, he had a tie to Christianity difficult if not impossible to cut.

The myth of Greece did not become vitally important in his literary works until the middle or late 1780's.[1] Schiller's teacher Abel is said to have referred his students repeatedly to

Winckelmann,[2] but the image of Greece in the early poems is made up of Ovidian and rococo elements. Similarly, his frequent references to Elysium are *topoi*, not to be connected with a specific intellectual movement.

By contrast, Schiller's "Letter of a Danish Traveler (The Hall of Antique Statues in Mannheim)" of 1785 is drenched in reminiscences of Winckelmann.[3] These occur primarily in descriptions of the individual statues; Schiller's general statements, on the other hand, are more characteristically his own. Though Winckelmann is not mentioned, Lessing is; the fictitious Danish traveler is aware that he has been on holy ground. In his evocation of the Farnese Hercules, Schiller uses the archaeologist's device of illustration through allusion to a familiar myth: "I see a figure such as this fall upon the Nemean lion, and terror and astonishment overwhelm me." [4] He makes the almost obligatory reference to the paradoxical beauty of the tortured Laocoön. (The statue must have attracted him as another example of the pleasure which the tragic can afford. Here, too, "the form must annihilate the material.") It is in the description of the Apollo Belvedere that he follows his model the most closely. Like Goethe, he is struck by Winckelmann's emphasis on the light, soaring quality of Apollo's stride;[5] like Winckelmann, he attempts to interpret the emotions expressed by specific parts of the statue. Like Winckelmann, too, he tries to express in words the central intention or "idea" of individual works of art.[6]

It would be easy, and boring, to cite further parallels. Yet obvious as Schiller's borrowings are, his deviations from his predecessor are equally important. First of all is the rococo, more or less Wielandian, tone of certain important passages: "two thousand years disappear before your step; suddenly you stand in the midst of fair, laughing Greece, move among heroes and Graces and pray, as they do, to romantic gods." [7] In this context the word "romantic" inevitably makes the gods seem less real, less actual; we are in the world of mythology, of aesthetic semblance (*Schein*). But though the Greek divinities were fictions, they reflected the ethical nobility of real human beings. "The Greeks depicted their gods only as nobler men and approximated their men to the gods. They were children of one family." [8] Greek art testifies to a faith in truth as well as beauty, and remains a "challenge" to all the peoples of the earth. Typically, Schiller ends on the note which Jacob Burckhardt called *agonal*: like Klopstock and Herder, he held that the Hellenic achievement should stimulate rivalry rather than imitation. [9]

Thus there is not much originality in the Mannheim essay. Schiller's creative involvement with Hellas does not begin until about three years later. Then a number of experiences and activities suddenly testify to the strength of his interest: the first version of "The Gods of Greece," his reading and discussion of Goethe's *Iphigenia*, the experience of Homer, and his translations of Euripides. All of these manifestations occur within a surprisingly short time. It is no accident that Schiller's really Hellenist period began in Goethean territory and at a time when he was in contact with friends and admirers of Goethe — Herder, Wieland, and the Lengefeld sisters, one of whom he was to marry. From this time onward, Goethe and Greece were to be linked concepts in his mind, as they were (with a difference) in Heine's. How closely he associated Goethe and Greece is apparent also from his rather sharp comment in a letter to his close friend Körner of November 1, 1790: "I don't wholly like his philosophy either: it draws too much on the sensuous world where I draw on the soul. Generally his way of imagining things [*seine Vorstellungsart*] is too sensuous and *touches* things too much for my taste." [10] The inclusiveness, the totality, of Goethe's interests compensates however for this earthiness, and Schiller proceeds: "But his spirit searches actively in every direction, and strives to build up a whole — and that makes him a great man in my eyes." Like Greece, Goethe is criticized for his sensu-

ousness, his physicality; but, again like Greece, his universality
exerts an increasing appeal.

So much has been written about "The Gods of Greece" and
the significance of the poem that one is hard put to add further to the discussion. It is the extreme, intensely emotional
statement of the Hellenist position, more violent, more Rousseauistic than anything in Winckelmann's writings:

> Ach, da euer Wonnedienst noch glänzte,
> Wie ganz anders, anders war es da! [11]

Using mythological references with great cumulative effect,
Schiller conjures up an Eden of joy, art, beauty, love — and,
rather surprisingly — virtue. Ascetic Christianity, eighteenth-
century deism, and Newtonian physics have destroyed this
paradise. Unlike Shelley, the poet does not hold that the
world's great age will begin anew; he laments an irretrievable
loss.

In content, the poem is a mixture (rather than a synthesis)
of themes and arguments, given force and unity of tone by
its heavy rhetorical emphasis. Not every sentiment expressed
here reflects Schiller's personal conviction, but two lines of
the original version (of 1788) state a tenet of German Hellenism which Schiller was repeatedly to express later:

> Da die Götter menschlicher noch waren,
> Waren Menschen göttlicher. [12]

In its famous evocation of death as a beautiful Genius [13] the
poem is completely within the orthodox Winckelmannian
tradition; elsewhere, it draws on a whole stock of ideas and
references. Even a Dionysian note is included in Schiller's
vision of Hellas, though his "great joy-bringer" is probably
closer to a rococo Bacchus than to Nietzsche's divinity. A
typical Enlightenment thrust at the Roman Catholic Church
was eventually eliminated:

> Nach der Geister schrecklichen Gesetzen
> Richtete kein heiliger Barbar. [14]

Particularly the first version strikes one as a versified philosophy of history, apparently dashed down on paper in an ecstasy of enthusiasm.

On closer reading, one sees that Schiller's attitude is more critical than is often realized. More than once he presents the Greek gods as aesthetic constructs, creatures of myth, almost of fairy tale: "Schöne Wesen aus dem Fabelland." [15] If they ever truly existed — and throughout most of the poem Schiller leaves little doubt that they did — they have long since perished:

> Was unsterblich im Gesang soll leben,
> Muss im Leben untergehn. [16]

As has been pointed out, Schiller liked to state an extreme intellectual position to stimulate the dialectic process. His very defensive statement to Körner seems to imply that something of the sort was involved here:

The god whom I place in the shade in the "Gods of Greece" is not the god of the philosopher or even the beneficent illusion of the many, but he is a monster composed of many frail, distorted images. — The gods of the Greeks, whom I place in the light, are only the attractive characteristics of Greek mythology, combined in a single image. Briefly, I am convinced that every work of art must be held accountable only to itself, that is, to its proper law of beauty, and is subject to no other claim. [17]

The sentence last quoted appeals persuasively to aesthetic rather than philosophic criteria. A few years later Schiller might well have pointed out that the Hellenic figures of the poem exist in the realm of "semblance" or *Schein*. The trouble is, as he himself came to feel, that aesthetic distance is not maintained. Quite possibly the rhythm of the poem had carried him further than he had really intended to go, if his later statement to Körner has any application here: "The musical element in a poem hovers far more often before me, when I sit down to write it, than a clear concept of its content, about which I am often hardly clear in my own mind." [18] In any case, it is pretty clear that Schiller is really celebrating beauty and art, not polytheism, in these much debated verses.[19] Much of the poem, particularly in its first version, is devoted to stressing the contrast between the beauty of the classical past and the drabness of the present. It is a point which as Christian a poet as T. S. Eliot has made more insistently if less flamboyantly than Schiller: "Where are the eagles and the trumpets?"

Surely, though, men like Fritz Stolberg and Franz von Kleist were not completely wrong, not merely narrowly orthodox or Philistine, when they objected to the tendency of "The Gods of Greece." [20] Interpret the poem as one will, one can hardly obscure its thesis that the world has become gray, gloomy, and ugly and that Christianity is largely to blame. Schiller's attack is of course one in a sequence: Winckelmann, Heinse, and on occasion even Lessing had made similar charges, though generally with more restraint. In the *Venetian Epigrams* and "The Bride of Corinth" Goethe would put the case with greater art, and perhaps with a clearer awareness of what was implied, than Schiller had done. Schiller's hymn came out at a strategic moment. Goethe himself was turning toward paganism; Heinse had just published his novel of "aesthetic immorality," *Ardinghello.* While Schiller's gods may be merely creatures of fable, there is a tremendous dynamism in the way he invokes them. Whatever the poet's conscious intention, much of the drive of the poem does lie in the direction of paganism.[21]

Schiller's unfinished discussion of Goethe's *Iphigenia in Tauris*, roughly contemporaneous with the poem, treats the whole "matter of Greece" judiciously; it contains some very significant comments. The classicism of Goethe's drama, he rightly implies, is Winckelmannian: "One can't read this piece without feeling the breath of a certain spirit of antiquity, which is much too authentic, much too vivid, for a mere imitation, even the most successful. One finds here the imposing, grand repose, which places every ancient work so above rivalry, the dignity, the lovely seriousness, even in the most highly pitched expressions of passion." [22] Schiller's insistence that the play is far more than an imitation is revealing. Rather, he puts it, Goethe has been wrestling or vying with the Greeks; the verb he uses, *ringen*, indicates how fiercely competitive his own attitude toward ancient literature essentially was. Equally characteristic is the phrase used to contrast modern with antique mores: "the more beautiful humanity of our modern customs." [23] Sensitive though he was to the appeal of Hellas, Schiller, even at his most enthusiastic, was not really a Graecomane of the strict observance.

In speaking of Schiller's rendering of Euripides' *Iphigenia in Aulis* (1788–1789) and of scenes of his *Phoenician Women* (1789), one is tempted to use the word translations — if at all — only in quotation marks. He employed "trots" in three languages, of which the Latin translation by Joshua Barnes seems to have helped him the most; he speaks of it as his "actual source." [24] There seems no reason to doubt his statement to Körner: "I had to *puzzle out* the original text or rather, I had to make one myself." [25] Schiller hoped, not without reason, to learn more "simplicity in plot and style" from this undertaking. Compared to Euripides, the most "sentimentive" of the Greeks, Schiller is wordy and even more rhetorical than his model. Possibly Schiller meant his *Iphigenia* to parallel Goethe's drama as a contribution to the renascence of the Greek spirit in Germany. [26] It seems much more likely, though, that the dramatic quality of Euripides' play and its classicality, rather than its Greekness appealed to him. [27] When Schiller includes a couplet to the effect that "training and instruction early guide the docile hearts of youth to virtue" [28] in his translation, we realize how far he was from being a Greek reborn. Yet one may assume that this dramatic exercise helped "form his hand," just as his later study of Aristotle did.

What concerns us in Schiller's poem "The Artists" is the question of the role of Greek art in the development of mankind which this long didactic poem sketches out. The evolution is now seen positively, the notion of progress having replaced Rousseauism as the historical point of view. The artist has played a decisive part in the rise of culture: he has guided mankind through beauty toward truth. But even when that is attained, art retains an eternal function. Ultimately art and knowledge, truth and beauty, are one.

Since he has turned away, in the "The Artists," from any sort of cultural pessimism, Schiller can no longer regard the Greek achievement as absolute. It remains exemplary, however, for the Greeks are the first and greatest of artists. At one point at least, their aesthetic principles are expressed in Winckelmannian terms:

> Die Kraft, die in des Ringers Muskel schwillt,
> Muss in des Gottes Schönheit lieblich schweigen.[29]

It is, however, the artist as a type, not bound to any age or nation, who is central to the poem. Indeed, with its repeated references to harmony, "The Artists," like so many of Schiller's works, owes more to Leibniz and Shaftesbury — and thus indirectly to Plato — than to Hellenism.

In "On Grace and Dignity" (1793) as in "The Artists," Greek art and mythology afford Schiller his most telling evidence. In addition, Greece has begun to function, as the example of Goethe was to do, as a force to help modify Kant's Draconian rigorism. Above all, the Greeks are the exemplars of totality, uniting sensuality and freedom, passion and calm, grace and dignity. The following passage is Winckelmannian in descriptive method as well as in content:

If grace and dignity . . . are united in the same person, then the full expression of humanity is found within him. . . . With muted splendor, reasoned freedom [*die Vernunftfreiheit*] rises in the smile of his mouth, in his gently animated glance, on his serene brow; and in a sublime parting, natural necessity sinks in the noble majesty of his countenance. The ancient statues were shaped after this ideal pattern of human beauty, and we recognize it in the god-like form of a Niobe, in the Apollo Belvedere, in the Borghese Winged Genius, and in the Muse of the Barberini Palace.[30]

Elsewhere, Schiller follows Winckelmann's description of Laocoön in describing the ideal of serene suffering, though he mentions neither the archaeologist nor the statue by name. Laocoön occurs again and again in the literature of the later eighteenth century as a saint of *Humanität*, a pagan St. Sebastian, as it were. The Greeks began to appear in Schiller, as they already had appeared in the writings of so many of his contemporaries, as archetypes of noble humanity. Again, however, the Greek element should not be stressed too much. The ideal of harmony which is basic to Schiller's "beautiful soul" is fundamentally Leibnizian. And as Schiller himself noted, the idea of basing morality on inclination or love rather than on duty or the law is basically Christian.[31] *Ama et fac quod vis!*

"On the Expression of Suffering" (*Über das Pathetische*), a lesser essay of the same year, is closer to the line of Winckelmann and Lessing. The Greek poet, unlike the French, shows his heroes uninhibited by etiquette or convention, just as the Greek sculptor does not hamper his figures with clothing. Thus both humanity and beauty are achieved.[32] The examples which Schiller cites — Philoctetes, Hercules, Iphigenia, Laocoön (here he quotes some sixty lines of the *History of Ancient Art*) — and the dogmas he upholds had long been familiar, in the main, to his public.[33] The most important advance marked by the essay was in its further formulation of what Schiller meant by the aesthetic; much of the rest of it was distinctly "old hat" by the 1790's. Friedrich Schlegel's cruel remark that Schiller's early education left much to be desired was not unjustified. But how rapidly Schiller caught up!

Since Schiller's *On the Aesthetic Education of Mankind*

(1793–1794) has been interpreted very differently by various critics, and since it is of crucial importance to any treatment of his thought, it seems best first to state my own general reading of it. As the product of a period of transition, the *Aesthetic Education* is, naturally, not a completely consistent work. As late as 1793 Schiller had written, in a marginal comment on Humboldt's "On the Study of Antiquity, and Especially of the Greek," that the culture of the Greeks was "merely aesthetic";[34] but so rapid was the evolution of his thought that the aesthetic element was soon to become the keystone of this, his most important philosophical work. His political views were also changing. Although he takes the French Revolution as the starting point of his discussion, and implies throughout most of the essay that aesthetic education will eventually solve the practical problems of great nations, he admits resignedly in his last paragraph that the true "state of fair semblance" will actually exist only in "some few select circles." [35]

Yet with the important exception discussed below, the general drift of the work is clear enough. Schiller keeps the term "aesthetic education" very broad. Quite possibly, though he relies on the fine arts for his examples, he intends also to include "the best that has been thought and said in the world" in his curriculum. In view of the strictures of the late Irving Babbitt,[36] it should be pointed out that Schiller was not recommending the kind of aestheticism often connected with the name of Oscar Wilde.

There is one all-important crux: is aesthetic education the way to moral and political betterment, or does the former of itself imply the latter? [37] Again, Schiller is not completely consistent: for much of the essay he treats aesthetic training primarily as a means to an end, but he does state, in the twenty-fifth letter, just as he had in "The Artists," that the possession of beauty involves that of truth.[38]

Struggling as he does with a monstrous terminology, Schil-

ler defines and redefines in a dogged and at least partly successful effort to make clear his concept of the aesthetic. Art
is an autonomous realm, the kingdom of "disinterested pleasure," but though as "play" it is nonpurposive, it does subserve,
indirectly, an aim beyond itself and thus has a moral aim. For
the aesthetic experience restores (or creates) the proper balance between material and intellectual drives: "melting"
beauty can tame the savage breast; another type of beauty
(the "energetic") can invigorate the lax or the decadent. One
is reminded of Plato's comments, in the *Republic*, on the varying effects of different modes of music. While true art cannot move us to act or read us a moral lesson, it brings about
the proper harmony (again Schiller's key concept emerges)
in man and clears the way for moral or political action. Thus
Schiller vindicates, after and despite Kant, the "improving"
function of art which the Enlightenment had upheld.[39]

Toward the end of the *Letters*, Schiller, his enthusiasm increasing as his thought moves further and further away from
concrete political matters, attributes more and more power to
the aesthetic instinct. It becomes the potential creator of that
"Third Kingdom" dreamed of by mystics since Joachim a
Fiore.[40] This is the religion of art with a vengeance. The word
"utopia" springs to mind, but realizing that Schiller's analysis
is now oriented on the individual, we may feel that *On Aesthetic Education* actually has more affinities with the *Bil-
dungsroman* than with the literature of the state.

As one would expect, the Greeks are to play the part of
aesthetic educators. They are *the* artistic people; their statues
are the touchstones of beauty, and the existence of the Olympian
gods is the highest symbol of the realm of "semblance." Most
important of all, perhaps, the Greeks, as individuals, have
cultivated the totality of their powers to a degree which
modern men cannot emulate. Anticipating Hölderlin, Schiller
speaks of the fragmentary, distorted, and one-sided development of contemporary man.[41] Unlike Hölderlin or Heinse,

however, he does not give the palm to Greek society as a whole; he has no desire to be a citizen of any other age than his own.[42] But the Greek person — to Schiller, as to Winckelmann, the Athenian was the representative Hellene — was more harmonious, more roundedly human, in a word more aesthetic, than the man of the eighteenth century.

It can hardly be emphasized too strongly that Schiller's concept of the aesthetic was not that of the 1890's. It included the categories of the noble, the grand, the sublime, even the heroic. How are men to be educated? "Wherever you find them, surround them with noble, with great, with meaningful [*geistreichen*] shapes, encompass them with the symbols of excellence, until semblance overcomes actuality and art vanquishes nature." [43] Schiller follows Lessing in finding evidence of ethical superiority in the restrained silence of the Greek army before Troy.[44] In his characterization in the ninth Letter of the ideal modern artist, he conjures up the image of a man who has been formed on the timeless norms afforded by Greek culture. Thus educated, he will "return, an alien figure, to his century, not to delight it . . . but, terrible as the son of Agamemnon, to purify it." [45] (Clearly Schiller has Goethe in mind though he does not mention him.[46]) Central to Greek art, as Schiller evokes it here, are the concepts of severe beauty and stern moral dignity. The pretty, rococo Greeks (or *Graeculi*) of his early works have vanished. Art, as in Gautier's poem, has survived all else; but it has survived to ennoble, and indeed to chastise, the men of lesser ages. Ethics and aesthetics are inextricably fused.

In the Greek games — bloodless, unlike the gladiatorial contests which succeeded them — both the humaneness of the Hellenes and their realization of the importance of play (*Spiel*) is evident.[47] (Here a perhaps involuntary play on the words *Spiel – Spieltrieb – Kampfspiel* is revealing.) Another verbal association moves the reader smoothly from Olympic games to Olympian gods.[48] Free of care and toil, they represent play at its most sublime —

Ewigklar und spiegelrein und eben
Fliesst das zephyrreiche Leben
Im Olymp den Seligen dahin.[49]

— as Schiller put it in "The Ideal and Life." Here too it is
hard to keep all thought of the Olympian of Weimar out of
one's mind.

Winckelmann's Greece has been modified, for Schiller, by
the writings of Herder and Humboldt and by his experience
of Goethe. In a curious and rather touching way, the influence
of the archaeologist has been combined with that of Kant.
Since beauty is "the consummation of mankind" and is an
integral part of man's nature, there exists the categorical imperative: "beauty *shall* exist." [50] Here, as in the whole concept of an education through beauty, Schiller is carrying out
implications of the work of Winckelmann, the first great
aesthetic pedagogue of the Germans.[51] Similarly, when Schiller praises the Olympian gods above the "divine monster" of
Oriental imagination,[52] accepting anthropomorphism as a step
toward *Humanität*, he is very much in Winckelmann's tradition. Schiller would judge even music by classical criteria:
"Music, at its noblest peak, must become form and influence
us as does the calm power of the ancient world." [53]

It was thus appropriate that a twentieth-century Hellenist
like George should single out the *Letters* for special praise.
His general estimate of Schiller was not a high one, but, he
conceded: "as teacher of beauty and educator, as author of
the *Aesthetic Education* . . . Schiller will again be celebrated
in a brilliant resurrection." [54] Taking up this hint, Miss Gerhard has argued eloquently that Schiller's greatest contribution lies not in his dramas, but in his Hellenizing aesthetic
theory. Yet it is still possible to believe that individual insights
of the work — the concepts of aesthetic semblance and of the
play impulse, the passage cited above, describing the role of
the artist as the judge of his age — are more satisfying than
the essay as a whole.[55] However this may be, one must be careful not to ignore the non-Greek aspect of Schiller's argument.

Human totality must be found not by a return to Greece but
by an advance to a third stage, surpassing both the ancient and
the contemporary world.[56] Man must dare to be bold as well as
to be wise, must shun imitation and proceed "with bold simplicity and quiet innocence" [57] to attack the complicated problems of his time. This variation on Winckelmann's famous
formula of "noble simplicity," occurring as it does in the last
sentence of the *Letters*, is as significant as it is typical of
Schiller.

"The Ideal and Life," a poem of 1795, marks an important
change: here the aesthetic realm is sharply separated from the
practical. Schiller seems to have abandoned the idea of any
bridge between the two; only a demigod can pass from one region to the other. In a series of fifteen contrasting strophes,
he sets off the Olympian serenity of the ideal against the struggles of life. Knowing that Schiller understood Olympian existence as a symbol of the aesthetic, we may infer that the great
work of art, and perhaps the great artist, live in the kingdom
of the eternal:

> Aber frei von jeder Zeitgewalt,
> Die Gespielin seliger Naturen,
> Wandelt oben in des Lichtes Fluren
> Göttlich unter Göttern die *Gestalt*.[58]

Thus Laocoön's human sufferings rightly stir us to protest
against the injustice of life, but, from the viewpoint of aesthetic contemplation, his misery is forgotten and only beauty
remains. At the close of the poem, Laocoön gives way to the
divine sufferer Hercules, who rises from earth and is welcomed among the gods. Surely Thomas Mann was not too
daring when, in the most moving of his essays, he associated
Hercules, at last triumphant after all his labors, with Schiller
himself.[59]

The decisive letter of August 23, 1794, had put things differently: Goethe, despite his "Greek spirit," was a Northerner

and was therefore forced "from within and intellectually, as it were, to give birth to a [new] Greece." The image is tortured indeed. What seems significant is that the Greek note remains in these references of the 1790's, whether Goethe is associated with Orestes or with the Olympians, or depicted, in the brief poem "Fortune," as the favorite of all the Hellenic gods. In the letter, as Rehm well points out, Goethe plays the same role of Northern pagan or German Greek that Winckelmann was to take in Goethe's famous essay of 1805.[60]

As Schiller's very poignant epigram "The Antique Statue to the Northern Wanderer" is generally printed, it seems to reflect a skeptical attitude toward the whole "German-Greek encounter," as it has been called. The statue speaks to the Northern traveler who has crossed the Alps to see it:

> Und nun stehst du vor mir, du darfst mich Heil'ge berühren,
> Aber bist du mir jetzt näher, und bin ich es dir?[61]

In the original version, four additional distichs made it clear that the fault lay solely with the Northern wanderer: "Den verdüsterten Sinn bindet der nordische Fluch."[62] Generally Schiller was far from feeling that communication with the classical past was an impossibility. His sense of continuity, of linking tradition, enables him to end his elegy "The Walk" on a note of consolation and resolution. Nature is timeless, the generations are bound together:

> Unter demselben Blau, über dem nämlichen Grün
> Wandeln die nahen und wandeln vereint die fernen Geschlechter,
> Und die Sonne Homers, siehe! sie lächelt auch uns.[63]

As Greek art served as the norm of excellence in the *Aesthetic Letters*, Greek literature is repeatedly drawn on to provide examples in *On Naïve and Sentimentive Poetry* (1795–1796). There is one great difference: the Hellenic hegemony in art is absolute, whereas it is limited, in literature, to the "naïve." The reasons are not far to seek. The fine arts, in

Schiller's view, depend on clearly marked, limited contours; [64] they are finite by hypothesis; in literature, of course, the reflective or sentimentive [65] moderns aspire to the infinite. It would be absurd, he pointed out, to base one's concept of literature on the ancients alone. Closely linked is a more personal and perhaps more potent reason: Schiller was after all writing a manifesto, almost a magna charta, for sentimentive poets, not least for himself.

In his celebrated essay, Schiller describes nature — the great source of the naïve — in terms reminiscent of Winckelmann's Greece: "When you approach her [nature] from your circle of artificiality, she stands before you in her *grand repose*, in her naïve *beauty*, in her childlike innocence and simplicity." [66] In one of his most penetrating *aperçus*, Schiller remarks that our feeling for nature does not resemble the antique "nature sense": it is rather akin to our feeling for the ancients. [67] Thus he has marked out the longing for nature and for Hellas as two great aspects of sentimentive poetry; without mentioning them by name, he has aligned Winckelmann and Rousseau. German Hellenism, the implication would be, is romanticism before the fact. We recall the passage in the *Thoughts on Imitation* comparing a young Athenian gymnast to an athletic Red Indian. [68] It is hardly necessary to add that Schiller shares the enthusiasm for the naïve in culture — primarily represented by the Greeks — as fervently as for that in nature. But inventing classifications and drawing distinctions have generally a cooling effect; Schiller has relativized the glory of Hellas by virtually confining it to one of the two great aspects of artistic achievement.

Similarly, he writes with a great deal of distance, with a certain condescension, of the Greek gods: being of a limited, human quality they are ideally suited for use in literature; "joyous imagination," not reason, gave them birth. [69] Born under that "happy sky" which the German Hellenists never tired of mentioning, the Greeks were a fortunate race; but are not "we moderns," with our multiplicity of problems and our infinite goals, more interesting and more mature? Every genius must be naïve, as the Greeks were; when Schiller describes the genius in the poem of that name, he uses Winckelmannian language: "Einfach gehst du und still durch die eroberte Welt." [70] At his best, the modern genius is naïve and something more. Schiller has moved far away from the mood of "The Gods of Greece"; the nimbus has vanished, and one recalls his remark that Greek culture was "only aesthetic."

What is Goethe's position in this new critical hierarchy? One might expect that his prestige, so closely linked to the Greeks, would sink, but such is not the case. As in the *Aesthetic Letters* and in the letter of August 23, 1794, he is one of those strangers to his own age who are the wonders and the terrors of the time. "The stamp of the ruler reposes on their brows." [71] But Goethe is not merely naïve, not merely "a Greek"; he has treated sentimentive materials, above all in *Werther*, in a naïve way, and represents the triumphant synthesis, the ultimate ideal. [72] Thus, though the essay ends with a vindication of the sentimentive, Goethe's own position is not negatively affected. "The Greeks," however, are affectionately and respectfully put in their place. It is a very high one, but it is no longer at the absolute peak of human achievement. They make their own great contribution to literature and to the human ideal, but it is only one component. [73] Similarly, in sketching out the new "Elysian" idyl to surpass the Arcadian idyl of the past, Schiller combines a modern, dynamic element with Winckelmannian calm:

> Thus calm would be the controlling impression made by this genre, but calm of perfection, not of lassitude, a calm which flows from the equilibrium, not the stagnation of energies, from abundance, not from emptiness, and is accompanied by the sense of an infinite power. The highest unity must exist, but it may take nothing from multiplicity; the spirit must be made peaceful, but striving should not cease on that account. [74]

On the whole, the *Xenia* and the other minor poems of the 1790's do not significantly change the picture. Allied with Goethe, Schiller assumes a very definitely classical stance but stops one step short of complete Hellenism; one receives the impression of a certain balance. Schiller realized all too well, even in his most classicistic mood, "Dass das Schöne vergeht, dass das Vollkommene stirbt." [75] It may nevertheless seem not quite fair for the Schiller of this period to reproach Friedrich Schlegel for "Graecomania," [76] but apparently he felt that Schlegel deserved to be treated with particular severity. He joined robustly, in the *Xenia* and elsewhere, in chastising the Stolbergs and the other representatives of fanatic or orthodox piety. Nothing could be allowed to reflect adversely on the classical heritage; it seemed to him simply a blunt fact that German art and literature would have produced nothing significant without it:

Muss der Künstler nicht selbst den Schössling von aussen sich holen?
Nicht aus Rom und Athen borgen die Sonne, die Luft? [77]

While Schiller thus accepted the validity of the classical tradition, he regarded the myth of Greece with considerable skepticism in his last years. In his well-known letter to J. W. Süvern, Schiller writes that his admiration of Sophoclean tragedy as a manifestation of its own age is "absolute," but that it would be absurd to adopt it as a criterion today. "Beauty is for a happy generation, but we must try to stir an unhappy one with sublimity." [78] Even more significant is the change in his attitude toward Goethe's *Iphigenia*. Like Goethe himself, he now finds the drama "astonishingly modern and un-Greek." The reason he gives is the decisive point: after his study of Aristotle's *Poetics* he finds that the work lacks the specific qualities of the drama, "force, life, movement" — in a word, action.

Indeed, the study of the Greek tragedians themselves and of Aristotle had gradually pushed Winckelmann's concepts into the background. Schiller's increasing fascination with the idea of fate and with techniques used by the Greek dramatists is a matter tangential, at the most, to this study.[79] With one great exception, the debt of the late dramas to the Hellenist tradition consists primarily of verbal reminiscences.

In the fine arts, however, the situation was a different one. Submitting an opinion for a competition sponsored by the journal *Propylaea* in 1800, Schiller adopts the standards of its editors. He warns against the sentimentive bent of the Germans and of the present time, which may lead to the ruin of the plastic arts, and praises the "lovely naïve emotion" of one of the competitors.[80] Feeling that these matters were not really Schiller's forte, one should perhaps discount this brief essay. More interesting is the fragment "Tragedy and Comedy," which is analogous in more ways than one to *On Naïve and Sentimentive Poetry*.[81] Comedy, he writes, raises man to a loftier condition than does tragedy: "Our condition vis-à-vis comedy is calm, clear, free, serene, we feel ourselves neither active nor passive; we are spectators, and everything remains external to us. This is the condition of the gods, who concern themselves with no human affairs, who soar freely above the world, whom no fate touches, whom no law constrains."[82] But if comedy makes us gods, tragedy makes us heroes, godlike men, Titans. Prometheus, Schiller well points out, is to some extent himself a symbol of tragedy.[83] Again, his deeper sympathies are clearly not with the Olympians.

Perhaps the most important part played by the myth of Greece in Schiller's last years is the role it assumed in his admirably clear apologetic essay "On the Use of the Chorus in Tragedy" (1803). Here, where Schiller proposes "openly and honorably to declare war on all naturalism in art,"[84] the function of "the Greeks" is very important indeed. It was not from Winckelmann, of course, that Schiller had drawn his notions of aesthetic distance and noble play. But when the dramatic artist strives to give his figures and his tragedy the proper ideality, he needs the serenity and loftiness which only a chorus of the Greek type can provide. The rich lyric style, "within which the persons of the plot move freely and nobly, with a controlled dignity and lofty calm," [85] is like the classically draped clothing of the sculptor. Similarly, the chorus, mainly because it destroys vulgar illusion, gives the action itself the quality of calm or repose — "the fair and lofty calm, which must be the character of a noble work of art." [86]

We are convinced, more by the essay than by the drama which it served as a preface. If *The Bride of Messina* has disappointed most of its readers, perhaps the last paragraph of Schiller's theoretical discussion betrays one of the reasons. He notes that he has employed Christianity, the myths of the Greek gods, and "even Moorish superstition" in a mixture. [87] The words used, *vermischt angewendet*, seem unintentionally derogatory. Schiller appeals to the Enlightenment notion of a pure religion superior to all specific religious forms; but that concept is more fruitful in theological debate than in the drama, as Lessing's example might have shown him. [88] Actually, in its use of concepts like *hubris* and Nemesis, *The Bride of Messina* is more "Greek" than, say, "The Gods of Greece." But the ancient and modern elements are not combined as successfully as in *Iphigenia*, nor does the drama convince us of its inherent tragic necessity.

A sketch for a poem, found in Schiller's literary remains, brings out the contrast between the ancient gods and modern *Humanität* with an almost Nietzschean sharpness; it stands in harsh contrast to most of his other comments. To quote it in part:

The Ocean King calls his gods together and takes counsel with them, [to learn] how they intend to maintain their ancient divine freedom against human ingenuity, because mechanization is becoming too much for them. Everything divine is disappearing from the world, and the old gods are yielding their place to men. "I always hear people praising humaneness, they want to introduce it everywhere, and thereby everything great and divine is being torn up by the roots." [89]

The notion of the decadence of the gods anticipates Heine's
"The Gods in Exile"; the revulsion against humanitarianism
recalls certain moods of Goethe. Schiller has strayed far away
from the world view of the Enlightenment.

Two major conclusions suggest themselves: Schiller's relation to the myth of Greece was a stimulating and productive
one, yet his own affinity to the Greeks was not particularly
close.[90] To discuss the second conclusion first: his grasp of the
language was very weak, and his knowledge of the literature
uneven at best. In his last years, to be sure, his own dramas
were greatly affected by his study of Sophocles and the *Poetics*. But the bulk of his work had been produced before he
had much real knowledge of Greece. As late as December
1795 he complained to Humboldt about the lack of "beautiful
womanliness" in Greek tragedy [91] — a strange judgment in
view of the *Antigone*. When he called himself a "barbarian
in everything concerning the fine arts" [92] he was obviously
exaggerating, but his statement to Humboldt seems broadly
true: "Alas, Italy — and Rome especially — is no country for
me; the physical conditions would weigh on me, and its aesthetic interest would afford no compensation because I lack interest in and taste for the fine arts." [93] The Greek gods and
heroes furnished Schiller with some of his most impressive
symbols, just as Winckelmann's prose gave him the raw material for such magnificent lines as "Einfach gehst du und
still durch die eroberte Welt." Yet when he describes works
of art in primarily aesthetic terms, as in the "Letter of a
Danish Traveler," the attempt seems to go against the grain;
he is clearly derivative.

It would be crude and misleading to state flatly that Schiller was "anti-Christian." To be sure, he wrote to Goethe of
his joy that the motto "Remember to live" triumphed over
"the accursed Memento mori" in *Wilhelm Meister*;[94] and his
rejection of Kant's rigoristic dualism and of the doctrine of
original sin is common knowledge. Yet he himself was a dual-

ist of the dualists, deeply imbued with Christian morality and
metaphysics though certainly not with Christian orthodoxy.
As Rehm has convincingly shown, he was more of a Christian
than he knew.[95] Schiller planned a drama on Julian the Apos-
tate,[96] presumably in the mood of "The Gods of Greece"; it
may well be significant that he never wrote it. Eduard Spranger has brilliantly demonstrated that Schiller was not a consistent philosopher; he did not perform the (impossible) task
of harmoniously synthesizing Kant and Goethe, nor did he
choose finally and firmly, in his theoretical writings, between
the "idealism of freedom" and "objective idealism." [97] Thus
it is difficult, and to some extent idle, to speculate whether
Schiller accepted or rejected "the Greeks"; one must know
his position on particular features of Greek life and myth, at
a particular time.

One may instance two interrelated aspects of Hellenism
which particularly appealed to Schiller. Narrowing the gap
between gods and men did indeed increase man's stature. In
his essay on Winckelmann, Goethe summed up the impact
of this concept on later eighteenth century: "The god had
become man, to raise man to godhood. Men perceived the
loftiest majesty and were filled with enthusiasm for the loftiest
beauty." [98] And the myth of the laboring and finally triumphant Hercules, familiar in part from Winckelmann's description of the Torso, inspired him as no other did. With Hercules
and his myth of heroic toil, Schiller might well feel an affinity.
The demigod appears in the most varied contexts; [99] Schiller
hoped to show his deification, and his union with Hebe, as
an example of the highest type of idyl.[100] We may infer that
to him the Greeks served "to point a moral, or adorn a tale"
— in a sublime sense — but they were not ends and ideals in
themselves.

Thus Greece represented the great complementary factor
to Schiller, the "other" element needed to achieve totality,
just as sentimentive man needs the naïve. It was also, in his

later years, a source of discipline from which he hoped to learn simplicity and classicality. Winckelmannian Greece was closely allied to his old dream of Elysium. Thus he wrote to his fiancée that he expected from their marriage: "a lovely happy calmness . . . a uniformly joyous existence."[101] Increasingly he associated the concept of Hellas with the realm of the idea and the ideal, as in his letter to J. B. Erhard: "Stay in the serene and quiet region of *ideas*, and leave it to time to induct you into practical life."[102] More and more he came to realize that this concept did not represent any empirical reality, but that did not in itself detract from its value as a norm.[103] It fitted in well with his old notion of harmony and thus with that of the "beautiful soul." But to the Schiller of the late dramas, tragic Hellas had far more actuality than did "Iphigenian"[104] Greece. In his sarcastic epigram on a critical remark of Friedrich Schlegel's —

> Oedipus reisst die Augen sich aus, Jokaste erhenkt sich,
> Beide schuldlos; das Stück hat sich harmonisch gelöst —[105]

Schiller tellingly contrasts theory and reality.

To the mature Schiller, there is something beyond harmony: the tragic.[106] Ancient poetry exists "on a lower level" than modern;[107] similarly, ancient works of art are sensuously, not absolutely, ideal.[108] Schiller could not ignore what has been called "the Kantian destruction of the ancient world,"[109] but he typically preserved antiquity as an eternal norm. The Greeks may and must be surpassed, but they will remain as an irreplaceable element in the education of mankind.

Chapter IX

The Greek Gods and Christ: Hölderlin

In any account of German Hellenism, or of German poetry, Friedrich Hölderlin must occupy a central position. He is unique, at least among the major figures, in the intensity of his belief in "the gods." Whether his gods were the Olympians, or aspects of nature, or something else again, can be established only by a careful reading of his works. At any rate, his divinities represented aspects of reality to him, lived experiences which Hölderlin took with the utmost seriousness. (Indeed, he seems to have taken everything with such seriousness, never really to have relaxed his strong tensions and passionate devotions. Inevitably, his mind finally cracked under these unrelenting strains.) Goethe's admission that he was a polytheist only for poetic purposes [1] would have deeply shocked the younger poet. The world was one, Hölderlin believed: nature and spirit, Christ and Apollo, present and past, politics and love, must be sensed and interpreted as parts of a harmonious whole. If such integration could not be achieved — and he was far too sincere (to use a much abased word) to blink the difficulties — only collapse remained.

Hölderlin is so extraordinarily difficult a poet, at least in his later works, that there is no lack of conflicting interpretations, some of them at least as obscure as the most opaque of his writings. By following closely a few strands of his thought —

his "myth," especially his concept of the gods; the tension between the ideal of the past and present degradation; devotion to the ancient gods and a deeply rooted love of Christ — one may reach some insight into the meaning of his career and his fate. If he is difficult at times, he is at others almost startlingly lucid and direct. As a prologue to a discussion of his poetry, a few sentences about his personality, education, and background may be useful.

Until his breakdown,[2] Hölderlin's basic character seems to have changed very little. His essential purity is striking: he seems to have been remarkably free of meanness and selfishness, and amazingly single-minded in both his beliefs and his personal attachments. Thus when he was torn, in later years, between Christianity and a sort of pantheism, he went through not merely a philosophical and moral crisis, but an experience which threatened the roots of his existence. Closely linked to his purity was a will to believe, and believe the best. "For everything is good,"[3] "nothing is base,"[4] as he put it in a late poem. Extraordinarily intellectual — when a student he was an admired friend and companion of Hegel and Schelling — he was nevertheless, in an honorable sense, naïve. Like the hero of his novel *Hyperion*, he was first startled, then shattered by any encounter with human baseness. That men can behave falsely or cruelly, or fail to worship beauty and goodness, he could hardly endure. He demanded in literature the same genuineness he expected in life; his brief poem "The Sanctimonious Poets" expresses his anger at writers who degrade the gods by using their names as mere ornaments:

> Ihr kalten Heuchler, sprecht von den Göttern nicht!
> Ihr habt Verstand! Ihr glaubt nicht an Helios,
> Noch an den Donnerer und Meergott . . .[5]

Not surprisingly, Hölderlin, laboring under a tremendous psychological strain, was as labile as he was vulnerable.[6] In addition to his inner religious and intellectual conflicts, he experienced sharp disappointment at the neglect of his poetry; frustration of his "Platonic" love for Susette Gontard, whose husband was Hölderlin's employer at the time; disillusion with the events of his own times, and a sea of other troubles. Moods of exaltation were followed by depressions; moments of equilibrium seem to have been few. That he was able to achieve what he did is testimony to the quiet, unpretentious heroism of his nature.

For all his devotion to Greek gods and heroes, Hölderlin was hardly pagan in temperament. The robust sensuality of a Heinse, the serene self-containment of the mature Goethe, were not for him. His early ideal of Greece was derived mainly from Winckelmann, Rousseau, and Plato's Socrates; the Greeks he envisioned were impossibly pure and unselfish. Later, after his immersion in Pindar and Sophocles — he made striking translations of both — he became much more aware of the harder and wilder strains in Hellenic culture. He remained, however, generally optimistic in his concept of the gods: thus his Bacchus is an altruistic deity who awakens man to noble activity.[7] If Schiller was right in thinking the ancients natural and spontaneous, then Hölderlin was a modern of the moderns. He was "Greek," to be sure, in his sense of fate, his belief that nature, mythically represented by a galaxy of real, not allegorical gods, was divine, and that beauty was to be worshiped. Yet he was no aesthete in the pejorative sense; beauty was also goodness and truth, and poets and philosophers who neglected the stern facts of history and politics were doomed, in his view.

As a young student at the famous *Tübinger Stift* (Seminary),[8] Hölderlin was already exposed to the tensions which were to rack him until he became, perhaps mercifully, insane at the age of thirty-six. The Seminary was primarily concerned with training future pastors and theologians. Hölderlin himself came of a pious Protestant family; his mother, to whom he was deeply devoted, expected him to enter the church. But the Seminary, much influenced by the Enlightenment, was far from orthodox; and its curriculum included a "worldly" course in the Classics. Keenly aware of the new ideas of the time, Hölderlin worshiped Rousseau and Schiller, accepted Winckelmann's doctrines, and explored with Hegel and Schelling the still newer notions of German idealism. He quickly broke with Protestant orthodoxy, but never lost his sometimes tortured love of Christ, whom he regarded as a friend as well as a god or demigod. To spare his mother, he was as tactful as possible about his lack of faith; on the other hand, he was too honest, unlike many of his contemporaries, to accept a position in a church in which he no longer believed. Thus he was forced into the precarious and humiliating career of a private tutor.

Impressionable as he was, Hölderlin at first responded, with his eager enthusiasm, to a variety of influences. Greece was only one of the many ideals which inform his early poetry. He echoes the usual Enlightenment attacks on priests and nuns [9] — though he is generally Christian — expresses a Leibnizian belief in harmony, glorifies Rousseau, and sympathizes with the French Revolution. On the whole, the eighteenth-century literary revolution meant more to him than political stirrings. His youthful poems, derivative and eclectic, could not have been written without an immersion in Klopstock, "Ossian," Friedrich Stolberg, and Schiller. There is a strong utopian tendency. (Inevitably, Schiller, with his more abstract approach to poetry, his philosophical lyrics devoted to the "ideals of mankind," meant more to Hölderlin than Goethe did. *Werther* is an exception, and a significant one.) He makes use of a variety of myths: there are classical allusions, references to Germanic figures like Teut and Mana,[10] and to Jehovah.[11] The Winckelmannian triad of simplicity, calm, and grandeur is invoked in Hölderlin's early poem "To Perfection," [12] but the young poet has not yet found his own direction. Until he was about twenty, he displayed little originality;

aside from a consistent solemnity, a rather wearing insistence
on soaring, he can hardly be said to have a style of his own.
When he did "break through," it was, significantly, with a
poem about Greece.

Gradually, almost subterraneously, the Hellenic myth was
establishing its primacy; soon the other enthusiasms would be
pushed into the background. At the Seminary, as a student,
Hölderlin was praised for his diligence in the Classics, especially in Greek.[13] One of the two brief essays he submitted for
the degree of Master of Arts was entitled, ambitiously enough,
"History of the Fine Arts among the Greeks" (1790). It is
not remarkable in itself, and is in fact neither original nor well
organized. At this point Hölderlin knew far less about Greece
than did his contemporary Friedrich Schlegel; indeed, many
an undergraduate has submitted a more impressive essay than
this. Basing himself mainly on Winckelmann and Herder,
Hölderlin speaks of the "aesthetic people," and strikes the
usual utopian note: "Everywhere were freedom, joyous heroism, sensuous beauty, and the awareness thereof."[14] One point
is important in view of Hölderlin's later preoccupation with
"Mother Asia": the "free, serene Greek," repelled the "dom-
ineering, and in part terrible daemons" of the Orient.[15] If the
essay is of little value in itself, it has great significance as a
document of Hölderlin's beliefs. The Winckelmannian gods
and heroes served as a catalyst; the poet's will to believe, his
tremendous religiosity, could now crystallize. For years Hellas and its gods were to dominate his poetry. The experience
of Greece was a liberation for Hölderlin; he was now able
to focus his powers. At the same time it threatened him with
captivity to another time and nation. Eventually he struggled
to escape, but the attempt cost him dear.

In his "Hymn to the Spirit of Greece," probably written
in the same year, Hölderlin emerged as a poet in his own right.
Perhaps this is not a great poem — in part, it still depends
heavily on Schiller and others — but it contains a vision of

Greece which is authentically Hölderlin's own, and is marked
by a startling directness of statement which is characteristic
of his finest poetry. Lines like

> Im Angesichte der Götter
> Beschloss dein Mund
> Auf Liebe dein Reich zu gründen [16]

could have been written by no other poet. If there is nothing
new about his celebration of Greek freedom, joyousness, and
uniqueness ("Dir gleichet keiner/Unter den Brüdern" [17]), the
image of the "blessed generations" of Hellas is inimitable in
its simplicity and in the sincerity it conveys. This is no philosophy of history, still less aesthetic play; it has the quality of
religious faith. In his repeated assertion that Greece "founded
her realm on love," Hölderlin has gone far beyond the usual
eighteenth-century belief in the humaneness of Homer and
the Athenians. Of course there is precious little love in Thu-
cydides, say, or the myths of the Titans; but it was a subjective
necessity for the poet to believe that love was the foundation
of his ideal world. Perhaps he was, after all, an *anima naturali-
ter Christiana.*

The poem "Greece" (1793) shows a similar fusion, perhaps
unconscious, of ancient and Christian elements. Some of its
lines recall the longing of the weary church-goer for a promised Heaven:

> Mich verlangt ins ferne Land hinüber
> Nach Alcäus und Anakreon,
> Und ich schlief' im engen Hause lieber,
> Bei den Heiligen in Marathon . . . [18]

The soul longs for "the distant land" — a variant has "the
better land" [19] — and would rather be resting with the "saints"
in Marathon than active in the present world. Indeed, "my
Plato," we read earlier in the poem, created paradises. The
naïve intimacy of "my Plato" (later Hölderlin writes of "my
Hercules") [20] reveals the depth of his emotional attachment.

The poem is elegiac in mood: Attica has fallen, the marble halls lie in ruins. Inevitably we are reminded of Schiller's "The Gods of Greece," but Hölderlin is much more in earnest; where the older poet had written of a "fabled country," the younger presents a "piously believed reality." [21] Between the brilliance of ancient Hellas and its melancholy present there is a contrast almost unbearable for one of Hölderlin's temperament; it was to form a central theme of his *Hyperion*.

The Greek pantheon, in Hölderlin's mind, is closely linked with nature. It is not only, or primarily, that the gods may embody aspects of the physical world. Rather, both represent reality at its highest; both are pure, beautiful, friendly to man, and in a profound sense good. When Hölderlin writes of "Father Aether" [22] or the god of the sea he does so with both intimacy and reverence, and leaves no doubt that to him these figures are utterly, existentially real. His simple line "Im Arme der Götter wuchs ich gross" [23] expresses a sense of closeness to the divine which is characteristic.

But who, or what, are Hölderlin's gods? In his works, especially in the odes and hymns of his later productive life, the outlines of his belief begin to appear; it is not systematic but it does have a general coherence, a degree of overarching unity. Intuitively, he arrived at a concept very like Friedrich Schlegel's: the myth must fuse intellectual content and sensuous expression. The cosmos may be regarded either as eternal nature, independent of time, or dynamically, under the aspect of history. "Father Aether," for instance, is primarily a nature god; Christ and "the youngest daughter of time," Germania, are essentially in history, though they transcend it. The two realms are not absolutely separate: thus Poseidon is the eternal sea but is still conscious of the passage of time and mourns or rejoices at its changes. Unlike Stefan George, Hölderlin did not believe that men are or may become divine; when his Empedocles thinks himself a god, he is guilty of *hubris*. Nor are his gods simply aspects of nature; they are aware of man and generally sympathetic with him. In moments of exaltation the priest and the poet may communicate with the gods and to some extent comprehend them.

Karl Viëtor was surely right in stating that Hölderlin was not really polytheistic: his gods are aspects of "the father" or "the god." [24] It is also interesting that the poet became increasingly chary of using the traditional Olympian names like Apollo or Zeus. In *Hyperion, The Death of Empedocles,* and many of the poems, the ultimate god is nature; Viëtor speaks of "pantheistic religiosity." [25] In the last hymns, "the father" is supreme: he is not the omnipotent god of Christianity but is a loftier being than the Homeric "father of gods and men." These very late poems are difficult in the extreme and in some cases unfinished; absolute certainty about their meaning is unattainable.

That Hölderlin was not a polytheist does not mean that the lesser gods or demigods were in any sense unreal to him. They are never mere allegories or ornaments. He believed in them as a good Catholic may believe in the saints; if they are not in an ultimate sense divine, the divine is nevertheless in them. Furthermore, he was convinced of the need of mediators, in all religions.[26] Man cannot normally endure the full power of the godhead; it must descend to him as if "by a stairway (*treppenweise*)." [27]

Until very late, the gods of Greece dominated Hölderlin's pantheon; at least until his last breakdown, he felt a special emotional closeness to them. Certainly he believed in their essential reality, which is not to say that he accepted every myth of the gods as literal truth. The more frivolous amours of Zeus, for example, he simply ignored. To say that he regarded the Hellenic divinities as representations of the religious aspect of nature, expressed in perfect artistic form,[28] is misleading because it is too rationalistic: it neglects the fact that Hölderlin was first of all a poet. Each of his gods had his own physiognomy, his own personality. When Hölderlin wrote, shortly before his final collapse, "Apollo has smitten me," [29] he was not allegorizing but expressing his felt conviction that the gods are completely and sometimes terribly real.

Below the gods are demigods and heroes. The pantheon extends beyond Olympus: in some poems Christ is regarded as only partly divine, since He was subject to death; in "The Rhine," Rousseau, the modern culture hero, appears as more than mortal. In varying moods, Hölderlin regarded differently the gods' attitude toward man; there was a general darkening of his view as he grew older. At first, in his rapturous optimism, they seemed kindly, devoted to man's welfare. After his disillusion, Hyperion interprets their Winckelmannian calm and bliss as indifference to man's fate; but he draws comfort from the ultimate god, nature, as does Empedocles. The gods "need" men, at least poets and heroes, to celebrate them. [30] They may punish human arrogance terribly, as Sophocles taught Hölderlin, but never unjustly.

As examples of a lived ideal, a sort of concrete universal, the men of ancient Greece perhaps meant almost as much to Hölderlin as did its gods. Hellas was not merely a "theocracy of the beautiful" [31] but a society founded on love, not primarily on beauty. Patriotism, philosophy, and religion were at least as important as art; unlike Winckelmann and Goethe, he stressed the city-state as an organic whole. Later, indeed, the poet came to feel that an undue aestheticism had brought about the ruin of Greece:

> sie wollten stiften
> Ein Reich der Kunst. Dabei ward aber
> Das Vaterländische von ihnen
> Versäumet und erbärmlich gieng
> Das Griechenland, das schönste, zu Grunde. [32]

But in their greatest days, the Greeks were as devoted to civic ideals, as "pious," [33] as Vergil's Aeneas. As beautiful as the statues described by Winckelmann, they were also marked by beauty and grandeur of soul. Close to the gods, they were therefore close to nature. Unlike Hölderlin's contemporaries, they were rich in deeds [34] as well as in thoughts; their whole life was marked by the unity which modern man has lost.[35] In the first flush of his enthusiasm, he endowed Greek civilization, above all the Athenian, with the qualities of Elysium and with some of the radiance of the Christian heaven. Later he came to feel that the Hellenes, because of their very virtues, were likely to be guilty of *hubris*; still later, that they had to guard themselves carefully against an innate Oriental fieriness or wildness.[36] But Greece never lost its place in Hölderlin's affections or in his philosophy of history. The golden age had really existed; it would somehow return. It represented the highest actual flowering of human culture [37] and at the same time a timeless ideal model.

Against the background of this vision, Hölderlin's attitude toward his own age becomes understandable. He was convinced that he dwelt in a "world grown old," [38] a "shabby" [39] time. Actually he was living in one of the great periods of human history: one needs only to name some of his contemporaries — Goethe, Napoleon, Beethoven — to realize how far from shabby the age was. But "the old, blissful coasts," [40] the islands of the Archipelago, Athens, Elis, and Olympia, seemed more real to him than the present as well as more beautiful. Though he indeed was to gain profound insights into Greek thought, he was quintessentially romantic about Hellas. Like many of his German contemporaries, and like Shelley, he believed in a golden age in the past and another in the future. Hölderlin's concept is not really cyclical, however, for when the gods return, paradise or rather Elysium will have been forever regained. Rather, it is a secularization of Christian ideas: Eden, the Fall, and the final triumphant end of history are transposed into a myth in which the Hellenic gods are central. At the Seminary, Hölderlin, Hegel, and other ardent young students used the words "Kingdom of God" as a slogan or password to express their eschatological hopes.[41] For the poet, "Kingdom of the gods" might have been more accurate. In his last years he could believe in it only with part of his mind; his earlier devotion to Christ proved at least as strong as the fascination of Apollo and Zeus.

To turn back to specific works: *Hyperion* (1797–1799) centers on the contrast between the ancient glory of Greece and its present degradation.[42] Hyperion, the protagonist, feels the disparity as keenly as Byron did; he has Byron's (and Werther's) *Weltschmerz* but none of the Byronic robustness and verve.[43] The plot of this lyrical "novel in letters" may be quickly told: Hyperion, an impulsive, enthusiastic, labile young Greek of the late eighteenth century, is of course very much a portrait of the author. After experiencing friendship and love, he takes up arms to help liberate his countrymen from the Turks. Action frees him from his usual anxious melancholy, but he is soon disillusioned: the Greeks of his own time are cruel and vicious barbarians. In a complete failure of nerve he renounces both his political hopes and his beloved Diotima, who soon dies. (Diotima, who is also addressed in several of his lyrics, is Hölderlin's image of and tribute to Susette Gontard.) Having visited Germany, he denounces its inhabitants as warped, one-sided Philistines;[44] by classical standards, they are not human beings at all. Yet he is consoled by the beauty of the German spring. Friendship, love, and action have failed; nature remains. The beauty of the world is indestructible.

The contrast between ancient and modern life is expressed in a series of symbols. A jackal prowls among the ruins. "Five lovely columns stood mournfully above the rubble, and a kingly portal, crashed to earth, lay at their feet."[45] Yet nature has not changed, and Diotima incarnates both the beauty and the "holiness" of the Greece that has fallen.[46] Her calmness, serenity, and simplicity are repeatedly stressed; she derives from Winckelmann's ideal as much as from Plato's prophetess. Inspired by her and by a visit to Athens, Hyperion is to educate and inspire the people in the authentic Athenian spirit. "There will be only one beauty; and mankind and nature will be united in one all-embracing unity." [47]

After Hyperion's defeat, he expresses in his "Song of Fate" a view of tortured men and beautiful but indifferent gods which is far more Greek than his earlier enthusiasm. The gods are free of fate, marmoreal, indeed Winckelmannian:

> Und die seeligen Augen
> Bliken in stiller
> Ewiger Klarheit. [48]

Men, as in Goethe's poem "Song of the Spirits above the Waters," are dashed blindly from cliff to cliff, like an Alpine waterfall. While Hyperion's failure reveals a great deal about Hölderlin's own doubts in his poetic mission, it must not be taken absolutely. Greece cannot be revived by the direct action of any individual, however enthusiastic or pure, but the gods will return sooner or later. If the myth of their rebirth, expressed in a series of odes, hymns, and fragments, is a labored historical construction, it is nevertheless deeply felt.

Hyperion is not a great novel; actually it is rather an elegy expressed in lyrical prose than a novel at all. As an aesthetic whole it is far less impressive than the poetry of Hölderlin's maturity. Its "message" — and surely, despite the disclaimer in the preface, it is a didactic work — is one of unity: the individual, like society and the universe itself, must be a harmonious whole. Diotima, who symbolizes Greece, "trusts nature"; [49] the world is one, and there is no extramundane god. A pantheistic belief enables Hyperion to survive all his disasters; it satisfies his emotions as well as his mind.

Pantheism is even more central in *The Death of Empedocles*, an unfinished tragedy (1799). Empedocles is shown as a prophet particularly close to nature, and hence in Hölderlin's way of thinking to the ultimate spirit or *Geist* of the cosmos. His tragic guilt is arrogance: he feels that his words brought forth the gods themselves.[50] (One cannot help thinking of Fichte here.) In his defiance of the priests and the mob he reminds one of Prometheus but still more he recalls Christ:[51] he even has a last supper of bread and wine with his disciples before his sacrificial death. Typically, Hölderlin has tried here to reconcile opposites. To atone for his *hubris* Empedocles leaps into the crater of Aetna, literally reuniting himself with nature. In depicting his death as a religious action rather than as suicide, Hölderlin apparently intended to write the mythical drama of pantheism.[52] Although he achieved some extraordinarily beautiful passages, often reminiscent of Goethe's *Iphigenia*, he hardly succeeded. He was too ethereal, one feels, to write dramas; moreover the "problems" of the play do not really lend themselves to dramatic presentation.

A series of great poems written around the turn of the century deal with a cluster of interrelated questions, all having to do with the Greek past and its meaning for the godless present. In *Hyperion* Hölderlin wrote of his countrymen with the bitterness of disenchanted love; in "Song of the German" his mood is very different. Since Greece lay in ruins, his thoughts turn again to Germany, the "ripest fruit of time."[53] Throughout history, the spirit has moved from land to land. In what other modern country are there such poets and thinkers?

> Wo ist dein Delos, wo dein Olympia,
> Dass wir uns alle finden am höchsten Fest?[54]

For all his pride in German attainments, Hölderlin's mood is interrogative rather than boastful; he speaks more of hopes than accomplishments, and the new Delos and Olympia have not yet been erected.

Hölderlin's concept of the night of history is central in several crucial poems. Novalis had contrasted the night of Christianity and love to the day of antiquity; Hölderlin's symbolism is very different. To him too day is the era of the

Greek gods. Night, which set in after the crucifixion of Christ, is a time of sleep and of deprivation; the old gods have departed, and Christ is also far from man. Thus in the elegy "Bread and Wine" night is the time of forgetfulness and "holy drunkenness,"[55] but day is more beloved. The poem moves back and forth dialectically between present and past, night and day. Greece and its fall are invoked in the second main division, the center of the poem.

In the third section of the elegy, which like many of Hölderlin's poems is triadic in structure, resolution is achieved. We have been born too late; the gods seem indifferent to us but it is because they "spare" the weakness of modern men. (The lack of any bitterness or blame is typical.)

> Nur zu Zeiten erträgt göttliche Fülle der Mensch.
> Traum von ihnen ist drauf das Leben.[56]

Yet if the poet suffers in this "shabby time" he may still hope, like the priests of Bacchus, to live and work in the "holy night." The Father's face is averted, but a quiet spirit (*Genius*), Christ, has left us bread and wine as a consolation. They are a sign that he, and the other holy ones, will return; they link of course antiquity and Christianity, but the ancient gods remain dominant. Man today can feel "some gratitude" for the divine gifts, but not the highest, ecstatic joys:

> Denn zur Freude, mit Geist, wurde das Grössre zu gross . . .[57]

Christ is a comforting rather than a radiant figure. The poem ends serenely: the last word is "sleeps." Given its dialectical structure, the implication is that night will give place at the proper time to day — the return of mythical Greece and the old gods in all their glory. Hölderlin does not seem to mean that men will build temples again to Zeus or Apollo but that the aspects of life they represented will be worshiped;[58] joy and intellect will again be fused.

"The Archipelago," perhaps Hölderlin's greatest poem,

again sets off the present against the past. Now the hope of renascence is more strongly expressed, the tone is more urgent: "Blüht Ionien, ists die Zeit?" [59] Here Athens is the shining ideal. Just as the city rose again after its destruction by the Persians, the whole Greek world will return. The Athenians were particularly close to the Olympians: in a reciprocal relationship, the gods who aided them needed and expected human thanks. They were "the loving people" — what one might call Hölderlin's crypto-Christianity again appears. As in *Hyperion*, the barbarously industrious moderns, who have lost all sense of the divine, are evoked in contrast. In this hymn, however, rebirth is seen as certain: a god, the "spirit of nature," will bring back the age of beauty and the gods, despite fate, history, and devouring time (*die reissende Zeit*). Again, it is not a question of a rebirth of Greece itself, but of the return of the Greek spirit to inspire and shape some Western nation. This modern people must then look back to its great predecessor:

> Hin nach Hellas schaue das Volk, und weinend und dankend
> Sänftige sich in Erinnerungen der stolze Triumphtag. [60]

Naturally, it was Germany on which Hölderlin's hopes for "another Hellas" were fixed; the hymn "Germania" expresses his dream most explicitly. As so frequently, the poet begins with a lament for the old gods; he even speaks of them as dead, but though they have vanished, they will visit the earth again. Here the spirit which inspires one nation after another, symbolized by the eagle of Jupiter, flies from the Orient over Greece and Italy and comes finally to the virgin Germania, the "most quiet daughter of God." [61] She is young and timid, but "all-loving," and has hence been chosen to bear a "difficult happiness": she will be the center and inspiration of a new age. As a priestess, unarmed, she "gives counsel to the kings and peoples round about." [62]

Another late poem, "The Migration," also puts its main

stress on Hölderlin's hopes for the future rather than his laments for the past. As if to establish the stature of his countrymen,[63] he has constructed a myth of his own: in ancient times the Germans met, on the shores of the Black Sea, the "children of the sun"; from this union the Greeks were born.[64] The poet, with a typical leap of thought, imagines a journey to Greece. He does not intend to remain — the mood of *Hyperion* has passed, at least for the moment — but to invite the Graces to visit Germany. Some day, he concludes with a rare flash of irony, the Germans will ask the Graces how it was that they came to visit savages.

On poems like "Germania" and "The Migration," and on other evidence, a theory of Hölderlin's "turning to the West" has been erected.[65] It is quite true that he tried, though hardly consistently, to free himself from the "tyranny of Greece." A fragmentary essay of 1799 expresses his fear of losing his originality, indeed of being crushed, by the weight of an almost infinite past.[66] We must conceive of our own drive toward culture as springing from the same "common original ground"[67] as that of antiquity, he believed, or we shall be enslaved. The poet began to stress at this time, like Friedrich Schlegel, a fiery, Oriental, "aorgic" element in Greek culture, and to set up "Hesperia" — the West, not merely Germany — as a balancing ideal. Hoping to become a lecturer at Jena, he wrote to Schiller that he had attained a certain freedom vis-à-vis Greek literature; perhaps he could liberate students from bondage to the letter of the Greek tradition.[68] In his translations of Sophocles he was free indeed of the letter, rendering the name of Zeus as "father of time" and Eros as "spirit of love."

If this belief had clearly prevailed, we would have the familiar story of a young enthusiast modifying, in maturity, his excessive hopes, accepting the universe, and establishing a synthesis of "Junonian" sobriety and Hellenic fire;[69] the Greeks would have become, as in the late criticism of the Schlegels, only one cultural element, though an indispensable one. But this is only half the tale; its ending is neither happy nor banal. Along with Hölderlin's more "sensible" insights, the unique attraction, the almost irresistible magnetism, of the Greek gods persisted. Over against that developed a counterpull, all the stronger for having been long suppressed, the poignant emotional appeal of Christ. The poet's allegiances were hopelessly split: he struggled to reconcile the conflicting divinities into one great syncretic myth. This was a task at which a more robust and disciplined intellect might well have struggled in vain. It would be melodramatic to say that it caused his madness. Yet the schism within his religious beliefs was much more than a mere symptom of his disturbance; the opposition between Christ and Dionysus, *caritas* and beauty, was a profound emotional crisis. Hölderlin's struggle anticipates Nietzsche's of course; it is more moving than the philosopher's because the poet was singularly free of hatred and resentment. His attitudes toward Christ and toward the Greeks were both "founded on love," and his dilemma was thus a far more tragic one.

Again and again, Hölderlin tried to order his conflicting myths harmoniously. Individual poems do show that he had reached, for the moment, a resolution — which made his ultimate failure all the more crushing. The hymn to the Conciliator ("Versöhnender der du nimmergeglaubt") is a poetic syncretization of pagan and Christian myth; as in "Bread and Wine," the Greek element is still dominant. "Conciliation" refers first of all to the peace of 1801,[70] then to Christ, then to the supreme problem of joining the Olympian gods and Christ in concord. Three versions of the poem exist, an indication of how doggedly the poet wrestled with his task. The last is the most clearly articulated and the most pantheistic.

The "youth" (Christ) is to be welcomed, with the other divinities, at the great celebration of peace. Though the joy he brought was soon obscured by his early doom, his coming was not in vain. When he was first sent by "the Father," he could not reveal that a new age would begin, for he was sent "not to live but to die." [71] Now the new day, the great festival, is about to come. All religions will be reconciled; man will no longer "count" the gods.[72] Paradoxically, Christ will now be more divinely celebrated in the evening of his days — that is, now that he no longer reigns alone.[73]

In the final version Christ is designated as a son of the "All-living One" (*Dem Alllebendigen*) not *the* son of the Christian God.[74] At the price of relinquishing Christ's specific divinity, Hölderlin has "reconciled" the gods, but he soon found the sacrifice too heavy.

A letter to his brother of 1801 seems to express Hölderlin's basic conscious belief at the time. "Everything [is] infinite unity, but in this All [is] *a pre-eminently united* and unifying element, which *in itself is no 'I,'* and let that be, between us, God!" [75] The "pre-eminently united element" is Hölderlin's Father, or "All-living One," seen under the aspect of prose. But the formula ignores the figure of Christ, who was returning more and more insistently to his mind. Nor is it adequate to express the power of the Greek divinities, who were indeed aspects of "infinite unity" but far more than that to him.

The full sharpness of his dilemma appears in the hymn "The Only One" (1801–1803; three versions have been preserved or reconstructed; the poem was never completed).[76] Here no real reconciliation is attained. The poem begins with yet another tribute to Greece, expressed in keen, even painful paradoxes:

> Was ist es, das
> An die alten seeligen Küsten
> Mich fesselt, dass ich mehr noch
> Sie liebe, als mein Vaterland? [77]

The single word *selig* (blessed, blissful) contains much of Hölderlin's conflict: it denotes Elysium and the "blissful islands" of which his friend Heinse had written, but also the bliss of the Christian heaven. Apparently a sense of guilt is implied in loving the ancient coasts more than his native land. The poet envisions himself, "as if sold into heavenly captivity, there, where Apollo walked in kingly form." [78] The sense of enslavement to Hellas reinforces the image of being fettered; the contradiction is not resolved. This notion of bondage is new in Hölderlin's poems; other surprises are to follow.

Again the poem turns to the relation of the old gods and their "brave sons," [79] the Greek demigods and Christ. The poet loves Him as the youngest and last of the divine family, "the house's treasure." Suddenly he addresses Christ directly, with startling poignancy: "My Master and Lord!/ O Thou my teacher!" Why has Christ remained far away; why could He not be found among "the ancients/The heroes and/ The gods"? This is surely the breakthrough to consciousness of the religious faith of his childhood.

Fearing the jealousy of the other gods, he even admits guilt: "For too much/ O Christ, I cling to Thee." [80] With a dialectical shift, he tries to redress the balance, "boldly" proclaiming that Christ is the brother of Hercules and Bacchus. All three are demigods, born of mortal mothers. Yet this syncretizing myth no longer really satisfies the poet: "shame hinders/ Me from comparing with you/ The worldly men." [81] "Worldly men" is startling for Hercules and Bacchus. Beissner explains "men" as a reference to demigods, not full divinities;[82] this may be true as far as it goes but it is inadequate. The great contrast is between the spiritual Christ and the merely worldly ancient figures. And why should Hölderlin, if still a pagan, feel shame at making the comparison? Well might he admit that this song had too much expressed the feelings of his own heart — "too much" of course from the point of view of a believer in the Greek myth. Touchingly he asserts that he will "make good the mistake" [83] in other songs; but after this time he was never able to complete any poems in the pagan mode. The hymn ends not with a synthesis — that would be impossible — but with a comparison between the sadness of Christ before his ascension and the lot of heroes while they are still on earth, followed by the enigmatic statement that spiritual (Christian) poets must also be worldly. Looking back at the poem, one can conclude that its title does not mean that Christ is the sole god but rather that he is unique in the strength of his appeal and in authenticity. Apollo, Hercules, and even Dionysus have become pale figures compared to Christ.

"Patmos" (1801–1802) is one of the last complete, or virtually complete,[84] poems Hölderlin wrote before his serious breakdown in 1802. Again he felt compelled to deal with the night of the gods, and with the relation between past and present, paganism and Christianity. The poem is dedicated to the pious landgrave Friedrich V of Homburg, who had been pained by Enlightenment and aesthetic paganism.[85] Remembering the direction of "The Only One," one might expect a full avowal of Christianity in a hymn which takes its title from the island where St. John the Divine saw his apocalyptic visions; but Hölderlin was too divided inwardly, and too honest, to make any flat declarations. Though he is careful to spare the feelings of the landgrave, he nevertheless still speaks of Christ as a demigod and of "Heavenly Ones" in the plural. If on balance the poem is far more Christian than pagan, it is still marked by great tension. It is more controlled and unified than "The Only One," but its inner contradictions are sharp; one cannot read it without sensing the strains under which Hölderlin labored.

The first few lines at once create a sense of strain which becomes at times almost unbearable. God is near, yet hard to comprehend; where danger is, a saving power grows. Like eagles, like the "sons of the Alps"[86] who cross the abyss without fear, we must hope to face peril. Surrounded by a mythical mountain landscape, with "peaks of time" around us, where men are utterly cut off from those they love even though they live near, the poet prays for wings, hoping to "cross over and return." [87] The dangers of the poem are both religious and personal and they are intertwined: the difficulty of comprehending God and the sense of alienation are somehow one.

After contrasting the bareness of Patmos to the rich beauty of Cyprus and other classical islands, the poem moves on to Christ's farewell to the disciples and his death. It is the greatest of mysteries that the most beautiful of beings, the demigod, should die. He is the last of the divine beings; the Father averts his face; no longer can an immortal being be seen in heaven or on earth. The day of the gods is over; man's consolation, now that he lives in "loving night," [88] can only lie in simple wisdom, in memory, and in meditating upon the holy writings, [89] for the glory of the gods is no longer visible.

Adapting the Bible to his heterodox belief, Hölderlin uses the parable of the wheat and the chaff for his own purposes. The grain is preserved, and if some of it is lost — if God's speech is no longer heard in its immediacy — that is not an evil: God "does not wish everything at once." [90] In other words, it would be impious to expect the splendor of day during the era of night.

Christ and the other Heavenly Ones still live; day will return, not, one infers, as the Second Coming but in the form of a "mythic Greece" with a reconciled Christ included in the pantheon. [91] But that is inference; the poem is less definite. It closes with a direct but puzzling statement. Every divine being demands sacrifices: we have therefore served Mother Earth and "recently" the Sunlight "ignorantly." The Father desires first of all that we cherish the "solid letter" [92] of the sacred writings and the interpretation of existing tradition. That is the task of German poetry.

The final lines read like a disavowal of the classical myth. Clearly the cult of earth and sun is subordinated to that of the "letter" — which to Hölderlin's pious, and Protestant, patron could have meant only the text of the Bible. (Twice the poem mentions "holy writings" or "Holy Writ"; it is saturated with Biblical allusions and language.) Yet "holy writings" may also be taken to include myths of Zeus or Dionysus. Much depends on the overtones one assigns to "ignorantly" (*unwissend*): does the word suggest the innocent ignorance of men born before the Christian revelation,[93] or the inevitable perplexity of all those who dwell in the "night"? [94] If the former, how can the poet say that we have *recently* served the Sunlight?

Doubtless the poem meant one thing to the landgrave, another to a pagan, but Hölderlin would have been the last man to use Aesopian language deliberately. One can interpret the hymn as the avowal of a Christian *malgré lui* or as the attempt of a pantheistic poet to give to the beloved and heroic figure of Jesus the greatest possible role within a basically pagan myth. Neither interpretation is really satisfactory, though there is evidence in the text for each. Christianity seems to be getting the upper hand, but we shall be wise to keep in mind Guardini's repeated admonition that Hölderlin never reached a final resolution.[95] Up to the moment of collapse he was still struggling to reconcile the irreconcilable. The center of "Patmos" lies precisely in the struggle, the dissonance.

A true synthesis, after all, was impossible. If Hölderlin had succeeded in persuading himself that Christ was no more divine than Dionysus, it has been well pointed out, he would have had no serious difficulty in constructing a myth of reconciliation.[96] In his last known letter written before his breakdown, he wrote of the greatness of the ancients but also of the "incomprehensibly more divine character of our holy religion." [97] Unlike Winckelmann, Goethe, Schiller, Heine, and a host of lesser men, he had a specific, very strong love for Christ; indeed, a psychological bond to Him. For a worshiper of the Greeks, it was a paradoxical endowment. As Guardini says, one cannot even be sure whether

Hölderlin's gods were essentially pagan or rather served to prepare the way for an acceptance of the one god of Christianity, conceived of not as a bloodless monotheistic principle but as a living reality.[98] Certainly he had a *fibre adorative*, a genuinely religious temperament. Unlike his successor Stefan George, he reached no clear decision. Even the evidence of his long years of madness is inconsistent. He spoke of himself as orthodox and was, at one period, badly upset when visitors brought up pagan matters.[99] Yet the brief poem "Greece," written during the last year of his life, includes the lines:

> Mit Geistigkeit ist weit umher die alte Sage,
> Und neues Leben kommt aus Menschheit wieder.[100]

His poetic gift had fled with his sanity — the verses are signed "In submissiveness Scardanelli [a name he often used for these last pitiful efforts], the 24th of May, 1748" — but the myth of rebirth in the spirit of Hellas still returned, intermittently and perhaps dimly, to his distracted mind.

Generally, Hölderlin's impact has been mainly in the direction of paganism: it is his vision of Greece which has had the greatest appeal. In the nineteenth century he was largely ignored, though Nietzsche admired him intensely. Rediscovered in the first years of the twentieth century, he appealed particularly to George and the members of George's circle like his first important editor, Hellingrath, and Friedrich Gundolf; he was interpreted as the greatest prophet of the Hellenic ideal. Gradually he reached a wide audience, not limited to Germany. When the German reaction against all varieties of paganism set in after 1945, Christian as well as existentialist readings of Hölderlin gained considerable appeal. Often they are as tendentious as the Georgean image. A critic like Guardini, who did not hesitate, even in the Nazi period, to point out the poet's Christian aspect but staunchly refrained from exaggerating it, is highly unusual.

In German eyes, Hölderlin has himself become a mythical figure. Usually he has been seen as the charismatic "German-Greek youth," fusing in himself the essences of both cultures. Some writers use him as evidence for the claim of a special affinity between the two nations: only the Germans, the argument runs, understand Hellas in a truly "deep" way. Although there is to be sure an authentically Greek note in a poem like "Hyperion's Song of Fate," Hölderlin's reflective, idealizing manner of thought is very far indeed from Greek objectivity. A member of a highly self-conscious generation, like Hegel, Schelling, and Friedrich Schlegel, he shared the general orientation of his age and was in the broader sense of the term a romantic.

A countervailing myth makes him a martyr to the "tyranny of Greece over Germany," alienated from his own time and eventually driven insane by the spell of Winckelmann's gods. Here there is an element of truth; but in order to realize how greatly this view oversimplifies his predicament, one has only to ask oneself whether Hölderlin would have been sounder, happier, or better balanced if he had longed for the German middle ages or the days of Arminius.

Apart from his personal psychological problems, Hölderlin's fatal conflict derived from the impossibility of reconciling his deep devotion to Christ with a clashing belief. This conflict is as old as Christianity itself; it was his intensity, his very sincerity, which made it unbearable. When he wrote, in a late version of "Patmos," of the danger of mixing personal love with religious adoration, he was referring to the disciples' relation to Christ, but he may well have given us the clue to his own disaster:

> Zu viel aber
> Der Liebe, wo Anbetung ist,
> Ist gefährlich, triffet am meisten.[101]

Chapter X

Christianity versus Aesthetic Paganism: Some Romanticists

♪♪♪♪♪♪♪♪♪♪♪♪♪♪♪♪♪♪♪♪♪♪♪♪♪♪♪♪♪♪

One would expect that the German romantic writers, enthusiastic champions of the middle ages, the beauty of Christian ritual and belief, and so forth, would oppose any sort of aesthetic paganism; and this is roughly true. Over against Goethe's belief that romanticism was morbid, Friedrich Schlegel maintained: "Romantic poetry is the poetry of *life* (abundance, light, fire, flower); ancient poetry, that of *death* (gigantic or elegiac)." [1] A later romantic, Joseph von Eichendorff, challenged pagan belief by entitling a very Christian story "The Marble Statue." Here the statue of Venus, an archetype of the beautiful "lost" woman, is a symbol of sin and ultimately of death. The hero, deeply tempted, is saved when he hears an old Christian song.

Yet a certain subterranean paganism persists in the writings of the early romantics. These poets, aiming at universality, did not exclude Greek themes or proscribe the Greek spirit: the young Friedrich Schlegel, above all, was a devout and enthusiastic Hellenist. Aestheticism has an intrinsic tendency toward paganism, even when it uses Christian symbols. A religion of art has per se an anti-Christian thrust. And if a poet like Novalis makes his erotic images centrally important, not mere metaphors, he is to that extent a cryptopagan. This is perhaps the most heretical of the opinions expressed in this book.

I

Friedrich Schlegel is increasingly recognized as one of the most stimulating and original of the German romanticists. With the possible exception of Heine, he was the most brilliant German literary critic of the nineteenth century. For a long time, his reputation suffered from a variety of reproaches, mainly moral in nature: that he was lazy, that his novel *Lucinde* was voluptuous if not pornographic, that his conversion to Roman Catholicism was a betrayal of the humanistic and Protestant traditions of German culture. Ernst Robert Curtius was one of the first important modern scholars to defend Schlegel; René Wellek has recently reasserted his position as one of the major figures in modern criticism;[2] the new edition of his complete works, now in progress, is added testimony to his stature. Indeed, the volume of Schlegel's writings and the obvious breadth of his knowledge sufficiently refute the notion of his indolence; the eroticism of *Lucinde* seems mild to a generation acquainted with Norman Mailer and Henry Miller; and now that a less sectarian approach to German culture obtains, his Catholicism no longer affords grounds for reproach.

In the development of German paganism, Schlegel is important in a variety of ways: his early efforts to become "the Winckelmann of Greek literature,"[3] the strong aesthetic emphasis of his criticism around the turn of the century, his perception of a Dionysiac element in Greek culture, and his attempt, especially in *Lucinde* (1799), to vindicate the beauty and intrinsic value of sexual experience. It is obviously the youthful Schlegel who mainly concerns us: as the great theorist of romanticism, and later the leading German Catholic historian of ancient and modern literature, he drastically changed his earlier views. *Lucinde* he repudiated outright. Yet one finds traces of Winckelmann's style and view of the world in the most unexpected contexts, and the Greeks still play an important though no longer dominating part in his vastly influential *History of Ancient and Modern Literature* (1812). That this work should be made up of lectures delivered in archconservative Vienna, under the aegis of Metternich, is paradoxical enough. Schlegel, though no longer "the god-gifted brat," as his friends used to call him, must have appreciated the irony of the situation. One of his early interests continued, and is central to this book: his fascination with myth. The content of his mythology changed — Christianity became in his eyes not a variety of myth but revealed truth — yet the interest remained significant in his total view of literature.

Born in 1772, Schlegel was one of the remarkable generation born within the few years between 1767 and 1773:[4] his brother August Wilhelm, Wilhelm von Humboldt, Hölderlin, Novalis, Wackenroder, and Tieck. Jean Paul was born a bit earlier, Kleist a little later. Except for Humboldt, the whole group was romantically oriented; undoubtedly the sense of belonging together heightened their early *élan*. When Schlegel was about seventeen, he read Plato, the Greek tragedians, and Winckelmann;[5] at about the same age, he was amazed by the life and movement, as well as the beauty, of the famous antique statues at Dresden. With characteristic enthusiasm he turned from law to classical studies. He studied under Christian Gottlob Heyne, perhaps the most influential classical philologist of the later eighteenth century,[6] and learned much, somewhat later, from Friedrich August Wolf.[7]

In a series of essays and one incomplete book on Greek subjects, all written in the years 1794–1798, Schlegel appears primarily as the disciple of Winckelmann. Notes of originality appear, however, and in the later of these rather minor works Schlegel's growing concern with the "interesting," the modern, the romantic, becomes more and more apparent. The first of this group of Hellenizing works, "On the Schools of Greek Poetry" (1794), follows Winckelmann closely. Thus the morality of the Dorians was marked by "grandeur, simplicity, repose; peaceable and yet heroic, they lived in noble joy." [8] This is more utopian than Winckelmann himself; and the archaeologist's influence is evident also when Schlegel divides Greek literature (and Athenian taste particularly) into four stages which develop organically out of "severe grandeur" toward harmonious perfection, and then decline and fall.[9] Even the use of the term "schools" to designate literary groups or isms derives from Winckelmann, as does the stress on political freedom.

Yet a second brief essay of the same year, "On the Artistic Value of Greek Comedy," shows considerable independence. The emphasis on the joyousness (*Freude*) of the Greeks is Winckelmannian to be sure, but Schlegel goes well beyond his predecessor. Even at its most sensual, joy is good in itself.[10] The emotion has very little to do with the smiling serenity of the Olympians, still less with the somewhat bibulous gaiety of which the pseudo-Anacreontic poets of the early eighteenth century had sung. Rather, it has the character of release, of breaking the limits of individuality. Schiller's "Hymn to Joy" celebrates the same exuberant, overwhelming emotion, but presents it as universally human, not Greek. Schlegel derives Greek comedy from the rites of Bacchus.[11] In the following passage he obviously has the concept of the Dionysiac in mind, though he was not to use the word itself for some years: "Only sorrow (*Schmerz*) divides and isolates; in joy all boundaries disappear. With the hope of unhampered union the last veil of animality seems to disappear; man divines that complete enjoyment which he can only strive for, never possess." [12] Long before Nietzsche, Schlegel sensed a wild, ecstatic element in Greek literature and life; this element, stressed and exaggerated by Nietzsche and his successors, was radically to alter the whole myth of Greece.

At another point too Schlegel departed, perhaps unconsciously, from the inherited image of Hellenic culture. Winckelmann had stressed the political freedom of the Athenians.

Adducing this factor in his vindication of Aristophanes, Schlegel expands it to include the moral freedom of the individual and the "unlimited autonomy . . . to which it [art] is eternally entitled." [13] When he speaks of the free person who acts entirely according to his own choice and whim (*Willkür*), he is already anticipating the mood of his famous romantic declarations of the liberty of art and of the individual.

In this brief essay, then, important elements of a romantic image of Greece may already be discerned. It seems to have received little attention, partly because it is generally Winckelmannian in language and at times cautious in its manner of stating insights which actually have radical implications. Thus Schlegel is conservative in maintaining that the expression of joy in literature must be beautiful — though, he adds, beauty must not be judged by merely conventional standards.[14] He had not yet become the "Frédéric tout pur" who delighted to shock the public by his impudent paradoxes. But the seeds of later developments are there.

To treat each of Schlegel's treatises on Greek subjects separately would hardly be rewarding. As so often in his criticism, he oscillates between conflicting points of view, sometimes proceeding dialectically to a triumphant synthesis, sometimes wavering ambivalently. Usually, in these works of the middle and late 1790's, Greek literature, and the Greeks generally, remain canonical. "The study of Greek poetry is a *necessary duty* of all *amateurs* — connoisseurs — thinkers." [15] Self-contained, beautiful rather than characteristic, Hellenic poetry had the quality of objectivity which the moderns have lost. For the Greeks alone, art was an end in itself. *"For all barbarians* on the other hand *Beauty in itself is not good enough."* [16] As so often in reading these early works, one thinks of Schiller, and of Kant behind Schiller, but it is probably Winckelmann's frank aestheticism that was decisive here. In Winckelmann's tradition too is Schlegel's belief that one should not imitate Greek poetry "one-sidedly";[17] true mimesis requires complete knowledge, and above all possession of the objective spirit of Greek literature as a whole, especially that of the golden age.[18] Like Lessing and Winckelmann before him, Schlegel held that the Hellenes were more humane than the Romans; thus he admired the "cultivated" conqueror Alexander far more than he did Julius Caesar.[19] He singled out the democratic aspect of Athenian culture for particular praise, perhaps annoying a reader like Schiller, who had been profoundly shocked by the Reign of Terror.[20]

So far I have summed up what we might call Schlegel's thesis; his antithesis, equally important, is concerned with his own age, specifically with contemporary German literature. Largely independent of Schiller, but in general agreement with him, Schlegel was moving toward a vindication of modern poetry. Like Schiller, he felt that the poet of his own time had achieved less than the ancients, but had greater potentialities. It would be strange, he believed, if "our poetry" did not surpass the Greek in richness of content, in "interest," though not in beauty.[21] Contemporary poetry is in a state of crisis; it is groping its way toward a new objectivity. Once "the objective" is attained — "the universally valid, constant, and necessary,"[22] which Schlegel equates with the beautiful — the pinnacle will have been reached.

This of course brings us to Schlegel's synthesis, which is roughly the same as his famous definition of romantic "progressive, universal poetry," published in the journal *Athenaeum* in 1798.[23] Only an ever richer, all-embracing poetry which numbers classical objectivity among its infinite attributes can satisfy his demands. (As he perforce admits, this ideal can be only approximated, never completely achieved.[24]) The romantic Schlegel did not repudiate Winckelmann; rather he included him, in Hegelian fashion, in his broad synthesis. Similarly, Nietzsche, some seventy years later, while stressing the Dionysiac nature of the Greeks, was to preserve Winckelmann's dogma in what he called their Apollonian

aspect. The Schlegel of the late 1790's was full of revolutionary hopes and boundless optimism, primarily about the future
of German culture. Breaking with Winckelmann's rather
deterministic organic view, he wrote that aesthetic culture
(*Bildung*) need not "develop, ripen, sink again, and finally
perish" like a plant or an animal.[25] The many-sidedness of
German literature, its very lack of a clearly defined character,
gave him hope that it would progress toward the goal of universality.[26] For a while, Goethe's poetry, "the dawn of genuine
art and pure beauty," seemed to embody the ideal.[27] Though
Goethe's later works were comparable to Shakespeare's in
"philosophic content and characteristic truth," his true goal,
Schlegel was convinced, was objective beauty.[28] But Goethe
could not long satisfy his utopian criteria; he soon conceived
the "image of a super-Goethean poet." [29] The super-Goethe
failed to appear, just as the Hellas envisioned by the preceding
generation was never realized, but for the time being,
Schlegel's ardor was not diminished.

   In line with his growing emancipation from eighteenth-
century tradition, Schlegel discerned "the divine drunkenness
of Dionysus" as an element of Sophocles' poetry, along with
Athena's ingenuity and Apollo's calm self-possession.[30] As
Sophocles is hardly an orgiastic poet, one may infer that the
critic attributed to him a quality he sensed in Greek culture
generally. He came to feel that the "Orphic-Bacchic element"
was both the most antique and the most modern factor in ancient culture.[31] Increasingly, Schlegel saw Hellenic culture
through his own eyes; in his unfinished *History of Greek and
Roman Poetry* (1798) he cites from Hesiod a most unclassical
tale of the castration of a father by his son.[32] A note of the
preceding year, intended for his own eyes alone, runs:
"Winckelmann was my master in the historical study of antiquity." [33] The use of the past tense is significant. When
Schiller attacked the Schlegels for making a fetish of the ancients —

Kaum hat das kalte Fieber der Gallomanie uns verlassen
Bricht in der Gräcomanie gar noch ein hitziges aus — [34]

he was understandably irritated by some of the more extreme statements of Friedrich's thesis but ignored the whole movement of his antithesis. The misunderstanding may have been partly caused by personal dislike.

Even after Schlegel had recovered from the "fever of Graecomania," frequent turns of expression in his later works reveal how deeply he had been affected. Thus he compared one of the characters in Goethe's *Wilhelm Meister's Apprenticeship* to "a mighty structure . . . in the grand old style, of noble, simple proportions, of the purest, finest marble." [35] To find the stock phrase "quiet grandeur" and its variants turning up in the early essays is not surprising,[36] but when one reads of the "quiet grandeur" of Spinoza in a later, and very important, discussion of myth,[37] one realizes that the classical experience had contributed in subtle and lasting ways to shaping Schlegel's mind.

"Everyone so far has found in the ancients what he needed or wished; primarily himself," [38] Schlegel wrote in 1798. It may well be that Greece was most valuable to him personally as a stage in the long process of self-realization, the quest for a belief which he could accept absolutely. "Lacking nature, I have long loved the ancients," [39] he noted, even more revealingly, two years later. Underlying his superficial frivolity and cynicism was a genuine religious impulse; his character reminds one of some of the English metaphysical poets. He searched for an absolute in a series of beliefs and myths: in the Greeks, in a cult of sexual passion, in the middle ages, in ancient India, finally, and satisfyingly, in Roman Catholicism. Irving Babbitt's image of the romantic convert to the Church, "the jellyfish" clinging "to the rock," [40] may have its relevance in some cases; it cannot help us in dealing with a mind of Schlegel's caliber.

When Schlegel wrote that the pinnacle and goal of philology was "to live classically, to realize antiquity in one's own self," [41] he afforded some insight into the motives which led him to write *Lucinde*. If you really admire the Greeks, behave like one! We may smile or be offended, but can hardly deny that a Hellenist who tries to be "noble and nude and antique" is at least consistent. There was also the example of Goethe's *Roman Elegies*.

Unlike Winckelmann, Schlegel had long had an enthusiastic interest in Greek woman. His essay "On Diotima" (1795) is devoted to celebrating a type of woman equally far removed from the bourgeoise and the hetaera. Free from prudery, keenly intellectual, a woman like Diotima could compete with the most brilliant Athenian on equal terms. To Schlegel, she was a reproach to his own time's ideal of domesticated femininity: "What is uglier than overemphasized womanliness, what is more repulsive than the exaggerated manliness which prevails in our mores, our opinions, yes even in our better art? . . . Only self-reliant womanliness, only gentle manliness, is good and beautiful." [42] This vision of Diotima fitted perfectly with the romantic belief that every true individual, like poetry itself, should be as universal as possible. When Schlegel, after a protracted and apparently rather miserable adolescence, [43] finally experienced happiness in love, he felt called upon to express his insights. *Lucinde* was the result.

This short novel may be described as a celebration of the "religion of love," [44] a vindication of sexual expression as a value in itself and of "romantic" living generally, and a hymn to the "new" woman, who is intelligent and intellectual as well as uninhibited. As Paul Kluckhohn has noted, *Lucinde* is a novel not of "free love" but of romantic marriage: the lovers welcome the coming of a child, [45] and fidelity, though not regarded as a virtue in itself, is a concomitant of genuine love. [46] A comparison with *Lady Chatterley's Lover* seems inevitable. Aside from Lawrence's warnings against the conscious mind and his concern with class differences, the two books are roughly similar in intention. Schlegel has more range and intellectual sophistication; Lawrence far more literary skill, and achieves more verisimilitude, particularly in the erotic passages.

Parodying Schlegel, one may say that his heroine is romantic because she is the "progressive, universal" woman; "the tenderest lover and the best company and also a perfect friend." [47] Lucinde is active, gifted, and imaginative, as well as passionate; there are no limits to the communication and sense of harmony which the lovers enjoy. [48] The individuality of each is strengthened though they are one; [49] in Lucinde there is none of the subservience of a Gretchen or Klärchen. (Goethe's women are real while Schlegel's is a synthetic construction, but that is another matter.) Julius' passion for Lucinde does not decrease his need or his capacity for masculine friendship. [50]

In establishing his cult of love — "it is the oldest, most childlike, simplest religion to which I have returned" — [51] Schlegel like Lawrence comes close at times to outright worship of sex, the "holy fire of divine voluptuousness." [52] Plato's Diotima, he now finds, revealed only half the nature of love; it is "sacred enjoyment" [53] of the actual present as well as longing for the infinite. "Beauteous life" — a more consistent pagan, Stefan George, was also to make an ideal of *das schöne Leben* — must become a "sacred festival." [54]

In his *Roman Elegies* Goethe had evoked lovers who have the white beauty of Greek statues, and written that only when touching the lovely body of his beloved could he really understand marble. [55] Similarly, Schlegel's protagonist Julius cannot stop "touching and caressing the swelling contours" of his mistress; his own body seemed "firm and solid as marble." [56] There may well be an overtone of parody here; Friedrich's theory and practice of romantic irony implied that an author should regard his work with a smile, even when he was most serious about it.

Certainly other parts of the book are parodistic. When Friedrich celebrated impudence he was baiting his readers, and his "Idyl on Indolence" seems to have been found more outrageous than his glorification of sex. Here, ironically quoting Winckelmann for his own purposes, he suggests that a pair of sleeping lovers would be an excellent subject for an artist who wished to represent "grandeur in repose." [57] A few pages later he imagines a figure of Prometheus, creating men out of clay; he finds the deified Hercules with Hebe on his knees a far more attractive symbol, for man must be able to enjoy idleness and love after labor.[58] It is the lusty Hercules of Goethe's farce who figures in the little allegory. Prometheus is described as "the inventor of education and Enlightenment," [59] and Schlegel delights in ridiculing these ideals of the eighteenth century and the middle class. Hoping presumably to shock the reader, he even remarks that Priapus had a sounder approach to "creating men" than did the industrious Titan.

Basically, however, the intention of *Lucinde* is serious, though the mood from which it sprang did not last long. Perhaps Schlegel is most in earnest when he turns from the glorification of enjoyment to another aspect of love: the longing for night, death, and rebirth. After thoughts and fears caused by an illness of Lucinde's, Julius knows "that death can also be sensed as lovely and sweet." [60] He understands that man can long for release from existence and interpret death as a state of higher freedom; the thought of dying then appears "like a morning sun of hope." Rest is found in longing, longing is found in rest; Lucinde is the "priestess of night"; the day is cold and hard.[61] "But finally the fruitless yearning, vain dazzling of day will sink and cease to be, and a great night of love be eternally, peacefully experienced." [62]

Clearly Schlegel is close here, in imagery and thought, to Novalis' "Hymns to Night." [63] He is at his most romantic in rejecting the day, light, and the sun, those central symbols of the Enlightenment, for the mystic night of the senses, the emotions, and death. In Novalis, religious symbolism makes the "Hymns to Night" the expression of (highly eroticized) Christianity; Schlegel does not commit himself to any religion, but the otherworldliness, the fascination by the thought of death, of key passages of *Lucinde* make his later conversion easier to comprehend.

Thus *Lucinde* has two aspects: a paganism of enjoyment and an equally erotic cult of death as the "night of love." Appropriately, it exerted a double attraction: the rather earthy Young Germans of the postromantic period took it as a confirmation of their doctrine of the emancipation of the flesh.[64] To Thomas Mann, as presumably to Wagner before him, *Lucinde* was primarily important as a work in which the romantic ideal of the *Liebestod* (love-death) was eloquently expressed.[65]

A bizarre variation on this theme is central to Heinrich von Kleist's *Penthesilea* (1808). The protagonist, a warlike but beautiful Amazon, in the mistaken belief that her chosen lover Achilles has deliberately humiliated her, takes a hideous revenge. Literally mad with frustration and shame, she slays him and then tears at his dead body with her teeth. When consciousness returns, she kills herself by sheer effort of will.

The play is a striking instance of that "confusion of the emotions" which Goethe found so objectionable in Kleist's works. Penthesilea is a classic case of ambivalence, of love-hatred. To Kleist she was admirable not pathological: in some other sphere than the unnatural Amazon state she would have lived nobly and beautifully. But objectively she is a sister of Strindberg's Miss Julia, Wilde's Salome, and Hofmannsthal's Electra: the heroine as hysteric.

Penthesilea is not pagan in the usual sense — Kleist was pleased that his friend Adam Müller did not think it antique

— and in its furious dynamism it is obviously anything but classic. Yet to express his most burning emotions, his hypertension, Kleist had to have recourse to ancient myth or Germanic legend; Christian symbolism was out of the question. *Penthesilea* is literally Dionysiac: the protagonist is as much the prey of the passions which blot out individuation as are the maddened women of Euripides' *Bacchae*. Besides *Penthesilea*, Friedrich Schlegel's theoretical interest in the Dionysiac is pale indeed.

For Schlegel was not really very like Tristan, still less like Penthesilea; the love-death could not satisfy him very long in his search for a myth. His "Speech on Mythology" (1800) is more characteristic and makes points which are still relevant today. Every contemporary poet, he feels, is handicapped by having to create each new work out of nothing, since "we have no mythology," and poetry thus lacks its needed center.[66] Only in myth can one view, both sensuously and intellectually, truths of which we should otherwise be unconscious; only in myth can our most profound insights be "hieroglyphically"[67] expressed. In Sanskrit as well as in Greek literature, in contemporary physics[68] as well as in Spinoza, elements of the desired new mythology may be found. Dante is the only poet who has, by his own gigantic efforts, created an integrated synthetic myth of the sort the present needs.[69]

This is not the place to pursue further Schlegel's enormously suggestive remarks on myth.[70] Some sentences in his "Letter on the Novel" of the same year seem to point toward the amalgamation of the finest "romantic" literature — Shakespeare, Cervantes, some of Italian poetry, certain medieval romances, and the fairy tale — with the classic. "Only these eternally fresh blossoms of fantasy are worthy of crowning the statues of the ancient gods."[71] In his tragedy *Alarcos* (1802) Schlegel tried to write "universal poetry" based on the combination of Spanish material, the Christian concept of God, and the ancient idea of fate, and including trimeter, *terza rima*, and even sonnets in his battery of metrical forms. Dorothea Schlegel compared the "dramatic marble" of *Alarcos* to the Laocoön,[72] but she was hardly an impartial critic. Actually, Friedrich was even less of a dramatist than a novelist or lyric poet; the laughter of the Weimar audience was the disappointing reward of this literary experiment.

From about the turn of the century, Schlegel seems to have conducted his search for myth in a rather sophisticated way, looking for a body of material useful to poets, not a set of religious beliefs. To put matters differently, he separated his metaphysical from his poetic quest. This of course is contrary to the dogmas of universal poetry, but leads toward clarity — and sanity. Hölderlin's desperate attempt to bring the Greek gods back to actual life was not for Schlegel.[73] However warm his enthusiasm about Norse, or Sanskrit, or medieval German poetry, it is not marked by quite the fine careless rapture of his Winckelmannian days; and his adherence to Roman Catholicism inevitably bore him out of the current of aesthetic paganism. The mature Schlegel is in some ways a better, if a less exciting critic than he had been in his youth; he figures hereafter in this account mainly as the opponent of tendencies which he had himself once supported. His later judgments on the Greeks and on neoheathenism generally can be quite briefly summed up.

Like Herder before him, Schlegel came increasingly to view the Greek accomplishment historically, and thus, inevitably, to relativize it. After his conversion, in 1808, his judgments on moral and religious matters became more severe than Herder's; the aesthetic point of view no longer satisfied him. In *On the Language and Wisdom of the Indians*, which appeared in that year, Schlegel's interest in myth was still strong. Sanskrit mythology is superior to the Hellenic in two ways, he held: originally more "gigantic and savage," it was in part even more gentle and charming in its later development than the works

of Pindar and Sophocles.[74] Four years later he wrote that
though Greek myths surpassed all others in "external" formal
beauty, they embodied theological concepts far inferior to
those of the *Zend Avesta* or the *Edda*.[75] No longer can he accept the belief in Hellenic joyfulness. Novalis had sensed
deep melancholy underlying the existence of the Greeks:
they could not face death with any hope.[76] And Schlegel now
found the Greek poets basically tragic: serene on the surface,
they lacked, for the most part, the "light of hope and true
joy." [77]

The *History of Ancient and Modern Literature* (1812) is
perhaps the most influential of Schlegel's later works. Writing at the height of the European revolt against Napoleon, he
employs a strongly patriotic, though not chauvinistic tone.
His emphasis is moral rather than aesthetic; except in matters
of detail, he is virtually independent of the Winckelmannian
tradition. Greek culture was "immeasurably fruitful *in good
as in evil*, and therefore doubly instructive" [78] (italics mine).
Greek depravity is sharply pointed out; Schlegel's youthful
enthusiasm for a joyous culture, for beautiful youths and
woman naked and without shame, has evaporated. Whereas
Schiller had felt that in ancient times men were more divine,
gods more human and humane, Schlegel found anthropomorphic concepts of the gods immoral. Too good a critic to become anti-Greek, he adopted a middle position. Greece affords a splendid example of a "fortunately developed literature" [79] but is no longer canonical. Though its culture, as a
whole, grew independently, the real origin of human civilization is Oriental; the Greeks were simply unaware of their
predecessors.[80]

In his consideration of recent and contemporary German
literature, Schlegel deplored the fact that "a merely artistic
and aesthetic point of view" had become dominant almost
everywhere.[81] Yet he held that "the mistaken antique business"

(*das falsche antikische Wesen*) in art and literature was beginning to decline.[82] It was not Winckelmann's fault, but it
was due to his influence, that the cult of the ancients had un-
duly flourished. The archaeologist himself was one of the few
first-rate minds of his generation and a great interpretative
critic; [83] his "Platonic enthusiasm" is duly noted.[84]

Clearly, a criticism of the "great pagan" in Weimar, who
stood unmoved either by the Christian or the patriotic fervor
of the day, is implied here. Similarly, Schlegel's description
of an exposition of contemporary German art (held in Rome,
in 1819) is a defense of Christian and "old-German" tendencies. The painters he praised especially were the so-called
Nazarenes, whom Goethe rejected as much for ideological
as for aesthetic reasons. Again, Schlegel is fair to Winckelmann; his enthusiasm was "splendid," but the neoclassicism of
painters like David is an "utterly false tendency." [85]

As a young man, Friedrich Schlegel was one of the most
fervent of the apostles of the Greeks, and far more original
than most. His short-lived cult of sensuality was not unnatural
in an admirer of Hellenic joy and Dionysiac release. After a
few years he came to regard Graecomania with critical detachment; he abandoned the cult of sensuality completely.
The search for an aesthetic myth was left to others and took
different directions.

II

Like Friedrich Schlegel, his elder brother August Wilhelm
was fascinated by Greek literature and knew a great deal
about it; he too was convinced of the importance of myth.
While Friedrich was largely the man of new insights, the
intellectual pioneer, August Wilhelm was the synthesizer, the
writer of judicious surveys. As the cofounders of romantic
criticism, the Schlegels complemented each other admirably.
To an "extreme" movement like aesthetic paganism, however,

the daring and adventurous Friedrich naturally had more to contribute; August Wilhelm's position is more moderate, more consistent, and less stimulating.

A student of Heyne's at Göttingen, August Wilhelm Schlegel was soon attracted to Greek mythology;[86] several of his early poems are devoted to figures like Prometheus, Arion, and Pygmalion. As a young man, he largely accepted the Winckelmannian view of Greek literature and art: thus he wrote that the Hellenes treated any theme, in either medium, with the maximum of beauty appropriate to it.[87] The intensely tragic quality of Sophocles' dramas does not detract from their "noble simplicity and quiet grandeur." [88] In the *Athenäum* fragments and his dialogue "The Paintings" (1798), Schlegel appears as rather an aesthete, though not in the thoroughgoing sense of a Heinse or even a Winckelmann. And even in his most Hellenist moods, he realized that ancient art would never completely return: a factor which comes from life would always be missing in any imitations or revivals.[89]

In a word, A. W. Schlegel was never a fanatic; he crusaded for neither paganism nor Christianity, for neither aestheticism nor a harsh morality. There is a certain classic restraint in his criticism, even in the works which became basic documents of romanticism. As Wellek puts it, his voice was "often that of the historian, the man of detachment, of tolerance, of universality." [90] The defects of these virtues he displayed too: he had little fire, little imaginative brilliance. Yet he was one of the critics who did the most to establish the general nineteenth-century attitude toward the Greeks and, by extension, toward classical paganism — as well as toward Shakespeare, Dante, Gothic architecture, and a host of other cultural entities. It is not necessary to discuss his views in great detail, partly because many of them have been so widely accepted that they have become clichés, partly because they changed far less than those of his erratic brother. Their general outlines at least should be drawn. If a more or less Winckelmannian Hellas became, to educated Europeans and Americans, one of the leading voices in a great cultural chorus (no longer the dominant voice), this was as much Schlegel's doing as anyone's. It is typical of him that his solution represented a sensible compromise.

He could not have reached such a compromise without sympathy for both the ancient and the modern, and if one judged by isolated remarks, one could be misled into thinking Schlegel a true believer in aesthetic paganism as forever exemplified in Greek art.[91] Hellenic statues possess "visible, eternal blessedness";[92] they simultaneously express emotion and sovereign calm.[93] In the "lofty purity" of sculpture, the ancient gods were raised not to morality but above it.[94] Untroubled by any conflict between flesh and spirit, they embody perfect harmony. Such statues are of unrivaled beauty;[95] the moderns have no alternative to following the ancients both in subject matter and in the spirit of their treatment.[96]

Despite such statements, which are sincere enough as far as they go, August Wilhelm's admiration of the antique had definite boundaries. Splendid as the classical achievement was, the modern is at least as great. "The poetry of the ancients was that of possession, ours is that of longing,"[97] he wrote in a famous sentence which recalls Schiller's great antithesis. The Greeks outstripped us in the realm of the tangible; they were the masters of the sensuous. Thus it is no accident that their absolute hegemony is limited to sculpture. In poetry their achievement was different in kind from the modern, but not greater.[98] Following their lead in painting has caused much harm, as Schlegel ventured to point out to Goethe even in 1805,[99] when the poet was in his most hyperclassical mood. Above all, Christianity is "deeper" than the Greek view of life, and it has, unlike any pagan cult, a relation to the infinite.[100] To Schlegel's romantic audience the last point was decisive.

While many of his contemporaries, like Schelling, ranked Christian above heathen art, Schlegel generally held that an-

cient and modern, classic and romantic, were equally important. The ideal critic would take a position midway between
the two poles.[101] Can one compare in excellence the Pantheon
and Westminster Abbey, Sophocles and Shakespeare? [102]
Rather, one must acknowledge and describe the unique quality of each. Aiming at an objective distinction, he noted that
"Greek religion strove to deify mankind; the Christian teaching on the other hand is based on the deity's becoming
man." [103] Yet he points out paradoxical weaknesses in Greek
religion (and none in Christianity). The revolt of Prometheus
and the idea of fate reveal a tragic aspect of all antiquity.
Furthermore, in being Promethean, ancient religion was itself
irreligious! [104] Schlegel's own position was generally that of
a liberal, "enlightened" Protestant. Though he wrote of
Christian myths and mythology, as we shall see, he used the
terms as a literary critic might today, not in the mood of a
Baylean skeptic.

Similarly, though A. W. Schlegel was keenly sensitive to
aesthetic values and emphasized them continually, he believed,
as Hölderlin came to, that they are not the ultimate values.
He made his conviction unmistakably clear in a review of
Wilhelm Heinrich Wackenroder's *Heart-Outpourings of an
Art-Loving Friar* (1797).[105] Wackenroder was himself a member of the "original" romantic school. His brief tract is as
emotional as its title implies, but it is an important document
in the history of modern aesthetics. Rejecting all systematic
approaches to art, and indeed any intellectual element in appreciation, he emphasizes inspiration, enthusiasm, and empathy
exclusively. At the same time, his tone is extremely pious;
there is a strong Catholicizing tendency, though he was never
converted: one finds here one of the first examples of the
predilection of the artist for the church of Rome. It has recently been argued that Wackenroder's "religion of art" was
a sort of aesthetic pietism: in his view the completely passive
artist is inspired in a way literally comparable to inspiration

by the Holy Ghost.[106] Such aesthetic religiosity has little in common with authentic Christianity. Schlegel's judgment was less severe, but he shrewdly remarked that the author not only compared religious with artistic inspiration; he tended to confuse the two. The tone of the review is sympathetic, but Schlegel's disapproval is clear at this point.

Clearly, Schlegel himself was not a mythopoeic writer, or a man who reacted to life in mythic terms. From the point of view of a Hölderlin, he was one of the "sanctimonious poets" who did not "believe in Helios." Yet his own discussion of myth, particularly in his important *Lectures on Literature and Art* (1801–1804), is significant and discerning. Since he was the most influential popularizer of the ideas of the German romantic generation, his ideas on myth were bound to have a considerable effect, especially as they tended to reinforce those of Friedrich Schlegel. Aesthetic paganism is hardly thinkable without myths and an intellectual climate in which they can flourish. Whether the particular myth deals with Apollo, Dionysus, the Great Mother, or for that matter with the love-death, it must find acceptance or at least a "willing suspension of disbelief" if it is to arouse more than curiosity. If the Schlegels and their allies had not rehabilitated myth,[107] the tone of German literature in the nineteenth and twentieth centuries would have been different: cooler, saner, and perhaps less exciting. Wagner, Nietzsche, and George could be completely accepted only by a "mythophile" culture, and only in such a culture could Hölderlin have celebrated his triumphant return.

As one would expect, the elder Schlegel referred often to Hellenic myth; he felt in fact that Greek statues show "the mythical ideal" at its highest.[108] Yet they represent, after all, a "world of gods who have died." [109] In a poem of 1800 he states that the arts have been in decline since the collapse of the Olympian reign; they are to be saved by devoting themselves to religious purposes.[110] Schlegel is not usually so pious, but generally he holds that artists, except for sculptors, will fare better by drawing from Christian mythology "figures of a still existing, active faith," as one of the characters in Schlegel's dialogue "The Paintings" puts it. To do so need not imply religious commitment: the artist can regard the faith aesthetically, as a "lovely, free poem" (*Dichtung*).[111] Although Schlegel echoed, rather vaguely, his brother's call for a new mythology, he did not believe that a single individual could create an authentic myth.[112]

That the Greek gods are dead is also the point of an episode in the anonymous novel *Bonaventura's Vigils* (1804). In a museum, a "little dilettante" pays enthusiastic if grotesque tribute to the Medici Venus. The author is moved to reflect on the contemporary cult of ancient art: "our modern religion of art prays in critiques and has devotion in its head, while genuinely religious persons have it in their hearts."[113] The dilettante should choose between genuine adoration of the old gods and reburying them. At the end of the scene the whole group of mutilated statues seems to come to life:

angry Jupiter was about to rise from his place, earnest Apollo reached for his bow and sounding lyre, mightily the dragons rose up around struggling Laocoön and his falling sons, Prometheus formed men with the stumps of his arms . . . only, deep in the background, there stood, without illumination, a chorus of Furies rigid and petrified, and gazed darkly and terrifyingly at the throng.[114]

A. W. Schlegel's own judgment about the proper attitude vis-à-vis myths is more balanced if less interesting. They are emphatically not mere ornaments for decking out a poem. The artist or poet must make the myth an organic part of his creation, but he need not believe in it. In a passage from the first version of "The Paintings" he seems to imply that one myth is as good as another, for aesthetic purposes:

Waller: You are in danger of becoming a Catholic.
Louise: As, now and then, a pagan. There's no danger in it, when Raphael is the priest.[115]

Probably it is revealing that Schlegel cut this passage in a later edition. In the already cited review of Wackenroder's *Heart-Outpourings* he again implies that it is a matter of indifference whether an artist seems to believe in the "mythological dreams of antiquity" or in "Christian legends and rituals"; it is an aesthetic not an intellectual or religious question.[116] Yet there are special reasons for Schlegel's apparent neutralism here.[117] More typically, he holds that the myth must be appropriate to the given art: classical subjects are ideal for sculpture, Christian for painting.[118] Schlegel seems not to have taken seriously enough the danger that a poet's lack of belief in the myth he treats may reduce his work to the level of a school exercise. His own drama *Ion* (1803) is a case in point: it is a cool, correct, skillfully versified, and completely academic treatment of a Greek theme.[119] At times he did see that a myth may be deprived of its magic powers by the passage of time, but he is hardly consistent on this point.

Schlegel was too moderate, too "sensible," to have been an ardent follower of the pagan belief or perhaps of any other. His review, in 1812, of Fernow's edition of Winckelmann's works[120] is evidence of how rapidly taste had changed in a few years. While he admires the breadth of Winckelmann's synthesis, his tone is reserved and at times condescending and even hostile. Schlegel notes that Winckelmann's favorite statues were late, and protests sharply against his suggestion that the heads of Amazons be used as models for statues and paintings of the Virgin: the archaeologist had no grasp of Christian ideals and was apparently ignorant of the achievements of Christian art. His own intellectual horizon had become so broad that he realized the insufficiency of any simple dichotomy between antique and modern. In his case, though not in Humboldt's or Goethe's, admiration of Sanskrit literature proved a relativizing force: Greece was not the only ancient culture to have left us immortal poetic masterpieces.[121]

Receptive as he was, August Wilhelm absorbed and restated most of the doctrines of German Hellenism. His fresh insights were few; his most original perception was that he observed an element of tragedy in the religion of the "happy" Greeks. In our context, his main contribution was that he subjected Winckelmann's paganism to the full dialectical treatment. In Hegelian terms, it was *aufgehoben*: simultaneously "overcome"; "raised up" (by inclusion in the broader perspective of world literature); and "preserved" within this wider perspective.

III

Like most of the young intellectuals of his generation, Novalis was acquainted with Winckelmann's doctrines.[122] He was never a Graecomane however, but a devout if unorthodox Christian. Apparently his acquaintance with Greek art and literature was limited. His comments on antiquity are in part derivative, in part marked by a subjectivity reminiscent of Fichte, whom he greatly admired. It is his poetry, especially his "Hymns to Night," which is mostly important to this discussion. Characteristically, he opposes Christian belief to the aestheticism of the Hellenic world. Yet in the eroticism of his writings — and in that respect alone — a pagan note is sounded.

Relatively few of the thousands of Novalis' aphorisms and notes which have been preserved deal with Greece, antiquity, and similar matters. In only a handful of these does he follow the standard Winckelmannian line. To be sure, he does note in early fragments that "the ancient statues compel us to treat them as sacred objects";[123] that they appeal not to "one sense but to all, to humanity as a whole."[124] Later, he remarks that everything was more poetic in the antique than in the contemporary world,[125] but it is clear from his work as a whole that his true allegiance was to the middle ages. Most revealingly, he stated that the "veil of the Virgin" surrounds perfection of every sort, including the antique world.[126] In other words, we perceive everything in a Christian ambience. In arguing that his contemporaries should "imitate" the ancients only to become artists themselves, he is in general agreement with the Schlegels' mature views: the Greek and Roman writers excelled in form; the moderns in content. If we can equal them in matters of style, he adds, going beyond his mentor, we can achieve a truly classical literature, "which the ancients did not possess themselves." [127] They would have had to study our writings!

Novalis' fragmentary defense of Schiller's "The Gods of Greece" [128] is especially interesting in view of his later "refutation" of that poem in the "Hymns to Night." He defends the older poet against charges of atheism "and I don't know what all." It seems most unlikely that he would have taken an extreme pagan position; quite possibly he would have drawn the distinction, less obvious in his time than in ours, between poetic and religious truth.

In other comments, Novalis is close to Schlegel's notion of universal poetry which should transcend but include the classical. Thus he mentions the "idea of the transition of one energy to the other (of their successive and simultaneous existence). (Synthesis of the ancient and modern.)" [129] This bold leap from physical science to the humanities is typical, and the suggestion of simultaneous existence casts light on Novalis' own myths. In the allegorical fairy tale in his *Henry of Ofterdingen*, Fable demands: "Life for the ancient world and clear form [*Gestalt*] for the future!" [130] A rather cryptic paragraph seems to call for the coalescence of Christianity and paganism: "Absolute abstraction — annihilation of the present — apotheosis of the future, this true better world is the heart of Christianity's demands — and with this it joins the religion of the friends of antiquity, the divinity of the ancient world, the restoration of antiquity, as the second main wing — both hold the universe . . . eternally soaring." [131]

While still a young man, Novalis was exposed to the contagion of Fichte's philosophical egoism; he was by no means immune. In fact, in his comments on antiquity, as elsewhere, he appears more subjective than even Friedrich Schlegel. Fichte had attempted to establish the supremacy of consciousness — the collective "ego" — over the external world; Novalis, like other enthusiastic Fichteans, tended to make the individual ego supreme. Thus he wrote in 1798: "Only now, antiquity is beginning to be born. It is coming into existence before the eyes and the soul of the artist. The remains of the ancient world are only the specific stimulants to the formation [*Bildung*] of antiquity. Antiquity is not made with hands. The spirit brings it forth by means of the eye — and the carved stone is only the body, which gains meaning and becomes manifest only through them." [182] There is a considerable element of truth in this emphasis on the subjective element of German Hellenism, but it is characteristically exaggerated. Nothing could be more unpagan — or for that matter un-Winckelmannian — than to use the words "only the body" to refer to a Greek statue. Elsewhere Novalis speaks of ancient works of art as "*products* simultaneously *of the future and the past*" [183] — a less extreme expression of his subjectivity.

Such scattered comments on the interpretation of antiquity are of secondary significance, though marked by occasional intuitive insights. In his fifth "Hymn to Night," as we have seen, Novalis attacked the widely accepted belief that the Greek image of death was more beautiful and noble than the Christian. Of concern in this chapter is his use of sexual imagery. "Night" in these hymns stands for a whole cluster of ideas not usually associated with one another: death, sleep, eternal life, Christianity, heaven; but at the same time earthly love as well as divine. No reader can help being struck by the prevalence and strength of such images; [184] his heaven is a very voluptuous place. (The whole cycle was inspired by a vision experienced at the grave of his fiancée.) This is most explicitly expressed in the verses at the end of the fourth "Hymn," which begin:

> Hinüber wall' ich,
> Und jede Pein
> Wird einst ein Stachel
> Der Wollust sein.
> Noch wenig Zeiten,
> So bin ich los
> Und liege trunken
> Der Lieb' im Schoss.[135]

At the end of the last hymn, profane and heavenly love become one; the images of his beloved and Christ merge:

> Hinunter zu der süssen Braut,
> Zu Jesus dem Geliebten.[136]

It is not too much to speak of Christian Dionysianism here; along with amorously expressed mysticism there is a mystique of sex; not only death and heaven are celebrated. A sentence like the following inevitably recalls the key passages of Schlegel's *Lucinde*, which indeed it presumably inspired: "Now I know when the last morning will be — when light no longer frightens away night and love — when slumber will be eternal and only *one* inexhaustible dream." [137] In some of Novalis' "Religious Songs" [138] and, less hectically, in *Henry of Ofterdingen*, the erotic note is similarly strong.

I am naturally aware that highly erotic metaphors were often used by medieval mystics — and that their contemporaries at times found them objectionable.[139] To what extent such metaphors are "mere" imagery is not a question which falls within the scope of this book nor of my competence; but it would be as naïve to ignore or underrate the sexual aspect of Novalis' poetry [140] as to read the Song of Solomon as an allegory of Christ's love for the Church. It has been well observed that some of Tieck's sophisticated fairy tales are "closer to Freud than to the Brothers Grimm";[141] similarly, I am convinced that Novalis' "Hymns to Night" are at least as close to D. H. Lawrence as to Mechthild von Magdeburg. In Novalis' case, there is the added point that he may well have drawn on "lived experience" as one source of his erotic symbols:[142] he was never confined in a monastery. What I am suggesting is that in Novalis, even in his vindications of Christianity, there is a celebration of sex which one would more naturally expect to find in "this-worldly" writers. Perhaps one can say that in this respect Novalis subverted Christianity from within — though certainly without any conscious pagan intent.

IV

Of all the German romanticists, it was Jean Paul Richter, digressive and sentimental though his fiction is, who wrote the most balanced and sensitive treatment of the myth of Greece in its relation to the contemporary world. In a passage of his *Introduction to Aesthetics* (1804), "Jean Paul" discussed aesthetic paganism with empathy and eloquence,[143] showing at the same time that any effort to imitate the Greeks was doomed.

Here Jean Paul wrote of the achievements of the Greeks, "this beauty-intoxicated people," [144] with as much fervor as any Hellenist. He stressed the central importance of the Greek belief in mythology. Borrowing arguments from Winckelmann, Herder, and Schiller, he wrote eloquently about Hellenic nobility, serenity, and repose, citing climate, freedom, and the other usually adduced causes of this unique cultural flowering. The Greeks could portray life simply for the reason that the Olympian world had an "abundance of meaning"; they did not have to strain for effects.[145] That Northerners are moved to such violent emotion by ancient perfection indicates the poverty of their own attainment.[146]

As the last point indicates, Jean Paul regarded the ancient

world with some historical sophistication. Imitation of the Greeks, in the nineteenth century, was not a sensible program, he felt; if even the Romans could not vie with them successfully, modern Europeans could still less follow their example.[147] Like the Schlegels, he conceded the first place for all time to classical sculpture; painting and poetry, arts characterized by a relation to "romantic infinitude," were a different matter.[148] For men of his generation, the Virgin was a far more significant figure than Venus. Aesthetic paganism was a beautiful dream; Christianity, to the romantics, was a vision of the truth.

Chapter XI

Aesthetics and Culture: Humboldt

Like the Schlegel brothers, Wilhelm von Humboldt was trained in the classics by the formidable Heyne of Göttingen,[1] who seems to have taught many if not most of the classicists of Humboldt's generation. Heyne stressed the importance of studying all aspects of Greek life, at the same time insisting on close knowledge of the literary texts. Undoubtedly Humboldt owes much of the breadth of his concept of antiquity to his teacher; like him, he came to combine the historical with the strictly philological approach, being interested in social and political questions as well as in literature and art. Unlike most of the Hellenists of his day, he did not filter his notion of Greece through a neoclassic sieve; the austerity of Aeschylus and the obscenity of Aristophanes were as authentic to him as Sophocles or Homer. Above all, Hellas was to him a shining ideal, a norm, and a myth; otherwise his name, however important in the history of scholarship, would not figure in this book. Occasionally he called himself a pagan, and claimed in fact to receive personal religious consolation rather from Homer than from the Bible.[2] He was a highly complicated person, and it would be misleading to call him a pagan, *tout court*, but still more so to claim him for Christianity.[3]

Humboldt was perhaps the most learned figure in an age of vast learning. In him, versatility and scope indicated not dilettantism but genuine universality. As a scholar, he was probably most significant as one of the founders of comparative philology, but he also made contributions to aesthetics, literary theory, archaeology, and political theory, among other fields. He translated from the classics and wrote quite a bit of poetry, most of it bad. In practical life, he was at different points in his career a statesman, diplomat, administrator, and educational reformer; he was primarily responsible for founding the University of Berlin, in 1810, and attracting a brilliant faculty to the new institution. Like Goethe, he had the means to devote himself primarily to cultivating his own personality; service to the state was important but secondary. It is typical of Humboldt, with his relative indifference to the public and to success, that his letters, especially his correspondence with Goethe, Schiller, and F. A. Wolf, rank among his most important writings.

In his relation to antiquity, Humboldt again recalls Goethe. There is real tension between his almost universal interests and his special predilection for the Greeks. He was torn, on occasion, between Indian philosophy and the Hellenic view of life; between a basically Winckelmannian attitude and Schiller's belief that the modern ideal is after all a loftier one. Sometimes he seems to have regarded Greek culture more as a part of the humanistic curriculum than as an absolute value. Interpretations differ; my own view is that he was basically a true if rather sophisticated believer in a Hellenic ideal both aesthetic and ethical. Certainly he did not relativize the Greek achievement in the fashion of the Schlegels. As we shall see, the evidence does not all point in one direction.

In his complex personality, Humboldt combined very abstract intellectuality with sensuality, and a much-noticed coldness with sensitivity and generosity. It has been well argued that his own temperament was far from classical:[4] he stressed longing, the creative value of loneliness, and self-awareness. In youth he created his own ideal of the ancient world because, like Winckelmann, he was unhappy in the contemporary one.[5] Later in life, looking back on his early days, he wrote to his wife that his love of antiquity, the only force to which he had a really vital relation, must have deeper roots than his early study of the classics.[6]

Many though his gifts were, literary talent was not among them. Nor was Humboldt a great or even an influential critic; he had ideas as well as knowledge but his style is often stiff and sometimes obscure. His impact then did not manifest itself primarily through the printed word, but it was still important. Through his connection with such scholars as Wolf, he helped to define the goal of classical studies generally accepted in German universities, and not only there. As the main architect of the curriculum of the Prussian humanistic Gymnasia, later extended to all Germany, he placed his concept of the classical ideal at the very center of the nation's educational system. Perhaps this was a dubious boon, both to the ideal itself and to the students; one hears a multitude of complaints about the coldness, dryness, and dustiness of this academic tradition. At any rate, Zeus and Achilles, not Wotan and Arminius, were the standard ideals of the classroom; but possibly this gave the latter the nimbus of the unofficial.

Humboldt's early concept of Greece appears clearly in his "On the Study of Antiquity, Especially the Greek" (1793). This short essay exists only in rough, partly schematic form. Yet it exerted some influence: Schiller read it carefully, adding his own comments, and Wolf quoted from it in his programmatic "Exposition of the Science of Antiquity" (1807), a work important in establishing the direction of classical studies in the universities.

In its general tendency, the essay is about what one would expect from an enthusiastic young man who had learned from Heyne and Wolf. As Ernst Howald put it, Humboldt did not have to struggle for his humanism: he was born into Winckelmann's tradition.[7] He wrote at the time that his knowledge of the Greeks was abstract and idealized (*idealisch*), but his later acquaintance with Aristophanes and other earthy writers did not change his image in any decisive way.[8] Most striking is Humboldt's interest in the Hellenes as human beings. He focuses on "the Greek man" as a type or model; moderns, by studying him, may attain the *"highest, best proportioned development of man."* [9] The Greek, especially the Athenian, combined physical and intellectual beauty; indeed, beauty was basic to his culture as well as to his "sensuous" religion.[10] The aesthetic component is important in Humboldt's image, but it is not central. Nor is the ethical: he notes without comment, in fact with approval, that the existence of slavery made it easier for the free citizens to devote themselves to culture, and that "ideas of morality . . . did not put fetters on the spirit." [11] But Humboldt does not emphasize this pre-Nietzschean immoralism; what really attracts him is the all-sidedness or "totality" of the Hellenes. (Again one recalls Friedrich Schlegel's remark that men find what they want in the ancients, mainly themselves.) It is this universality, plus their originality, which uniquely fitted the Greeks to serve as models; probably they will remain norms forever.[12] Their great sensitivity and sensuousness, one infers, would not be assets in certain other peoples, but are valuable components of Greek wholeness. They embody the original character of mankind,[13] refined but not inhibited or emasculated. As so often, a Rousseauistic note blends with Winckelmannian dogma.

From one aspect, it might seem that Humboldt was deflating the myth by using it as a means to a pedagogic end. Essentially though, he is discussing not a mere curriculum but preparation for life. The Greek has become the paradigm of man himself. It is inconceivable that Humboldt would have given such a function to the Hebrew or the early Christian — or for that matter to the early Teuton.

An essay on Pindar (1795) stresses another aspect of Greek life: sheer grandeur or greatness "of existence, of being, of life generally." [14] Anyone who possesses this greatness enjoys untroubled calm, as Pindar did.[15] No fanatic, Humboldt did not

imply that *all* Greeks possessed this Zeus-like serenity — which
of course is Winckelmann's "quiet grandeur" — but considered it representative of Hellas at its highest and hence normative.

In "On the Male and Female Form" (1795) the stress on
serenity and on totality continues.[16] Here Humboldt struggles
at repetitious length with a difficulty created by his idealistic
aesthetics. Since the highest human beauty is by definition
general or typical, it can obviously not be completely represented within the limitations of one sex or the other; yet the
artist has to confine himself to the masculine or feminine body.
How then can he embody the Platonic idea of man? Humboldt worries his "dilemma" with almost comical seriousness,
and concludes that the Greeks had reached a partial solution.
Ideal figures of Diana and Apollo, for instance, have the appropriate sexual beauty and something which rises into the
realm of the purely human as well.[17] And Olympian figures
manage to appear simultaneously human and superhuman.
Taking his cue more directly from Plato, Friedrich Schlegel,
in "Diotima," had speculated more amusingly on similar questions. It is revealing that Humboldt turns to the Greeks for a
solution to so abstract, and so farfetched, a problem.

In the mid-nineties a new influence modified Humboldt's
cult of Greece: that of Schiller and Goethe. At the time Schiller's fondest hope was to establish modern poetry as at least
the equal of the classics. From one point of view, his "sentimentive" poet, as we have seen, is superior to the Greek, ancient or reborn. Humboldt saw Schiller daily for several
months and then carried on a long correspondence with him.
Through the poet, he became a friend of Goethe's, who was
grateful for his admiration, respected his gifts, and even turned
to him for help in checking the correctness of the hexameters
of *Hermann and Dorothea*.[18] Humboldt devoted a book-long
"aesthetic essay" to Goethe's epic, which he presents as the
model of its genre and indeed of poetry in general. Here, it

seemed, a contemporary had learned all that any poet could from the ancients and had added to this the philosophical self-awareness of modern thought. For a time, the theory of Schiller and the practice of both poets impressed Humboldt so greatly that he thought the German accomplishment at least the equal of the Greek. He never abandoned "his" Greeks, but during the some three years of his most intimate relation to the Weimar poets and sporadically in later years, he tended to stress the depth and ideality of German poetry. He was not, however, won over to the "modern" side for very long. While he did not waver in his admiration for Goethe and Schiller as individual geniuses, his Hellenism went too deep to be permanently displaced. He was not one of those who felt that a Gothic cathedral was as beautiful as the Pantheon or that Shakespeare was Sophocles' brother. His attachment to Hellas was ultimately based on emotion; in the long run it was to prove stronger than his allegiance to any other ideal.

Humboldt was more fortunate than many of his contemporaries in that his image of the ancient world was not based exclusively on books. Traveling in Spain, he examined and described the remains of the Greek theater at Saguntum. Later, as the Prussian resident minister, he spent some six years, from 1802 to 1808, in Rome. Apparently his diplomatic duties were not crushing; there was time to associate with artists and scholars, to read, to look at works of art, even to attempt poems of his own. If living in Rome was not the epoch-making experience to him that it was to Goethe, it nevertheless seems to have given solidity and vividness to his notions of the South and of antiquity. Prussian though he was, Humboldt was no admirer of the state, and the Roman ideal did not attract him, though he respected it. It was rather the living physical reality of the city and the sense of Greek beauty shining through the Roman accretions which were the experiences really important to him.

Rome seemed to epitomize the totality of human history.

Humboldt's reactions have been compared to Gibbon's,[19] but it was really the decline and fall of Greece, not Rome, which made him melancholy. The surrounding landscape, the climate, and the vegetation claimed his attention,[20] along with less tangible factors. He wrote to Schiller of the "quiet grandeur" of the city and the mountains around it,[21] and maintained, in a letter to Goethe, that the Italian landscape created a sense of serenity — "One always remains in a clear, equable, objective mood" — whereas the German evoked restlessness or gloom.[22] The typical note of the "aesthetic traveler" is heard: Humboldt enjoys picturesque disorder and writes that it would be horrible if the Campagna were cultivated or an efficient police force installed,[23] but this attitude is not dominant. The essence of his views is found in a letter, a poem, and an unfinished essay.

The letter, already twice cited, is one of the most remarkable he ever composed. It was addressed to Goethe, who as the most renowned of contemporary visitors to Rome could be expected to understand Humboldt's rather complex reactions. Considering the attitude one should take toward antiquity, he wrote: "it is only an illusion if we wish to have been citizens of Athens and Rome ourselves. Antiquity must appear to us only in the distance, only freed of everything common, only as past." [24] This is the polar opposite to Hölderlin's youthful "my Plato" and his early dream of an Athens reborn here and now. Humboldt is very realistic about his romanticism. The ideal must not be confused with empirical reality. To determine what is objective in the impression Rome makes, Humboldt attempts a historical explanation:

A line of Homer, even an insignificant one, is a sound from a land which we all recognize as a better one and yet not strange to us . . . Many factors coincide to produce this effect . . . But in my eyes the real reason lies in the Dark Ages. Through Christianity and the state of wildness in society (the Greeks knew only a wildness in nature), man was so worn down that natural calm, undisturbed inner peace, were eternally lost to him; nowadays, one has to reconquer them by a hard-won victory. Man's nature was split, sheer spirituality was opposed to sensuality; he was filled up with notions of poverty, humility, and sin which never left him. If he then, rendered contrite within by a mixture of gnostic subtleties and fanaticisms and narrow-minded, horrifying Jewish concepts, frightened and tormented without by arbitrary power . . . if then he could look up for the first time to those [classic] nations, who had lived under quite contrary conditions, if he moreover saw their works surrounded by all the magic of imagination, he had to fall to his knees as if before the figures of the gods; and since we still live in the same inner and outer discord [*Zwiespalt*] — it is less only here and there — we must continue that adoration.[25]

Humboldt seems to be saying that if we make a myth of the ancients, we do so for the soundest historical reasons: it is an essentially true myth. In his heavy, even clumsy language he is urging charges against Christianity which Nietzsche was later to make familiar. Possibly his reference to poverty, humility, and sin consciously echoes the complaint against the "unnatural" virtues of poverty, chastity, and obedience which Goethe's Brother Martin, in *Götz von Berlichingen*, had voiced a generation before. It has been rightly pointed out that this explicit attack on Christianity is by no means typical of the author,[26] but there is no reason to doubt his sincerity. On the contrary: in this private letter to the great pagan of Weimar, he did not have to express himself with his usual circumspection.

The poem "Rome" (1806, in *ottava rima*) is less striking than the letter, but it is revealing. While it owes something to August Wilhelm Schlegel's elegy on Rome and Schiller's "The Gods of Greece," it is essentially independent in its views. Humboldt discusses the historic role and "idea" of Rome with hundreds of classical allusions and little fire. (As poetry, "Rome" is about on the level of Macaulay's *Lays* but less clear and vigorous.) Without the Romans, we would have neither Homer nor the Laocoön;[27] the preservation of Hellenic culture was their greatest contribution and the only one which seems really to matter to the author. There is real warmth only when he shifts to the theme of Greece. The poem ends with reflections on the philosophy of history which are not entirely lucid, but antiquarianism is clearly rejected and the necessity of change admitted.[28] Somewhat in the mood of Gautier, but with arguments of a very different sort, Humboldt holds that only aesthetic form is eternal. The gestalt embodies that sheer truth which the mind, according to Kant, cannot grasp:

> Was dem Geist entflieht, als reine Wahrheit,
> Strahlt aus ihr in hoher Sinnenklarheit.[29]

Beauty is not its own excuse for being; it is the authentic expression of truth.

Quite typically, the unfinished essay "Latium and Hellas," of the same year, barely mentions Rome. Though there would be no point in analyzing in detail all of Humboldt's arguments, he does make statements which constitute almost a religious commitment, and these should be noted. Antiquity seems "a better home" for the human spirit; based there, one can understand all the varied aspects of man.[30] As if to confute A. W. Schlegel, Humboldt states that the Greek gods are the "children of infinity"[31] — a quality the romanticists generally reserved for themselves. They are above the "dreary seriousness of knowing good and evil, from which arises the concept of guilt."[32] Whereas Novalis had argued that paganism collapsed because it could not deal with the problem of death, Humboldt held that the Greeks faced courageously all the sadness of human life, which yet, to them, was simultaneously rich in joy. It is better to draw comfort, as Homer does, from the fact that even the greatest hero must die than to pretend, with the Christians, that the misfortune of death is intrinsically a good.[33] (Similarly, Hegel maintained that the Greek view of death was the more honest: "For them, mis-

fortune was misfortune, pain was pain." [34]) The idea of fate
gave depth to Greek thought; it is ultimately a consoling concept. The man who has accepted his destiny is not concerned
with vulgar "happiness."

This is the most extreme statement of Humboldt's Hellenism. Along with conventional comments about the Greeks'
love of proportion and their uniquely rich cultural and
public life, [35] there are others more typically his own: that
their striving was always of an ideal, spiritual sort; [36] that the
national character was rich in "polar," apparently contradic-
tory, traits — it was marked by a longing for loneliness, for
instance, as well as gregariousness. [37] Again, Humboldt seems
to have projected parts of his own personality upon the
Greeks, to have made them an unexpectedly Faustian people.
Very explicitly, the Greek view is contrasted to the Christian
and made to seem philosophically and ethically far superior
to it.

Above all, Rome appeared to him as the greatest concrete
expression of the classical world; as a symbol, in Goethe's
sense, of antiquity. Paulsen was right, I think, in speaking of
Greece as Humboldt's religion, and claiming that he found
in Rome "the visible presence of the divine." [38] It is in this light
that we must understand Humboldt's startling sentence about
Goethe's "Winckelmann": "There are passages in it which
are among the greatest ever uttered." [39] In this essay, as has
been noted, Goethe had infuriated the romantics by glorify-
ing the archaeologist's pagan and antique characteristics; it
was a barely veiled declaration of his own position. This must
have moved Humboldt very profoundly; for his praise, even
of Goethe's works, is not normally so sweeping. Where
Greece was concerned, the calm, well-balanced diplomat
could become very laudatory indeed.

What were the effects of Humboldt's stay in Rome upon
him? In later life, there are nostalgic recollections: thus a poem
of 1820 complains that in the North there is no sun, only its

shadow.[40] When he wrote of the sacred hills of Rome, suffused with quiet grandeur —

> . . . Verlangen nach den heilgen Hügeln
> um die ewig stille Grösse schwebt —[41]

he meant it quite literally. Most revealing of all are the lines associating the calm inspired by the grandeur of Rome with the more profound calm of the grave:

> Und aus der Grösse Gefühl spriesst Ruh des beschwichtigten Busens,
> Die nach tieferer Ruh drunten im Grabe sich sehnt.[42]

We recall that Humboldt had written of antiquity as a better land and a better home; again, the emotional basis of his commitment is evident.

After returning from Italy in 1808 Humboldt was at first extremely active in his service to the Prussian state. Under the leadership of Baron vom Stein he worked as one of a brilliant group dedicated to internal reform; later he was active as a diplomat at the Congress of Vienna and elsewhere. Yet he managed to keep his Greek studies alive. In 1819, after opposing the reactionary course of Prussian policy, he resigned from office and withdrew to his country estate in Tegel, near Berlin, where he could again devote himself to scholarship and self-cultivation. In this last period of his life his predominant interest was in linguistics, but there was ample time once more for Greek literature and ancient art.

Humboldt was always a complex person of varied attitudes and enthusiasms. He was also remarkably judicious. No churchgoer himself, he held that the newly founded University of Berlin should have a church of its own.[43] When Goethe sent him an essay including a violent denunciation of one of the great themes of Christian painting — "A woman with a suckling, even if not giving suck, is an indecent motif for higher art,"[44] he declared, ex cathedra as it were — Humboldt's reaction was characteristic.[45] On the one hand, he wrote that he was much pleased by the "passage against the Madonna," since he was attracted by everything pagan; on the other, he suggested that a Madonna giving suck might be unobjectionable in modern painting though not in sculpture. At times he seems to carry diplomacy too far, adopting a heathen tone to one correspondent, a Christian one to another.[46] Some verses of 1815, intended for his own eyes alone, express a frequent mood though it was not an attitude he made public:

> Ich bin ein armer heidnischer Mann,
> Der die Kirchen nicht leiden kann;
> Ich leb' in der alten vergangenen Zeit,
> Drum wähle ich mir die Einsamkeit.
>
> Die Menschen von jetzt, sie gefallen mir nicht;
> Sie holen vom Himmel ein wundervoll Licht;
> Die Alten, sie schöpftens aus eigner Brust,
> Und senktens in Lebens Wehmuth und Lust.[47]

This is by no means his only mood, of course. Particularly after the death of his wife, he struggled with the question of personal immortality, and he liked to quote from the Bible, in which he was astoundingly well read for a "poor pagan man"; but the non-Christian note is more frequently struck.[48]

Another rival to the Greek ideal arose in India. Humboldt plunged deeply into the study of Sanskrit, a fresh and exciting pursuit in the early nineteenth century, though he did not share in the general "Indomania" of the romantics. In 1823 he wrote to the philologist F. G. Welcker:

I find in the Greek [fairy tales, popular sagas, and legends] . . . such delicacy, lightness, yes I should like to say divineness, that even to be reminded of ours, in that connection, seems to me like mixing crude metals with precious ones. I am not more favorably disposed toward mixing in the Indian and Egyptian. For whatever one may say about the beauty and sublimity of the *Ramayana, Mahabharata,* the *Nibelungen* . . . it always lacks the one quality in which the whole magic of Greek lies, which one cannot completely express in any words, but which one feels deeply and infinitely.[49]

He goes on to say that in any crisis, even in the moment of death, some lines of Homer would afford him more comfort than "anything of any other people." [50] Homer's verses, even the catalogue of ships, would give the sense of passing from the human sphere to the divine.

In the following year, however, Humboldt was inspired to uncharacteristic enthusiasm by the *Bhagavad-Gita*, a long episode in the *Mahabharata*. It is easy to see that the praise of contemplation above action, and yet of duty, in this work, like its emphasis on profound absorption in ultimate questions, would have inevitably appealed to him. He wrote to Gentz that this was the deepest and loftiest poem in existence. [51] Yet his apostasy was brief; some of the sonnets he wrote in old age seem almost to apologize for it. Thus he felt that the sheer profusion of images (*Bildermenge*) of Indian art often crushes the imagination. One should shun such exotic temptations:

> so sollte man, da voll in Hellas Werken
> das Höchste ist des Irrdischen erstrebet,
> nicht mehr auf fremder Töne Lockung merken. [52]

Most characteristically he writes that only Greek literature "stills the heart's longing." [53] Again the term "religion" springs to mind. [54]

Yet a brief comment, written in old age, shows that Humboldt had at least one moment of radical heresy. In a sketch arguing that religion and poetry are intimately related to moral education, one unexpectedly encounters the following: "The religion of the Greeks was not more poetic than Christianity, it was only more sensuous. The Greeks did not exactly shine in perfection of moral education [*Bildung*]." [55] As his brother Alexander remarked, these few lines "stand like a fallen aerolite." [56] Their sarcastic tone is striking, but it would be risky to read too much into an isolated *aperçu*, a fragment of a fragment. The main current continued to flow in the opposite direction, as Humboldt's late sonnets clearly show. These poetic exercises (he wrote one a day for over three years) make up the rather ponderous key with which he unlocked his heart. They were not intended to be published, and indeed they are valuable not as poetry but as spiritual autobiography. Neither Jesus nor Christianity is directly mentioned. Immortality is a frequent theme but is not treated in a specifically Christian way.[57] On the other hand, Hellas, Greek art, and the nature of beauty appear again and again as subjects. In the last hour of his life, we are told, Humboldt quoted lines of Homer, Pindar, and Schiller.[58] The proportion is about right: the "modern," German element is represented but subordinate.

To attempt a quick summary: the most important attribute of Humboldt's Greeks is all-embracingness, totality. Everything must harmonize within the greater unity. In their culture sensuality and even obscenity have their place;[59] these are not Winckelmann's Greeks, still less Fénelon's. Though the Greeks did not ignore the existence of unhappiness, the dominant impulse of their lives was to be fully human,[60] to "enjoy human existence in serene joy," accepting all the gifts of the gods.[61]

Since Humboldt believed with Schiller that the Hellenes did not suffer from the modern division between consciousness and actuality, inner and outer life,[62] it is surprising that he attributes ideal longing to them.[63] It is a little difficult to see why one should yearn, and for what, if one is already total. Humboldt declares that Greek longing was devoted to representing in the symbolic form of art "the highest life . . . that is, the most human existence." [64] Somehow his heroes can be both aspiring and fulfilled: they have the romantic virtues as well as the classic. All this and Heaven too!

Quite consistently, Humboldt regards political freedom as an essential part of Hellenic life, though he elaborates upon the point in one fragment only.[65] Unlike Hölderlin, he did not condemn the Athenians for their exclusive devotion to beauty and culture. Like many another liberal, he admired ancient freedom, above all the freedom of the individual. Characteristically, in Germany at least, the romantic admirers of medieval art have upheld a strong, "organic" state; the classicists have been liberals (like Wieland and Lessing) or largely indifferent to politics.

To return to Humboldt's Greeks: they represent man per se. "They are for us what their gods were for them . . . flesh of our flesh and bone of our bone; [they knew] all the misfortune and all difficulties of life; but [had] a way of thinking which transforms everything to play and yet only smooths away the roughnesses of life while preserving the seriousness of the idea," he noted.[66] Nothing modern can be compared with them,[67] but the very fact that they cannot be equaled makes them the proper model. Antique man was irradiated by divinity.[68]

Rather than continuing to expand this anthology of praise, it is worth reminding oneself that Humboldt was far more interested in the idea of Hellas than in its empirical reality.[69] At times at least, he realized that his view was one-sided, or "too idealizing." Essentially, however, he was concerned with Greece as a norm, with establishing a myth embodying timeless and valid ideals.

Before trying to establish what Humboldt's impact may have been, we must briefly consider one more point: his notion of the proper relation between modernity and the ancient world. It has been shrewdly observed that for the German classical writers there were really only two historical periods: the Greek and the present.[70] Usually, though not always, the Greek emerges easily first in Humboldt's estimation. At times he held that they were not a "better, nobler race" in themselves, but were able in their own time to realize all their high qualities fully.[71] In the realm of sensuous form they are unsurpassed; the modern world excels in that of music and feeling.[72] Even assuming infinite perfectibility, a true synthesis of antique and modern is inconceivable.[73] Yet they are the unique incarnations of the idea of man, and education today must be based on their achievements. Since Humboldt shared the belief of the time that his countrymen understood the Greeks the most fully, and were closest to them,[74] he had a special reason to hope for the success of humanistic education in Germany. Accordingly, when he was put in charge of the Prussian Section for Culture and Public Education in 1809, he made the classics the very center of his reforms; and he was in a position of great influence.

In the curriculum he proposed for the Prussian Gymnasium, Humboldt appears as a thoroughgoing humanist, who looked down on utilitarianism even more than on a theological emphasis.[75] His two ideals, universality and individuality, complemented each other: [76] each person was to develop his powers to the fullest scope. Indeed, his own aristocratic background is apparent here: like the Greeks, he scorned any study which was basely practical and Philistine. The subjects most emphasized are Latin, German, Greek, and (for reasons which will be noted) religion; he also increased the requirements in the sciences. For all its humanistic orientation, the new curriculum did not stress Greek to a fanatical extent; it was third in number of total hours of instruction to be given during the ten-year course.[77]

Humboldt had not betrayed his own convictions; rather, realizing that administration, like politics, is the art of the possible, he aimed at attainable goals and he attained a great deal. He worked skillfully with colleagues of different beliefs — one of them, Nicolovius, was a devout Christian — and managed to strengthen his own emphasis without injuring their feelings.

In 1812, three years after he took office, Greek was made obligatory.[78] None of his educational directives stressed the content of Greek literature and philosophy; [79] rather, he emphasized that the form and structure of a language are educative in their own right. Since he shared the romantic belief that each language mirrors the spirit of the people which speaks it,[80] he was striking a blow for Hellas and at the same time neatly avoiding any overt propaganda. Humboldt's faith in the value of linguistic study was genuine, of course, but his ardor for the "content" of Greek was even greater. In discussing Humboldt's humanistic reform of the curriculum, Friedrich Paulsen wrote: "In the Greek ideal the new age found the image of perfection, instead of in Christianity: the image of the perfect man instead of the God who has become man . . . Hellenizing humanism is a new religion, the philologists are its priests, the universities and schools its temples." [81] Paulsen's words apply to Humboldt, Wolf, and others rather literally, but one suspects that in many cases using the term "religion" would be exaggerated; *Weltanschauung* would be nearer the mark. At all events, a new religion has to be introduced discreetly if scandal is to be avoided; compromises were inevitable.

In the nature of things, there were limiting factors, not least in the capacity of the students. In the first fine careless rapture, standards in Greek were set too high; as early as 1828, they had to be lowered.[82] Latin was so firmly entrenched that it continued to receive more attention than any other subject, though Humboldt was not alone in his belief that Roman literature was of secondary value.[83] Religious education was strengthened; Humboldt believed that religious faith held a nation together socially and therefore approved.[84] It is significant however that no theologian was a member of the special "deputation" which he convened to guide the reform of the schools.[85] Only future theologians were required to study Hebrew, which was apparently considered rather a "preprofessional" than a cultural subject.

In the nineteenth and early twentieth centuries, the Gymnasium became notorious for overburdening the pupils with too many and too varied requirements. Cultural critics like Nietzsche and Lagarde and novelists like the Manns and Hesse denounced it. Here Humboldt and the other humanists of his generation can hardly have been mainly to blame. The major trouble seems not to have lain in the classical emphasis as such but in the dualism of these schools; when the importance of science increased, they tried to eat their cake and have it too, to give the adolescent students a thorough humanistic and scientific education simultaneously.[86] Perhaps one could say that Humboldt should have foreseen this development and set up two different curricula, but it would be unfair to expect prophetic gifts even of a universal man.

To evaluate Humboldt's impact on German culture seems almost impossible. He was no proselytizer and can hardly have expected that classes in Greek would become hotbeds of extreme paganism, but rather that at least some of the students would receive a lasting impression of the grandeur and beauty of the Hellenic past. And while many pupils doubtless found classicism very stuffy — if only because they had to learn about it in school — we may assume that many others accepted it. Poets like George and Spitteler, cultural critics like Burckhardt and Nietzsche, would have found even smaller audiences in a public not exposed at all to the Greek myth. And there is another point: the humanism and aestheticism of Humboldt and his supporters, it has well been argued, affected the teaching of German literature as well as that of Latin and Greek.[87] Lessing, Goethe, and Schiller were established in the schools as the major "German classics" — not, say, Tieck, Kleist, and Jean Paul. Without this emphasis, the profile of German literature would now be very different; it would appear more eccentric, more parochial, and indeed even barbaric.

Chapter XII

The Return of Helen: Goethe

After the death of Schiller, Goethe appears to us increasingly as the unfathomable sage, the old man of incredibly varied interests and talents, of amazingly complex character and mind. Recalling the role of renunciation and of reverence in his late novels, or of "Grace from above" in the second part of *Faust*, we cannot think of him as the militant pagan he often was in his middle years. Yet we know that his fascination with Greece continued — though it became far less exclusive — and that many of his reasons for rejecting Christianity remained cogent to him. One can indeed say that his taste became more catholic, his ethical and religious views broader in the last decades of his life. There is no consistent, one-directional development, but a certain degree of reconciliation was achieved. Heathen thesis and Christian antithesis do not fuse into a neat synthesis: *Faust* points in one direction, *Wilhelm Meister's Wanderjahre* in another, and the poet's letters and conversations are full of remarks which cannot be harmonized. His mind, Ludwig Curtius has well said, had two focuses, the sensuous and the idea; we cannot relate everything in it to a single center.[1] The "Helen act" in Faust represents one great aspect of Goethe, the closing scenes of the work another. Before examining individual works, I shall attempt to show briefly how the conflicting strains persist in Goethe's religious and ethical beliefs as well as in his aesthetics. In searching a work of literature for such beliefs, one runs the obvious risk of distorting it; but, broadly speaking, Goethe's later works are in some degree didactic, and to read them as pure poetry would be as wrongheaded as taking them as exercises in moral exhortation. Fortunately his pervasive irony serves to warn us against the latter danger.

In the older Goethe's letters and conversations, as in his autobiographical *Poetry and Truth*, there is a new stress on religion and on an altruistic, self-denying ethic. Frequent references suggest that he felt a tendency to return to the mood of his youth, when even his resentment of Pietist intolerance [2] could not deprive him of the affection he felt for the Bible and for the figure of Jesus. The Christianity he constructed for his "private use" [3] plays a greater part in *Poetry and Truth* than the ancient gods or the "forest" of Greek statues he saw in the Mannheim gallery. The man whom so many thought — not without reason — an "old heathen" included in his autobiography a highly compressed but charming retelling of the book of Genesis.[4] Doubtless the intention was to show indirectly the importance the Bible had for him. For the child of a Protestant family, that was natural enough; it is amazing though to find an account of the Catholic sacraments,[5] written with great flair and apparent sympathy. Goethe holds that Protestantism has too few sacraments, and stresses that the ritual of the original church gives form and solemnity to life: "And so cradle and grave are linked by a radiant circle of equally dignified sacred actions, whose beauty I have but briefly indicated." [6] Broadly speaking, Goethe continued to resist Catholicizing in life and art, but at times he recognized the beauty and majesty of the Church. One can distinguish between his attitude toward authentic, historical Catholicism,[7] which in some moods he respected, and his consistent rejection of the romantic converts and the Nazarene painters of his own day.

Generally though it is the elements of "natural religion" in Christianity — reverence, piety, love, the worship of a single god — which evoked his admiration. His rhetorical question to Chancellor von Müller reminds us of his poem of 1784, "The Mysteries," and also of the "pedagogical province" in the *Wanderjahre*: "What gave the Christian religion the victory over all others, by which it has deservedly become the mistress of the world, except that it absorbed the truths of natural religion within itself?"[8] Christianity then is not the highest conceivable form of faith, but it most closely approximates that ideal religion of truth, reason, and love to which the great figures of the German Enlightenment paid tribute — the "archetypal religion," to use Goethe's language. In a somewhat different frame of mind he remarked to Eckermann that he could cheerfully accept the divinity of Christ or of the sun (taken as a symbol of light and of God's creative power) but not the sacredness of the thumb bones of the Apostles Peter or Paul.[9] As a child of the eighteenth century, Goethe was very much on his guard against superstitions, but "pure" Christianity was a very different matter. The human spirit would not surpass the "moral culture of Christianity as it gleams and shines forth in the Gospels," he told Eckermann in one of their last conversations.[10] Superficially this is very close to Stefan George's "Cross, thou shalt long remain the light of the earth," but in context George's line is condescending and rather regretful.

Goethe was annoyed at charges that he was not a Christian,[11] and even remarked to von Müller that perhaps he alone among living men was the kind of Christian of whom Christ would have approved.[12] Yet he drew the line at saints and apostles, implying to the same friend that they were probably no better "fellows" than Klopstock, Lessing, and himself. For all his devotion to the figure of Jesus, he found Him "problematic."[13] Christ had projected His own admirable character upon His concept of God.[14]

In his later years, then, Goethe is generally sympathetic to Christianity; but along with moments of skeptical insight, a

strain of outright paganism persists also. It is not untypical
that while he was writing *The Elective Affinities* — which
Thomas Mann called his "most Christian work" [15] — he repeatedly sounded a heathen note. Possibly it was only a kind
of teasing when he wrote his old, pious friend Fritz Jacobi
that it would be "most agreeable to live and die as the last
pagan," [16] but he used the same word to describe himself to
another correspondent,[17] and his references to the "modern
Christianity business" [18] and related matters are often very
cutting indeed. In this sphere Goethe seems as two-souled as
his Faust.

Around 1815 he became again sympathetic to Gothic architecture, shared in the patriotic effort to complete the Cologne
cathedral, and discovered great virtues in the religious paintings of the late medieval Rhenish masters. But as we shall see,
this was probably more a matter of aesthetics than of religion;
at any rate, the mood did not last long. To demonstrate
where his fundamental allegiance lay he published, in 1818, a
brief polemic discussion of the statue known as "Myron's
Cow." In its original Greek form, the cow, he deduced, had
been suckling its calf. To show animals giving suck is an
appropriate theme for art; human beings should not be shown
thus, gods least of all. "The intention and the effort of the
Greeks is to make man divine, not to humanize divinity." [19]
A swift association brings him to the theme of the Madonna:

A woman with a suckling, even if not giving suck, is an indecent
motif for higher art. Only the modern [*neuere*] age, which likes so
much to flatter our sensuality and drag it down rather than elevating
it, could, with a complete decay of the aesthetic sense, give high
nobility to such a subject: for what is it but displaying the joys of
copulation and the pangs of birth. Let whoever likes it take his delight
in it! [20]

Goethe could hardly have written more offensively, or more
coarsely. The passage quoted above was cut before publication, but enough was printed to stir up furious resentment

among some readers. These lines are too violent to be typically
Goethean, but it remains significant that he wrote them at all.
Although he had often praised Madonnas in earlier times, he
told Humboldt that he rejected all treatments of the theme,
even Raphael's.[21]

Yet Goethe's nature was basically conciliatory, as he himself noted, and he repeatedly attempted to bring the Hellenic
and the Judeo-Christian positions into harmony. Thus he
wrote of the "charming diversity of Greece and the dignified
unity of Israel." [22] There are only two real religions, he noted
in his *Maxims and Reflections*: one completely without forms
to represent holiness; the other employing the most beautiful
forms for worship. "Everything in between is idolatry." [23]
Again one is reminded of the "two focuses" of Goethe's
thought. Or he might attempt to dispose of the whole conflict
by stating that we are pantheists as scientists, polytheists as
poets, monotheists in moral matters.[24] He expressed sympathetic approval of the Hypsistarians,[25] a sect of the fourth
century which tried to combine the best elements of paganism,
Christianity, and Judaism. One senses the groping toward a
synthesis but agrees with Robert d'Harcourt that there are
"contradictions and also indecision, indecision in the face of
mystery." [26]

In the closely related sphere of aesthetics Goethe's views
show very similar tensions and resolutions, or partial resolutions. Characteristically, though not inevitably, classical taste
was linked with pagan *Weltanschauung* — "Myron's Cow"
is a case in point. Here too one has the sense of broadening
horizons. "Perhaps we have been too antique," [27] he admitted.
Much as he opposed the romantics, he partially shared most
of their enthusiasms, and learned from them — from Calderón,
India, even the *Nibelungenlied*. The great lyric cycle of his
old age, the *West-östlicher Divan*, is set against a Persian
background. The ideal of world literature supplements,
though it does not replace, belief in the hegemony of the
ancients.

That belief continues, and is brought into sharp relief when Goethe focuses his attention on the romantic school. Romanticism borders on the comic, classicism on the serious and dignified, he maintained.[28] Even when a romantic poem has grandeur, it lacks taste.[29] Exotic mythologies offended his humanistic sensibilities:

> Und so will ich, ein- für allemal,
> Keine Bestien in dem Göttersaal!
> Die leidigen Elefanten-Rüssel . . .[30]

And Chinese, Indian, and Egyptian antiquities are of little use in "attaining moral or aesthetic culture." [31]

In cultural matters a synthesis, or at least a compromise, was more easily attainable than in religion. Within the great chorus of world literature and world art, the Greeks have only one voice, but as it is the most beautiful, it should furnish the criterion. We should create like the Greeks, according to eternal, inherent norms. "Let each one be a Greek in his own way! But let him be one!" [32] Clearly this is not a summons to slavish imitation. As the closest modern approximation to the spirit and form of Greek tragedy, Goethe cited Milton's *Samson Agonistes*.[33] His choice, made in 1829, shows how far he had gone beyond the doctrinaire classicism of his middle years.

In *Faust I*, finally published in 1808, aesthetic paganism plays only a minor role; the balance was to be redressed in the second part of Goethe's greatest poem. The paganism of the first part is largely divorced from beauty and expressed mainly in the Germanic atmosphere of scenes like "Witch's Kitchen" and "Walpurgis Night"; it is linked with ugliness, superstition, crude sexuality, and a sense of guilt. Only in the classical world, Goethe seems to imply, do man's impulses appear natural and beautiful. The "Northern" atmosphere of *Faust I* makes the serene enjoyment of one's existence impossible; the world is hopelessly split in two; when the protagonist abandons Christian standards, he becomes the prey of witch cults and Satanism. In "Walpurgis Night," the soulless shape of Lilith appears, beautiful but demonic; she stands in contrast, if one takes the poem as a whole, to the "Eternal Feminine" of Faust's true aspiration, and to Helen. As an anticipation of Helen, as it were, Faust catches a glimpse of a beautiful woman in the magic mirror on the wall of the witch's dwelling; but she is, significantly, only an image. To the extent that Faust, even in the first part, incarnates man's dignity and freedom, he reflects the beliefs of such Renaissance figures as Pico della Mirandola; but this theme too is not fully orchestrated until the second part of the drama.

The novel *The Elective Affinities* (1809) is one of Goethe's most enigmatic works: its intention has been hotly debated.[34] Goethe uses marriage as the concrete instance of moral law, and the overwhelming passion of an "elective affinity" as the expression of natural law; when the two clash, tragedy is inevitable. The marriage of Eduard and Charlotte is doubly threatened when he falls in love with a young girl, Ottilia; his wife, with an older man. Things seem to be moving toward divorce and remarriage when the problematic Ottilia accidentally allows the infant child of Eduard and Charlotte to fall from her arms and drown, after which Freudian slip she is not unnaturally filled with a sense of guilt. She starves herself to death in expiation, and Eduard dies soon after. The last sentence of the "tragic novel" is a nice example of Goethe's tendency toward conciliatory closings.

Goethe has made matters more difficult for his interpreters by including a good deal of contemporary material of a romantic flavor — manifestations of Nazarene taste and of mysterious physical phenomena.[35] Moreover, Ottilia, after ending her days on a note of saintly asceticism, performs apparent miracles in death. It is no wonder that many readers have found *The Elective Affinities* a very Christian book.

Others, like Wieland, have taken the opposite point of view. The love of Eduard and Ottilia is never condemned; on the contrary. Even in Ottilia's last days the lovers are linked by an "almost magical mutual attraction" [36] which irresistibly draws them together. We are very far from orthodox Christianity. The sarcasm of Goethe's own remark speaks for itself: "I a pagan? Well, I had Gretchen executed and Ottilia starved to death; isn't that Christian enough for people?" [37] Although the sanctity of marriage is indeed upheld, the victory of the moral law is a Pyrrhic one. By the end of the book, all the sympathies of the reader are with Eduard and Ottilia.

In aesthetic matters Goethe's attitude was also a complex one. The relative tolerance and breadth of his views at this time (they were published in the journal *On Art and Antiquity*, 1816–1832) are largely due to the influence of Sulpiz Boisserée. [38] Boisserée, an enthusiastic collector of medieval art, seems to have been a man of great charm, humor, and tact; he managed to overcome the suspicions which Goethe inevitably had of a man of his outlook. This was no mean task: Boisserée noted in his diary the poet's assertion that Caspar David Friedrich's (romantic) paintings could be viewed just as well upside down, and that he smashed offending paintings and shot books to pieces. [39] However exaggerated this report may be, it contains at least a kernel of truth, and it is remarkable that the two remained on friendly terms from their meeting, in 1811, until Goethe's death. The young medievalist needed all his diplomatic skill, for he had to live down the extra handicap of his connection with the recently converted Friedrich Schlegel, whom Goethe had come to dislike intensely. Boisserée, though, was free of the hectic, "forced" character which Goethe found typical of the members of the romantic school. So great was his success in charming Goethe that the poet contributed to Boisserée's major project, the completion of the Cologne cathedral; mentioned him twice, with high praise, in *Poetry and Truth*; and even went some distance, for a while, toward accepting his views, though before long he found it necessary to lay down a firm boundary against them. Doubtless the enthusiasm stirred up by the so-called Wars of Liberation (1813–1815) had something to do with Goethe's temporary accommodation with German art. He was the least chauvinistic of men but could not remain entirely untouched by the national mood. At any rate, Boisserée could rejoice that "even the old heathen king has had to pay tribute to the German Christ child." [40]

The "old heathen king" twice visited the collection of medieval paintings which Sulpiz Boisserée and his brother Melchior had amassed. The brothers were particularly interested in the masters of the Rhenish School; Goethe traced its connection with Byzantine art. He wrote appreciatively of a Saint Veronica, though he mentioned the "dreadful Medusa-like face" [41] of Christ on the sudarium. Elsewhere he described certain paintings of Cranach the Elder with sympathetic admiration and even discussed a Crucifixion without implying his aversion to the theme. He mentioned also the interest felt by the patriotic German in his "holy architectural monuments." [42]

Yet one cannot feel that the change went very deep. There is none of the fervent empathy which Wackenroder expressed and Tieck affected, nor any statement that German art approached the quality of Greek. The essays are genial in tone, but Goethe treats Christianity as essentially no different in kind or value from other mythologies. In connection with the Nativity he wrote: "a *mésalliance* was approved on high, so that the newborn god might not lack an earthly father to keep up appearances and take care of him." [43] This is the tone one might use about the birth of a "natural son" to some eighteenth-century princeling. Intellectually Goethe was closer after all to Winckelmann or even to Voltaire than to Novalis or Chateaubriand. Boisserée must have winced, but he was sensible and good-humored, and Goethe after all was calling attention to German and Christian art, in his own fashion.

The charming essay "The Festival of Saint Roch at Bingen" is the product of an excellent mood, all-embracing tolerance — and a certain irony. The chapel of Saint Roch had been badly damaged in the wars with the French. In August 1814 it was reconsecrated, after a secular celebration at which heroic quantities of Rhine wine were drunk. Goethe made sketches for a picture of the saint which later was executed by the hyperclassical Heinrich Meyer and another artist and hung in the chapel. The "heathen king" could hardly have been more gracious. He was fond of the Rhenish landscape, had a keen sense of tradition and ritual, and loved good wine. His own distance from Catholicism is clear in the quietly ironical way in which he recounted the miracles performed by the saint, and in expressions like "to turn to the particular saint in whose professional competence [*Fach*, a very bureaucratic term here] the matter lay." [44]

Goethe's "catholicism" was written with a small "c." The careful reader, then, could never have confused his position with the romantic one, but most readers are not careful. Perhaps the disillusion which followed the patriotic rising of 1813–1815 was involved. At any rate, the benevolence of essays like "Heidelberg" and "Saint Roch" ebbed away. A manifesto, clearly re-establishing the absolute primacy of Greek art, was decided on; it was the polemic "Neo-German Religious-Patriotic Art," already referred to. Meyer wrote it, clearly speaking for his master, in whose *Art and Antiquity* it appeared in 1817. This programmatic statement is superficially polite but it manages to convey the scorn implied in the title. It is hard not to use the term "hatchet man" in describing Meyer's role in this affair.

After referring to the "respectable, naïve, but rather crude taste" of older German painting,[45] Meyer turns to a historical account of changes in taste since the latter part of the eighteenth century when "a non-Catholic, Protestant, not to say unchristian way of thinking still prevailed." [46] The impact

of nationalism, of Gothic taste, and of writers like Wackenroder is noted. Sentimentality has led to a decline in technique.[47] Though old German works should of course be
collected and preserved — here he bows ceremoniously to
Boisserée — it is "safest and most reasonable" to follow exclusively the Greeks and their heirs in art.[48] The distinction
is essentially one between antiquarian and aesthetic values.
Now that the fervor of the Napoleonic wars has subsided,
Meyer concludes, it is time for a less emotional approach to
art and a less demonstrative religiosity.

Despite the tone of this declaration of war, Goethe did not
revert completely to the militant one-sidedness of the 1790's.[49]
In 1818, the year of his notorious essay "Myron's Cow," he
published a very moderate statement of aesthetic belief, "Antique and Modern." Rejecting the imputation of a narrow
Hellenism, he praises any artist who produces naturally and
easily, fulfilling the entire potential of his talent. His prime
example is Raphael, who "never Grecizes but feels, thinks,
acts wholly as a Greek would." [50] It is revealing that Goethe's
example of the supreme modern artist is the same as Winckelmann's. In another article called "Of German Architecture,
1823," to distinguish it from his Storm and Stress manifesto
on the same theme, Goethe views his own past historically:
he is not in the least apologetic about his youthful defense of
the Gothic, but again praises the Cologne cathedral,[51] in a
measured way.

That Goethe studied drawings of the Elgin Marbles in 1817
and found "the law and the gospel" in them [52] reminds us
how much sounder was the evidence about Greek beauty
available in his old age than in his youth, to say nothing of
Winckelmann's. He suggested that every German sculptor [53]
should travel to London to study them and other collections
in the British Museum. Possibly knowledge of works of the
great period came too late to have much effect on his poetry.
Yet if one compares *Iphigenia in Tauris*, say, with the first

part of the Helen act in *Faust*, there is a real difference in the "Greekness" of the two: the later work seems more authentic.

The lyric cycle *West-östlicher Divan* (1819) is a symbolic flight [54] from the old conflict between Greek and modern elements, for it is neither pagan nor Christian in tone. It represents a fusion of monotheistic religious feeling — Goethe finds the Mohammedan attitude much to his taste — with the affirmation of life, expressed in part in Hafiz' devotion to love and wine, and with a stoic acceptance of the heavy burdens of daily existence.[55] Generally a serene rationality prevails, but there are expressions of the mysticism [56] Goethe thought typical of old men. [57] In "Holy Longing" he celebrates a vitality so intense that it is consumed by the desire to die and be born again:

> Das Lebend'ge will ich preisen
> Das nach Flammentod sich sehnet.[58]

It is the central mystery of any religion of resurrection and not specifically Christian. Elsewhere in the cycle we have a vision of paradise [59] which recalls Dante and anticipates the triumphant ending of *Faust*; but the prevailing imagery used to evoke heaven is naturally Mohammedan. In the *Divan* Goethe turns toward genuine universality; the day of his exclusive classicism is over.

As one might expect, tributes to Jesus are combined with rejection of a great deal of Christian dogma. Again Goethe could use the Mohammedan point of view as a convenient mask:

> Jesus fühlte rein und dachte
> Nur den Einen Gott im stillen;
> Wer ihn selbst zum Gotte machte
> Kränkte seinen heilgen Willen.[60]

In the same poem, he again expressed his dislike of the Cross. Boisserée had the courage to write to him that his hatred was so bitter that it appeared eccentric to the point of downright foolishness.[61] Equally characteristic but less vehement is the rejection of humility: if Allah had wanted the poet to be a worm, he would have created him in that shape! [62]

While the *Divan* is a beautifully shaped work of art, *Wilhelm Meister's Wanderjahre* (1821; revised edition 1829), is perhaps Goethe's least formed novel. At any rate, it is the most clearly and unambiguously didactic of his major writings. With its stress on renunciation, self-denial, and the primacy of conscience, it is also, with *Iphigenia*, his most nearly Christian work. To some extent the novel reminds us of the "Charlotte morality" of the days before Italy, but Goethe's concept of renunciation seems broader, and paradoxically less negative here than in a work like *Tasso*.

Renunciation is now the necessary precondition of adjustment to life, no longer to a little court society but to the expanding world of the early nineteenth century. That world is not evil: one should not flee from it but serve it, and this can only be done by becoming deliberately one-sided.[63] Society as a whole profits from the devoted specialization of each of its members, and harmony is no longer to be found in the universal cultivation of the individual, but in the group. Only through altruism may man attain happiness. Primarily then "renunciation" [64] serves positive, active ends — the social, indeed socialistic, ends of a collective.

At an equally far remove from paganism is Goethe's utopian account of the "Pedagogical Province," a school for boys where Wilhelm leaves his son Felix for a period of moral education. Reverence or awe (*Ehrfurcht*) is the cardinal virtue on which the youths' training depends. The three types of religion illustrate three sorts of reverence: the ethnic, based on veneration for what is above us, and including "all so-called pagan religions"; the philosophic, founded on veneration for the element which is like us; and the Christian, erected on veneration for what is below us. This is an ultimate: "Mankind cannot go back again," and Christianity will never disappear.[65] Only all three religions together make up the true faith; the three reverences produce reverence for oneself. Man at his highest may consider himself the finest creation of God and nature, and maintain himself at this sublime level without *hubris*. Theism is linked with humanism (in the sense of a cult of man).

Christianity would appear to be finally and completely established as the norm. The overseers of the Pedagogical Province embrace even the doctrine of the Trinity, which had been for years a particular aversion of the poet's. One soon discovers, however, a radical distinction between the interpretation of Christ's deeds and life, which make up part of the "second" religion, the religion of philosophers, and that of the Crucifixion, which symbolizes reverence for what is beneath us. The latter is treated with great reserve. To expose the last sufferings of Christ would be "damnable impudence," [66] and the religion which venerates what is repulsive, hated, and to be shunned is not imparted to the pupils until the end of their course of studies. Only then does the student learn of it, "so that he may know where it is to be found if such a need should stir in him." [67] In other words, the young alumnus is not to be guided to become a Christian, but he is made aware of the general outlines of the religion of suffering; should he feel the lack of such a belief, he will know where to turn. Any unaesthetic sort of Christianity is kept at a distance. A sharp line is drawn between the life of Jesus and the sort of Christianity which focuses its gaze on "blood and wounds."

Another part of the Christian heritage, the conscience, is vindicated. The theme appears most clearly in the amazing Makaria ("the blessed one"), a woman mysteriously linked to the stars, whose ordered progress symbolizes the moral law. Like a star, man must move in "constant course around some pure center." [68] Makaria is a seer, and a saint who lives to help others. Obviously she is a Christian figure, yet there is no trace of any doctrine of sin or the Fall in the conception of her character.[69]

This extraordinary work presents an aspect of the older Goethe which shows how far he was from being simply the "old pagan king." In earlier years he had condemned Stoicism with its stress on doing without, along with Christianity, as a philosophy for slaves.[70] Yet not only is there a large Stoic element — appropriate in a book of renunciation — in the *Wanderjahre*; Goethe himself liked to repeat the Stoic *Sustine et abstine*.[71] In his *Maxims and Reflections*, as in certain late poems, one can find similar sentiments; and very different ones as well. An epigram, for instance, glorifies the early German warriors for their hatred of Christianity; it attacks Charlemagne's Christianizing activities, praises Luther's translation of the Bible for its idiomatic quality, and ends with the famous lines, usually quoted out of context:

> Freiheit erwacht in jeder Brust,
> Wir protestieren all mit Lust.[72]

The anti-Western element in the German tradition played a minimal part in Goethe's thought, but like almost everything else, it is represented there. Goethe's complexities are inexhaustible, and not all the contradictions in his thought can be reconciled by an honest logic. In the second part of *Faust* still other aspects of his mind appear. The tension between neopagan and Christian (or post-Christian) is not resolved in this, his last work; but it is reduced and made managable.

In a speech of acceptance made on receiving the Nobel Prize in 1957, Albert Camus spoke of the situation of the artist as "that ceaseless oscillation from himself to others, midway between the beauty he cannot do without and the community from which he cannot tear himself." [73] The words could be applied to Goethe and to his Faust after his symbolical journey to Greece is over, for the effort to gain new land from the sea, however ill-fated and ambiguous, at least implies that the aged magician has belatedly recognized that society does after all exist. In Goethe's poem Helen is no phantom conjured up by Mephistopheles but the quintessence of the Greek spirit as well as of beauty, and as such is completely out of Mephisto's reach. Throughout the first three acts of *Faust II* she becomes increasingly more real, transcending the realm of allegory to appear, for a moment at least, as actual. The quest for Helen is the most arduous of Faust's labors, for the poet who had come to realize the "un-Greekness" of his own *Iphigenia* saw the difficulty, the near impossibility, of the search for the true antique.

This quest dominates the first three acts of *Faust II* and gives them a certain unity. It is a process of aesthetic education, and that, to Goethe and Schiller, was in itself a form of moral cultivation, as Beutler has pointed out.[74] Though Faust does not radically change — whatever happens in heaven, he is not perfectible on this earth — he has become, at the least, more mature. The experience of Greece has given him a criterion, a "possession for ever."

Even to see the shade of Helen, at the Emperor's court, is enough to inspire in Faust the irresistible desire to free her from Hades and to possess her. After having been literally stunned in his encounter with the image of Helen, Faust, still unconscious, is carried to Greece by Mephisto and Homunculus, a very Faustian bottle imp to whom we must return.

The long, amazing series of scenes which Goethe called the "Classical Walpurgis Night" — in a contrast to the lewd celebrations of the German witches on the Brocken — is devoted mainly to Faust's search for Helen and Homunculus' related endeavor to be reborn as an organic, truly living creature. Faust's quest concerns us the more: can the problematic modern man, the intellectual as rather questionable hero, find health in the sphere of ancient paganism? The beginning is auspicious: on touching Greek soil Faust recovers his strength.

Throughout this second Walpurgis Night he seeks, and finally discovers, a guide who will lead him to Helen.

In the course of the night's adventures he encounters a whole series of mythological creatures. Not all of them are beautiful or benevolent; Goethe no longer saw Greece exclusively through Winckelmann's eyes, and he had long since grown away from an "Iphigenian" view of antiquity. Like Winckelmann though, he stressed the greatness or grandeur of the ancients: "Gestalten gross, gross die Erinnerungen." [75] In another connection, he once remarked that everything great is formative or educative as soon as we really perceive it.[76] Faust begins his higher education, so to speak, in the school of the Greeks. So much does he gain in dignity and stature that the prophetess Manto can refer to him, without incongruity, as a demigod.[77]

The classical figures or gestalten are characterized by a three-dimensional genuineness. Usually, as in the *Italian Journey*, the word connotes beauty as well; thus Helen is the archetype of all beautiful women, "die Gestalt aller Gestalten." [78] The term, which serves as a leitmotiv throughout much of the action, also has overtones of shaping, reshaping, and metamorphosis when it is applied to the figure of Proteus. Thus Goethe is able to link one of his favorite scientific concepts with the idea of Hellas, just as he tied Homunculus' quest to Faust's.

While still lying in a swoon, Faust dreamed of Leda and the swan; during the Classical Walpurgis Night this vision of the begetting of Helen is repeated.[79] His search for her is not merely what the Germans call a "culture journey," still less is it only an allegory of the endeavors of the German Hellenists from Winckelmann down. Above all it is the pursuit of a beautiful woman by a man who has fallen violently in love.

In its way Homunculus' enterprise is equally impassioned. A product of the laboratory, the sprite must "die and be reborn" if he is really to live. At the end of the Walpurgis

Night the scene shifts to the shore of the Aegean: the demi-goddess Galatea is to be celebrated as the queen of love. Water appears as a symbol of death and rebirth, of fertility, and as the feminine element.[80] (Goethe's word *Lebensfeuchte* recalls the waters of life.) As the scene nears its end, the tension mounts higher and higher. Homunculus has been told to unite himself with the ocean; in ecstasy he dashes his bottle to bits at the foot of Galatea's throne; the flame within it flares up in an "erotic climax";[81] he has joined organic nature and is ready to work his way up through thousands of forms to man. The sirens sing of love: "So herrsche denn Eros, der alles begonnen!"[82]

It may seem at first that with Homunculus we have digressed far from Faust's search, and from paganism. Yet in his career as a living being, he will develop according to "eternal norms,"[83] as we are told; Faust will discover aspects of the same norms in Hellas. Fairley has argued persuasively that Goethe is not concerned with "the classics" in isolation, but only as they are linked with natural science;[84] certainly the two are tied closely together here. Another bond between the two spheres is the erotic, conveyed in Homunculus' case largely through the imagery, in Faust's, by the myth itself. There is almost nothing in the Classical Walpurgis Night of the crude sexuality of the first Walpurgis Night, and what little there is is presented comically, in connection with Mephisto's desires. The scenes do unmistakably convey, however, the central importance of sexual love, on every level of organic nature and of culture as well. It appears inextricably linked with the *élan vital* of Faust and Homunculus, and later of Faust's son Euphorion. To the extent that Christianity had opposed or repressed this element, it necessarily appeared to Goethe as a hostile force.

Helen herself appears, rather suddenly, at the beginning of the third act. In this extraordinary play within a play, one of Goethe's boldest literary experiments, he has combined elements of Euripidean drama with romantic opera, Greek myth with Germanic legend and history; the action ranges over thousands of years, and ends in a Dionysiac orgy. The first section, predominantly "Greek," is written in trimeter and classical lyric meters; in the second, which represents the union of Faust and Helen, the verse shifts significantly to modern forms; the third section is devoted to their child Euphorion, his death, Helen's return to Hades, and the collapse of the Graeco-Germanic idyl; here ancient meters mingle freely with a variety of types of rhymed verse. Form mirrors content: Goethe well described an earlier version of this act as a "classic-romantic phantasmagoria." [85]

Here Goethe's classic and pagan ideal is at its height. The relationship of Faust and Helen is the archetype, as it were, of the "fulfilled moment," a state which cannot be permanent but which the poet preserved like a sculptor in the eternity of art. Faust of course had wagered that he would never call a moment fair or wish it prolonged, but that bet was the product of a dim, Northern, indeed pathological world. It has no meaning in Hellas, where the present exists in its own right, untroubled by fears arising from the past or impatience about the future. To exist is a duty, Faust says, even though such fullness of life may endure only for a moment. He himself appears finally worthy of such an experience, as if he had undergone a metamorphosis; love of Helen has "heightened" his personality.

Above all, classical life appears as natural, actual, sound. "How true, how really existent!" Goethe had exclaimed, during the Italian journey, and more than once he made his famous contrast between the health of the classic and the illness of the romantic. In Greece the union between well-being and beauty is achieved. In such a region the boundary between gods and men is not absolute. The poetry reminds us, in tone as well as in theme, of George Meredith's "Phoebus with Admetus." "I too was in Arcadia," is the motto Goethe gave his *Italian Journey*, and in Arcadia Faust and Helen live together — briefly.

For Goethe seems to have believed that the synthesis of present and past, romantic and classic, is as fragile as it is splendid. Euphorion has the faults as well as the virtues of his parents. In his rashness he shares the fate of Icarus, and of Lord Byron, who serves as an objective correlative, a specific example of the fusion of classic and romantic. Returning to the underworld, Helen leaves her veil and garment as a talisman for Faust.[86] Santayana's witty comment —

> Helen, to be sure, leaves some relics behind, by which we may understand that the influence of Greek history, literature, and sculpture may still avail to cultivate the mind . . . Perhaps in the commonwealth he is about to found, Faust would wish to establish . . . professorships of Greek and archaeological museums . . . Faust would have won Helen in order to hand her over to Wagner —[87]

is not really adequate; the "relics" have meaning for poets as well as for pedagogues and scholars.

Helen, Euphorion, and lesser figures distinguished by special devotion are in some sense immortal; but what of persons of no sharply defined character or talent? From a moral point of view, Goethe's position is markedly aristocratic and as such unchristian. Ordinary, "faceless," beings are not real entelechies and cannot exist after death:

> Wer keinen Namen sich erwarb noch Edles will,
> Gehört den Elementen an: so fahret hin![88]

"So to the elements!" The captive Trojan girls who form the chorus are not personalities. Only the matter of which their bodies was formed is immortal; transformed, it will be shaped into trees, brooks, and vines. In a wild Dionysian dance the captives take their leave of individuality, and the act ends.

Faust's first love, Gretchen, was not one of those whose individuality could perish. Returning to the North, Faust remembers her love as his most precious experience; despite all its incomparable qualities, the ancient world finally sinks into the background, the modern prevails. Goethe was no Hölderlin; he did not dash himself endlessly against the granite walls of time and fate.

Leaping forward to the difficult, antithetical, but immensely stimulating fifth act, we encounter many intellectual tensions: Faust reaffirms his secular beliefs in magnificent lines, but is about to be projected into a Christian, or seemingly Christian, heaven; he does at last labor for others but remains as self-centered and ruthless as ever; his defiance of the allegorical figure of Care is splendid, but she has the power to blind him; and so on. As we shall see, the action shifts back and forth, to and fro, in a really Hegelian pattern. Goethe does not blink the contradictions of man's nature and the dilemmas of life. Thus Faust's treatment of Philemon and Baucis is indefensible. The old couple is touchingly portrayed,[89] but Goethe does not conceal the fact that both husband and wife are superstitious and unwilling to accept change; needless to say, this circumstance is not presented as an excuse for liquidating them.

Perhaps the best way to establish the intention of the fifth act will be to examine the action from the point of view of the tension between secular and Christian elements which informs it. What happens to the this-worldly, humanistic, more or less pagan hero? When are we to take the Christian imagery seriously, if not literally? Clearly the treatment of Mephisto and his minions in the burial scene is comic; against this we must note that the act is saturated with Biblical references, often explicit, but some less obvious, like the similarity between the deaths of Faust and Moses.[90] To put essentially the same question in different words: how is one to interpret Faust's salvation, his ascent to heaven? Goethe called the drama a tragedy; does this mean that the hero must "fall" (presumably because of *hubris*) and suffer final defeat, or merely that the action is serious, of proper magnitude, with a hero of real stature?

Turning back to the text, we find a veritable tug of war between Faust's still potent will and the forces of time and circumstance which oppose it. (Although a hundred years old, he has learned neither prudence nor circumspection. The "aesthetic education" of Greece has given him dignity and a certain nobility;[91] it has not changed his basic character.) Immediately after the killing of Philemon and Baucis,[92] Faust is attacked by four "gray sisters." Care (*Sorge*) is the only one of the four with power to harm him. Against her he passionately reasserts his faith in this world, in human knowledge, in his own dynamism:

> Dem Tüchtigen ist diese Welt nicht stumm!
> Was braucht er in die Ewigkeit zu schweifen?
> Was er erkennt, lässt sich ergreifen.
> Er wandle so den Erdentag entlang;
> Wenn Geister spuken, geh er seinen Gang,
> Im Weiterschreiten find er Qual and Glück
> Er, unbefriedigt jeden Augenblick![93]

Though Care can blind Faust, she cannot break his spirit. When Faust claims that an inner light shines in his blindness, he is not wholly deceived, for as will appear, the last scene is a vindication of the Faustian drive; with all its inevitable errors, his unquenchable dynamism appears as one aspect of the force which saves the world from falling into drab stagnation.

The amazing scene "Mountain Ravines" is devoted to the translation to heaven of the secularist Faust. Goethe has been blamed, by Santayana and others, for using Christian imagery at the climax of his non-Christian poem; and the ending of the Classical Walpurgis Night does appear more appropriate to the whole thrust of the work. There seem to be two main reasons for his choice. The first is aesthetic: "Also you will admit," he said to Eckermann, "that the ending, where the rescued soul is borne upward, was very hard to make, and that I could very easily have been lost in vagueness if I had not given a beneficially limiting form and solidity to my poetic intentions by using the sharply outlined Christian-ecclesiastical figures and ideas." [94] This is the philosophically neutral statement of the practicing poet. For "the love which came to Faust's aid from above," [95] moreover, Goethe could hardly have found a more appropriate symbol than the Madonna. In the days of hyperclassicism he had harshly rejected this symbol, but that period lay far behind. The last scene is focused on love: love is in Faust's "dark striving" and, in a loftier sense, in the penitent Gretchen as well as the Virgin. That love appears in polar forms, with the feminine seen as the higher, the object of masculine aspiration, is in harmony with Goethe's view of the world. Quite as literally as in Dante, it is love which moves the sun and the other stars. "Love" includes *élan vital*, *amor*, *amor dei*, and Christian *caritas* — and even, at the other extreme, the lust of Mephistopheles. It is close to Schiller's "joy" in his famous ode. Thus a Christian element is included in the final apotheosis of Faust. [96] It is far from being dogmatically Christian. Goethe's heaven is no place of contemplation; and remarks like his reference to "the old Lord's" — or even "old gentleman's" — right of pardon [97] show that it is very much a matter of metaphor, imagery, poetic machinery. The one great exception is precisely in the concept of love; there Goethe is serious.

In this last scene the upward movement of the action reflects and symbolizes Goethe's notion of *Steigerung* (heightening and intensification). The universe, now transparent as it were, reveals the workings of love everywhere. Even the wild waterfall and the lightning are its messengers. [98] It is the power which forms and cherishes all life:

> So ist es die allmächtige Liebe,
> Die alles bildet, alles hegt. [99]

The word *Liebe*, alone and in constantly varying combinations, sets the tone of the entire scene.[100] Here any dichotomy of Christian and pagan has been transcended. It would be absurd to affix labels; one can only say that altruism, forgiveness, "love for what is beneath us" have fused with all the other meanings and aspects of love.

There can be no neat summing up of Goethe's relation to the questions discussed in this book. One can say that he always rejected the notion of original sin; always scorned those aspects of Christianity which seemed barbarous to a loyal son of the eighteenth century; never, even at his most "mystical," looked down on this world. His sense of the order, harmony, and beauty of the universe does not align him with any particular sect. It is equally true that he could not have written works like *Iphigenia*, *The Elective Affinities*, and *Faust* or great lyrics like "Harz Journey in the Winter" or "Ilmenau" unless he had been the offspring of a Christian culture. Perhaps his phrase "decidedly a non-Christian"[101] applies to most of his career; "anti-Christian" would be far too much. That he is moved by pagan as well as Protestant currents, that he did not achieve a consistency of religious belief, makes Goethe all the more representative of the modern epoch.

Notes

Index

EDITIONS FREQUENTLY CITED

Goethe, Johann Wolfgang von. *Gedenkausgabe der Werke, Briefe und Gespräche*, ed. Ernst Beutler. 24 vols. Zurich, 1948–1954.

Heinse, Johann Jakob Wilhelm. *Sämmtliche Werke*, ed. Carl Schüddekopf and Albert Leitzmann. 10 vols. Leipzig, 1902–1925.

Herder, Johann Gottfried. *Sämmtliche Werke*, ed. Bernhard Suphan. 33 vols. Berlin, 1877–1913.

Hölderlin, Friedrich. *Sämtliche Werke*, ed. Friedrich Beissner. 6 vols. in 10. Stuttgart, 1946–1961.

Humboldt, Wilhelm von. *Gesammelte Schriften*, Section 1: *Werke*, ed. Albert Leitzmann. 9 vols. Berlin, 1903–1912.

Lessing, Gotthold Ephraim. *Sämmtliche Schriften*, 3rd ed., ed. Karl Lachmann and Franz Muncker. 23 vols. Stuttgart, 1886–1924.

Schiller, Friedrich von. *Sämtliche Werke*, ed. Eduard von der Hellen. 16 vols. Stuttgart and Berlin, 1904–1905.

Winckelmann, Johann Joachim. *Sämtliche Werke*, ed. Joseph Eiselein. 12 vols. Donauöschingen, Germany, 1825–1829.

——— *Briefe*, ed. Walther Rehm and Hans Diepolder. 4 vols. Berlin, 1952–1957.

Notes

I. Winckelmann and the Myth of Greece

1. See Camillo von Klenze, *The Interpretation of Italy in the Last Two Centuries* (Chicago, 1907).

2. See Walther Rehm, *Das Werden des Renaissancebildes in der deutschen Dichtung* (Munich, 1924).

3. See Winfried Volk, *Die Entdeckung Tahitis und das Wunschbild der seligen Insel in der deutschen Literatur* (Heidelberg, 1934). On the relation between the cult of Greece and that of Tahiti, see Henry Hatfield, *Winckelmann and His German Critics* (New York, 1943), pp. 139f.

4. See "Die Insel als Symbol in der deutschen Literatur," *Monatshefte*, 41 (1949): 239–247.

5. Johann Wolfgang Goethe, *Gedenkausgabe der Werke, Briefe und Gespräche*, ed. Ernst Beutler (Zurich, 1948–1954), XIII, 846. This edition is hereafter cited as Goethe.

6. See K. J. Obenauer, *Die Problematik des ästhetischen Menschen in der deutschen Literatur* (Munich, 1933).

7. Erich Aron, *Die deutsche Erweckung des Griechentums durch Winckelmann und Herder* (Heidelberg, 1929), pp. 42f.

8. Jefferson owned a three-volume edition of the *Storia delle Arti*. See W. B. O'Neal, *Jefferson's Fine Arts Library* (Charlottesville, Va., 1956), p. 53.

9. See Winckelmann's letter of Sept. 22, 1764, *Briefe*, ed. Walther Rehm and Hans Diepolder (Berlin, 1952–1957), III, 55f.

10. See Carl Justi, *Winckelmann und seine Zeitgenossen*, 5th ed., ed. Walther Rehm (Cologne, 1956), esp. I, 129–136, 256–264, 270–272; Winckelmann's notebooks in the Bibliothèque Nationale; and Wolfgang Schadewaldt, "Winckelmann als Exzerptor und Selbstdarsteller" in *Hellas und Hesperien* (Zurich and Stuttgart, 1960), pp. 637–657.

11. Winckelmann uses this Vergilian tag in a letter of Dec. 8, 1762, *Briefe*, II, 274.

12. On his career in Saxony and the circumstances of his conversion, see Justi, *Winckelmann und seine Zeitgenossen*, I, and more recently Werner Schultze, "Winckelmann und die Religion," *Archiv für Kulturgeschichte*, 34 (1952): 247–260.

13. See Werner Schultze's useful, compact treatment cited above, and esp. Winckelmann's letter to Francke, Jan. 28, 1764, *Briefe*, III, 14.

14. See for instance his letter to Muzel-Stosch, Feb. 10, 1764, *Briefe*, III, 16.

15. Goethe, XIII, 418. See H. Stefan Schultz, "Winckelmanns Geschichtsbild und die neuere deutsche Literatur," *Deutsche Beiträge zur geistigen Überlieferung*, 2 (1953): 57–74.

16. See Winckelmann's letters of July 6 and 12, 1754, *Briefe*, I, 141–147.

17. *Sämtliche Werke*, ed. Joseph Eiselein (Donauöschingen, Germ., 1825–1829), I, 8. This edition is hereafter cited as Winckelmann.

18. See Humphrey Trevelyan, *The Popular Background to Goethe's Hellenism* (London, 1934), esp. pp. x f, 5f, 47, 61.

19. See Hatfield, *Winckelmann and His German Critics*, pp. 3–5.

20. On Winckelmann's position in the tradition of humanism, Horst Rüdiger, *Wesen und Wandlung des Humanismus* (Hamburg, 1937), pp. 156–191, is especially enlightening.

21. Horace, *Ars Poetica*, l. 268: "Pore over the Greek models night and day."

22. Winckelmann, I, 257f.

23. Winckelmann did, however, see the Doric temple of Poseidon at Paestum and reacted "properly" to the authentic work. Goethe, when he viewed the same temple, initially felt depressed, as he frankly admitted in his *Italian Journey* (Goethe, XI, 240).

24. See the essay "Winckelmann," especially the sections "Antikes" and "Heidnisches" (Goethe, XIII, 416–420).

25. See Wolfgang Schadewaldt, *Winckelmann und Homer* (Leipzig, 1941).

26. Winckelmann, V, 347f.

27. *Three Philosophical Poets* (Cambridge, Mass., 1910), p. 175.

28. Letter of Dec. 8, 1762, *Briefe*, II, 276.

29. Herder, *Sämmtliche Werke*, ed. Bernhard Suphan (Berlin, 1877–1913), VIII, 450–453. This edition is hereafter cited as Herder.

30. See Hans Zeller's keen analysis in *Winckelmanns Beschreibung des Apollo im Belvedere* (Zurich, 1955).

31. Winckelmann, I, 30f.

32. *Ibid.*, pp. 36f.

33. Cf. Walther Rehm, *Götterstille und Göttertrauer* (Bern, 1951), pp. 101–182.

34. Long before Nietzsche, Friedrich Schlegel distinguished three elements in Sophoclean drama: Apollonian, Dionysiac, and Minervan. (See Jakob Minor, *Friedrich Schlegel, 1794–1802: Seine prosaischen Jugendschriften*, Vienna, 1882, I, 140.) This casts doubt on E. M. Butler's claim that Heine was the discoverer of the Dionysian element; see *The Tyranny of Greece over Germany* (Cambridge, Eng., 1935), pp. 294, 299, 300, 307.

35. Winckelmann, I, 207.

36. *Ibid.*, p. 16.

37. Letter of Jan. 27, 1756, *Briefe*, I, 199f.

38. See *ibid.*, p. 201.

39. *Ibid.*, p. 27 (preface).

40. Winckelmann, IV, 56.

41. Winckelmann, I, 243.

42. Winckelmann, IV, 60.

43. See his letter of Jan. 26, 1762, *Briefe*, III, 14.

44. Cf. Hildegard Jersch, *Untersuchungen zum Stile Winckelmanns* (Calw, Germ., 1939), esp. p. 13.

45. See *The Tyranny of Greece*, pp. 262–264.

46. Justi, *Winckelmann und seine Zeitgenossen*, I, 144.

47. See especially Justi, I, 262.

48. Letter of June 24, 1759, *Briefe*, II, 8.

49. See *Briefe*, I, 284, and III, 169; cf. Schadewaldt, *Winckelmann und Homer*, pp. 19f. Other anti-Christian sentiments: *Briefe*, I, 151; II, 232f; III, 14.

50. Undoubtedly Winckelmann's cult of friendship has homosexual implications, but it cannot be reduced to its pathological element alone.

51. Letter of Sept. 17, 1754, *Briefe*, I, 151; see also II, 232f.

52. Winckelmann, I, 253.

53. See *Briefe*, I, 22, and II, 366; also Horst Rüdiger, *Winckelmann und Italien* (Krefeld, Germ., 1956).

54. Letter of March 10, 1766, *Briefe*, III, 169.

55. Cf. Horst Rüdiger, "Winckelmanns Persönlichkeit," *Der Deutschunterricht*, 8 (1956): 66–67.

56. The phrase "web of allegories" is translated from Fritz Strich's *Die Mythologie in der deutschen Literatur von Klopstock bis Wagner* (Halle, 1910), I, 107. Strich points out however that Winckelmann did show that Hellenic art drew strength from Greek myths.

57. See the *Versuch einer Allegorie*, 1766, especially its eleventh chapter (Winckelmann, IX, 246–270).

58. For a different point of view see Rudolf Sühnel, *Die Götter Griechenlands in der deutschen Klassik* (Würzburg, 1935), pp. 7f.

59. See E. M. Wilkinson, "Schiller's Concept of *Schein*," *German Quarterly*, 28 (1955): 219–227.

60. Winckelmann, I, 227.

61. *Ibid.*, p. 229.

62. *Ibid.*, p. 231.

63. *Ibid.*, p. 232.

64. See Hans Hafen, *Studien zur Geschichte der deutschen Prosa im 18. Jahrhundert* (St. Gall, Switz., 1952), pp. 51–57; also Hanna Koch, *Johann Joachim Winckelmann: Sprache und Kunstwerk* (Berlin, 1957).

65. Rainer Maria Rilke, *Sämtliche Werke*, ed. Ernst Zinn (Wiesbaden, 1955–1961), I, 557. C. F. MacIntyre (*Rainer Maria Rilke, Selected Poems*, University of California Press, Berkeley and Los Angeles, 1957) has translated it thus:

Archaic Torso of Apollo

Never will we know his fabulous head
where the eyes' apples slowly ripened. Yet
his torso glows: a candelabrum set
before his gaze which is pushed back and hid,

restrained and shining. Else the curving breast
could not thus blind you nor through the soft turn
of the loins could this smile easily have passed
into the bright groins where the genitals burned.

Else stood this stone a fragment and defaced,
with lucent body from the shoulders falling,
too short, not gleaming like a lion's fell;

nor would this star have shaken the shackles off,
bursting with light, until there is no place
that does not see you. You must change your life.

66. Letter of Aug. 18, 1759, *Briefe*, II, 23.

67. See I. Feuerlicht, "Vom Wesen der deutschen Idylle," *Germanic Review*, 22 (1947): esp. pp. 210–212.

68. Zeller, *Winckelmanns Beschreibung*, p. 80, speaks of Goethe's lines as an "echo." No conscious echoing need be assumed.

69. Goethe, I, 314:

He will walk as with feet of flowers
Over the mire of Deucalion's flood,
Slaying Python, light, great, Pythian Apollo.

70. Winckelmann, V, 221.

71. Winckelmann, I, 10.

72. *Ibid.*, p. 11.

73. See Diderot's "Salon de 1765," *Oeuvres Complètes* (Paris, 1875–1877), x, 417.

74. Goethe, VIII, 502.

75. See *American Journal of Archaeology*, 59 (1955): 116.

76. *Briefe*, II, 273, 283.

77. See Karl Borinski, *Die Antike in Poetik und Kunsttheorie* (Leipzig, 1914–1924), II, 205.

78. Goethe, XI, 166; see Walter Rehm, *Griechentum und Goethezeit* (Bern, 1952), p. 132.

79. Goethe, XXII, 642.

80. Winckelmann, VI, 22f.

81. Winckelmann, III, 61.

82. *Ibid.*

83. Winckelmann, V, 236f.
84. Winckelmann, VI, 365.
85. Goethe, I, 225f: "Eagerly the pilgrim wanders on: And will he find the saint? Hear and see the man who performed the miracles? No. Time disposed of him; you find only remains — his skull, a few of his bones preserved. All of us who seek Italy are pilgrims; we revere only scattered bones, credulously and happily."
86. *Briefe*, III, 302.
87. See Franz Schultz, *Klassik und Romantik der Deutschen*, I (Stuttgart, 1935), 65–138.

II. The Ancient Image of Death: Lessing and His Impact

1. Cf. Rehm, *Götterstille und Göttertrauer*, p. 191.
2. *Sämmtliche Schriften*, 3rd ed., ed. Karl Lachmann and Franz Muncker (Stuttgart, 1886–1924), XVIII, 116, letter to J. J. Eschenburg, Oct. 26, 1774. This edition is hereafter cited as Lessing.
3. In *Nathan the Wise*, the heroine symbolically describes the highly emotional Christianity of the fanatic Daja as a flower whose heavy, bittersweet fragrance makes her feel stupified and giddy. Lessing, III, 75.
4. See especially Gottfried Fittbogen, *Die Religion Lessings* (Leipzig, 1923), and Hans Leisegang, *Lessings Weltanschauung* (Leipzig, 1931).
5. See Heinrich Schneider's article "Lessing und Freund Hain" in his *Lessing* (Salzburg, 1950), pp. 245–248.
6. See Lessing's eighth "Literaturbrief," Lessing, VIII, 18.
7. Lessing, IX, 14.
8. Hatfield, *Winckelmann and His German Critics*, pp. 51–53.
9. Lessing, IX, 13.
10. *Ibid.*, p. 9.
11. Lessing, II, 373.
12. Lessing, XVII, 270; letter to Mendelssohn, Nov. 5, 1768.
13. For Lessing's side of the argument, see his *Antiquarische Briefe* (1768–1769). On Klotz, see Hatfield, *Winckelmann and His German Critics*, pp. 60–72.
14. Winckelmann, I, 162f.
15. Winckelmann, IX, 138.
16. Some of the winged figures which Lessing thought were genii are now held to be cupids. See *Lessings Werke*, ed. Julius Petersen and Waldemar von Olshausen (Berlin and Leipzig, n.d.), *Anmerkungen*, pp. 743f.
17. See Lessing, XI, 55.
18. See *Dichtung und Wahrheit* (Goethe, X, 348).
19. *Ibid.*, p. 349.

20. Herder composed two versions of this essay, published in 1774 and 1786 respectively.

21. Herder, XV, 431. As in Winckelmann, the image of the sea is linked with the idea of peace.

22. *Ibid.*, pp. 441f.

23. *Ibid.*, pp. 457, 481.

24. *Ibid.*, pp. 481–483.

25. Herder, V, 667–671.

26. Herder, XXVIII, 135f. See also "Die Liebe Im Todtenreiche," XXIX, 124.

27. See Harald Henry, *Herder und Lessing* (Würzburg, 1941), p. 94.

28. See below, Chap. X.

29. Schiller, *Sämtliche Werke*, ed. Eduard von der Hellen (Stuttgart and Berlin, 1904–1905), I, 158 (this edition is hereafter cited as Schiller):

> In those days no hideous skeleton came
> To the bed of the dying man. A kiss
> Took the last remnant of life from his lips,
> A spirit lowered his torch. The grandchild of a mortal held
> Even the stern scales of judgment in Orcus,
> And the soulful lament of the Thracian [Orpheus]
> Moved the Furies to pity.

30. *Ibid.*, p. 91: "He does indeed look charming with his extinguished torch;/But, gentlemen, death really isn't so aesthetic."

31. *Ibid.*, p. 258.

32. Schiller, II, 93.

33. Goethe, III, 233: "The touching image of death does not appear as a terror to the sage nor as the end to the believer. It urges the former back into life and teaches him to act; it strengthens the latter's hope, amid troubles, of future salvation. For both of them death is transformed to life."

34. Novalis, *Schriften*, ed. Paul Kluckhohn (Leipzig, c. 1929), I, 59–64. This edition is hereafter cited as Novalis.

35. Novalis, I, 60: "It was Death, who interrupted this banquet, with fear and sorrow and tears."

36. *Ibid.*: "A gentle youth puts out the light and is at rest — the ending becomes gentle, like the sounding of the harp."

37. *Ibid.*, p. 64: "Only *one* night of rapture — one eternal poem — and the sun of us all is God's countenance."

38. See Erich Schmidt, *Lessing*, 3rd. ed. (Berlin, 1909), I, 681.

39. Lenau, *Sämtliche Werke und Briefe*, ed. Eduard Castle, I (1910), 440–442.

40. Eichendorff, *Werke und Schriften*, I (Stuttgart, [1957]), 270f.

41. Heine, *Sämtliche Werke*, ed. Ernst Elster, II, 102: "Good is

sleep, death is better — indeed, the best would be, never to have been born."

III. Antiquity and Reason: Wieland

1. See Hatfield, *Winckelmann and His German Critics*, pp. 118–121, for Wieland's reservations.
2. Goethe, XII, 704.
3. See Friedrich Sengle's splendid biography, *Christoph Martin Wieland* (Stuttgart, 1949).
4. See the twelfth "Literaturbrief," Lessing, VIII, 26f.
5. On *Anti-Ovid* see Emil Ermatinger, *Die Weltanschauung des jungen Wieland* (Frauenfeld, Switz., 1907), p. 69.
6. Cf. the editions of 1773 and 1794.
7. Sengle, *Christoph Martin Wieland*, pp. 20f.
8. See Wieland's letter to Zimmerman, March 27, 1759, *Ausgewählte Briefe* (Zurich, 1815), I, 348.
9. See for example *Oberon*, Canto VII, stanza 15.
10. See especially Goethe's *Götter, Helden und Wieland*.
11. Cf. Friedrich Schlegel's essay "On Diotima," below, Chap. X.
12. See M. G. Bach, *Wieland's Attitude toward Woman and Her Cultural and Social Relations* (New York, 1922), p. 93.
13. *Ibid.*, pp. 79–89.
14. Cf. Emil Staiger in *Wieland: Vier Biberacher Vorträge 1953* (Wiesbaden, 1954), p. 50.
15. See Bruno Snell in *Die geistige Welt*, 2 (1947), 1f (cited by Sengle, *Christoph Martin Wieland*, p. 192).
16. *Wieland*, p. 51.
17. See Ermatinger, *Die Weltanschauung des jungen Wieland*, pp. 108–115; Charles Elson, *Wieland and Shaftesbury* (New York, 1913); and Herbert Grudzinski, *Shaftesburys Einfluss auf C. M. Wieland* (Stuttgart, 1913).
18. "Plan einer Akademie" (1758).
19. Lessing, VIII, 27.
20. See Otto Freise, *Die drei Fassungen von Wielands "Agathon"* (Göttingen, 1910), p. 94, but compare Erich Gross, *C. M. Wielands "Geschichte des Agathon"* (Berlin, 1930), p. 138.
21. Melitta Gerhard points out that in *Agathon* the validity of the moral norm is itself questioned. See her *Der deutsche Entwicklungsroman bis Goethes Wilhelm Meister* (Halle, 1926), p. 105; cf. p. 109.
22. Wieland, *Werke* (Berlin, n. d.), IV, 42: "The delightful philosophy which happily enjoys what nature and fate have granted us and gladly does without the rest, which prefers to see the things of this world in a happy light, is submissive to fate, and does not want to know what Zeus in his kindness hid from us in enigmatic night . . .

does not always *speak* of virtue nor *wax fervent* when speaking of it, but practices it, without reward, as a matter of taste."

23. In old age Wieland bought a "Sabine farm" at Ossmannstedt near Weimar but found snakes even in this Horatian paradise. See Sengle, *Christoph Martin Wieland*, pp. 493–502, 515–517.

24. Wieland's *Alceste* (1773) is paradoxically one of his most "Christian" works.

25. See *Sämmtliche Werke* (Vienna, 1812), XXVIII, 172. Wieland achieves a double perspective in this novel by often employing the point of view of Peregrinus' searching critic Lucian. Both Lucian and the hero appear sincere but one-sided; the two views correct each other. See also Lucian's *Sämtliche Werke*, trans. C. M. Wieland, III, (Leipzig, 1788), 45–110.

26. Wieland, *Sämmtliche Werke*, XXVII, 241.

27. The motif of the secret society occurs frequently in eighteenth-century and romantic German novels. See Marianne Thalmann, *Der Trivialroman des achtzehnten Jahrhunderts* (Berlin, 1923).

28. See Sengle, *Christoph Martin Wieland*, p. 488.

29. Wieland, *Werke* (Leipzig, 1799), XXXII, 376.

30. *Ibid.*, p. 382.

31. *Ibid.*, p. 385.

32. *Ibid.*, pp. 423f.

33. *Ibid.*, pp. 440, 445.

34. *Ibid.*, pp. 442, 453f.

35. *Ibid.*, p. 462.

36. *Ibid.*, pp. 463f.

37. See H. P. H. Teesing, "Wieland's Verhältnis zur Aufklärung im *Agathodämon*," *Neophilologus*, 21 (1935–1936): 23–35, 105–116.

38. Goethe, XII, 694.

39. Cf. Fritz Martini in *Festschrift für Kluckhohn und Schneider* (Tübingen, 1948), pp. 264f.

40. Goethe, XII, 703.

IV. The Greeks and History: Herder

1. See Eichendorff, *Der deutsche Roman des achtzehnten Jahrhunderts* (Leipzig, 1851), p. 239.

2. See Alexander Gillies, *Herder*, pp. 113f.

3. Herder, VIII, 441.

4. Herder, III, 187.

5. Cf. Herder, II, 140.

6. See Rehm, *Griechentum und Goethezeit*, pp. 104f.

7. Herder, I, 285–294.

8. *Ibid.*, p. 295.

9. Herder, II, 113.

10. *Ibid.*, pp. 114f.
11. *Ibid.*, p. 145.
12. Herder, I, 361f.
13. Herder does not, of course, condemn all literature in Romance languages.
14. Herder, III, 272f.
15. Herder, I, 426f. See also Strich, *Die Mythologie in der deutschen Literatur*, and Richard Chase, *Quest for Myth* (Baton Rouge, La., [1949]).
16. Herder, I, 440.
17. *Ibid.*, p. 444.
18. Herder, IV, 356–359.
19. *Ibid.*, p. 380.
20. Herder, III, 56f.
21. *Ibid.*, pp. 59f.
22. See Strich, *Die Mythologie in der deutschen Literatur*, I, 9, n.1.
23. Herder, III, 59.
24. *Ibid.*, p. 90.
25. *Ibid.*, pp. 242f, quoting Klotz.
26. Herder, III, 254.
27. *Ibid.*, p. 248.
28. *Ibid.*, p. 256.
29. Herder, XXIX, 303f.
30. Cf. *Die Mythologie in der deutschen Literatur*, I, 143f.
31. Herder, XVII, 376f.
32. Strich, *Die Mythologie in der deutschen Literatur*, I, 152f.
33. See the essay "Iduna," Herder, XVIII, 483–502.
34. See Robert R. Ergang, *Herder and the Foundations of German Nationalism* (New York, 1931); Carleton J. H. Hayes, *Essays on Nationalism* (New York, 1926); and Friedrich Meinecke, *Die Entstehung des Historismus*, 3rd. ed. (Munich, 1959).
35. See Rehm, *Griechentum und Goethezeit*, chap. iv; Hatfield, *Winckelmann and His German Critics*, chap. vi; Erich Aron, *Die Erweckung des Griechentums durch Winckelmann und Herder* (Heidelberg, 1929); A. E. Berger, *Der junge Herder und Winckelmann* (Halle, 1903); and Charlotte Ephraim, *Wandel des Griechenbilds im achtzehnten Jahrhundert* (Bern and Leipzig, 1936).
36. See Rudolf Haym, *Herder* (Berlin, 1954), I, 375; *Briefe an J. H. Merck* (Darmstadt, 1835), p. 4.
37. Herder, VIII, 17f.
38. *Ibid.*, pp. 13f.
39. *Ibid.*, pp. 35f, 53.
40. Herder, VIII, 45f. Cf. Winckelmann, IV, 245–301.
41. Herder, VIII, 65.
42. *Ibid.*, p. 23 (Herder's emphasis).

43. *Ibid.*, p. 24.
44. *Ibid.*, p. 26.
45. *Ibid.*, p. 63.
46. *Ibid.*, p. 62.
47. *Ibid.*, p. 63.
48. Herder, III, 297f.
49. Herder, IV, 349.
50. Herder, VIII, 485–558.
51. *Ibid.*, pp. 509f.
52. Cf. Herder, III, 297f, and Heinrich Düntzer, *Herders Reise nach Italien* (Giessen, 1859).
53. R. T. Clark in his *Herder: His Life and Thought* (Berkeley, 1955) well stresses the Enlightenment element.
54. Herder, VIII, 358.
55. *Ibid.*, p. 370.
56. *Ibid.*, p. 371f.
57. *Ibid.*, p. 373f.
58. *Ibid.*, p. 377.
59. *Ibid.*, p. 373.
60. *Ibid.*, p. 378.
61. *Ibid.*, pp. 443, 447. Cf. Schiller's poem "Die Antike an den nordischen Wanderer," Schiller, I, 151.
62. Herder, VIII, 481. Even if the variant *Heldenruhe* is accepted instead of *Heldenruhm* ("heroic peace" rather than "heroic glory"), the general drift of the passage remains the same.
63. Herder, VIII, 476f.
64. *Ibid.*, pp. 482f.
65. Cf. Herder, XIV, 147–149.
66. *Ibid.*, p. 91.
67. *Ibid.*, p. 108.
68. *Ibid.*, p. 105; see also pp. 99f, 108.
69. *Ibid.*, pp. 104f.
70. *Ibid.*, p. 104.
71. Düntzer, *Herders Reise nach Italien*, p. 81, letter of Sept. 17, 1788.
72. *Ibid.*, p. 117.
73. *Ibid.*, p. 189.
74. See Clark, *Herder*, pp. 354f.
75. Düntzer, *Herders Reise nach Italien*, pp. 220f, 225f.
76. *Ibid.*, p. 237.
77. *Ibid.*, p. 247, letter of Feb. 10, 1789.
78. See Clark, *Herder*, p. 356.
79. Herder, XXIX, 571: "Thus thanks to you, you divine Medusas, who have taught me that you are Medusas. Thanks to you, you dead arts, cold Muses, decayed walls, grave of vanity. If ever I have strewn

incense to the deceitful, the marble bosom, instead of to true hearts, then take from me the last toll here below, the toll of remorse, and let me go in peace."

80. *Ibid.*, p. 572: "Near by I saw thee, may name thee too, Thou inhumane, ancient and modern Rome! But who will not already know thee by name, thou Capitol and thou, St. Peter's Cathedral? Thou pit, whence, to burn the earth, an ancient and modern stream flowed out — once inhabited by warriors and senators, now inhabited by priests and monsignori."

81. Herder, XVII, 138.
82. *Ibid.*, pp. 150f.
83. *Ibid.*, pp. 161–170.
84. *Ibid.*, pp. 289f.
85. Herder, XVIII, 72–77.
86. *Ibid.*, pp. 77–80.
87. *Ibid.*, p. 80.
88. See *Faust*, ll. 575–579, Goethe, V, 161.
89. Herder, XVIII, 80f.
90. *Ibid.*, pp. 84f.
91. *Ibid.*, pp. 296, 301f.
92. See Goethe's letter to J. G. and Caroline Herder, June 7, 1793, Goethe, XIX, 213.
93. Cf. Rehm, *Griechentum und Goethezeit*, pp. 111–113.
94. Haym, *Herder*, II, 659, cites relevant letters of Schiller, Goethe, and Körner.
95. See Haym, *Herder*, II, 665, and Goethe's letter to Knebel, Jan. 1, 1791, Goethe, XIX, 176.
96. See Goethe, XII, 625f, and Haym, *Herder*, II, 673.

Chapter V. *Prometheus: Young Goethe*

1. Goethe, V, 200: "Where one foot on the treadle moves a thousand threads, the shuttles fly back and forth; the threads flow unseen; one move makes a thousand linkages."
2. Goethe, XVIII, 134; letter of Feb. 20, 1770.
3. Possibly there was only one visit; see Humphrey Trevelyan, *Goethe and the Greeks* (Cambridge, Eng., 1941), p. 38, n. 2.
4. Goethe, X, 548.
5. See his letter of October [?], 1771, Goethe, XVIII, 168.
6. Goethe, X, 550.
7. Goethe, IV, 388.
8. Goethe, I, 384.
9. Cf. Wolfgang Schadewaldt, *Hellas und Hesperien* (Zurich and Stuttgart, 1960), pp. 682f.

10. Goethe, XIII, 38f.

11. Goethe, X, 700.

12. *Ibid.*, pp. 194f:

> You are diligent and lazy,
> Cruel and kind
> Generous and niggardly:
> You are like all your brothers in fate,
> Like the animals and the gods.

13. *Ibid.*, pp. 195–197.

14. *Ibid.*, p. 125. Cf. Oskar Walzel, *Das Prometheussymbol von Shaftesbury zu Goethe*, Munich, 1932.

15. Goethe, XIII, 26.

16. Goethe, IV, 190: "To the gods' lot fell — permanence/And might, and wisdom and love."

17. See esp. *ibid.*, p. 206.

18. *Ibid.*, p. 213.

19. *Ibid.*, p. 124.

20. Of course much of Wieland's work, like his pedagogical novel *Agathon*, is not primarily indebted to the French tradition.

21. Wieland, *Sämmtliche Werke*, XXVI, 3–50.

22. This essay originally appeared in *Der teutsche Merkur* of 1773.

23. Goethe, IV, 216.

24. *Ibid.*, p. 220.

25. *Ibid.*, p. 223, emphasis added.

26. Here Goethe came as close to Heinse as he ever did; but where Heinse was utterly serious, Goethe was only half in earnest.

27. Goethe, IV, 225.

28. *Ibid.*

29. Needless to say, the caricature is less than just to Wieland, who very soon forgave Goethe for perpetrating it. A few years later, in *Iphigenia in Tauris*, Goethe himself committed Wieland's "offense" of Christianizing Greek myth.

30. See Thomas Mann's perceptive comments on Goethe's "laxness" in *The Beloved Returns*, and Paul Kluckhohn, *Die Auffassung der Liebe in der Literatur des achtzehnten Jahrhunderts und in der deutschen Romantik* (Halle, 1931), pp. 273–283.

31. Goethe, VI, 26.

32. Goethe, VII, 251.

33. Goethe's comment is cited in H. G. Gräf, *Goethe über seine Dichtungen* (Frankfurt am Main, 1901–1914), pt. I, vol. II, pp. 922f.

34. Cf. also Goethe's notes for a very earthy farce "Hans Wurst's Wedding," Goethe, IV, 247–259.

35. See in *Faust* (Goethe, V, 159), and the lyric "Zueignung" (Goethe, I, 11).

36. *Ibid.*, p. 322.

37. Goethe's debt to the Bible, like his reverence for it, was an enormous one; but that is indeed another matter.

38. Although Goethe included a graceful tribute to the world of Pietism in the sixth book of *Wilhelm Meister's Apprenticeship*, it is very clear that the "Beautiful Soul" there described is far from realizing the idea of genuine humanity which the novel presents.

39. Goethe, IV, 129.

40. *Ibid.*, p. 127.

41. See Goethe, XIII, 18.

42. Goethe, XIV, 157. Winckelmann was very fond of Gessner's work; even in Italy, his taste, like his vision of Greek life, was not completely free of the rococo element.

43. Goethe, XIII, 53, emphasis added. For Heinse's reaction to Rubens see Chap. VI.

44. On Goethe's relation to Pindar, see esp. Trevelyan, *Goethe and the Greeks*, pp. 53–56.

45. Goethe, XVIII, 173f, letter of July 10 [?], 1772. The same images occur in a famous passage in *Egmont* (Goethe, VI, 42f), but there the emphasis is on the power of fate; the role of human mastery is sharply restricted.

46. See the excellent essay by Johannes Urzidil, "Goethe and Art," *Germanic Review*, 24 (1949): 184–199.

47. Goethe, XIII, 21.

48. See especially J. M. R. Lenz, *Amerkungen über das Theater*, 1774.

VI. *Islands and Idyls: Heinse, Müller, and Forster*

1. See K. D. Jessen, *Heinses Stellung zur bildenden Kunst und ihrer Ästhetik* (Berlin, 1901), p. 16.

2. See Walther Brecht, *Heinse und der ästhetische Immoralismus* (Berlin, 1911), *passim*.

3. Quoted by Jessen, *Heinses Stellung*, p. vii.

4. See Jessen, *Heinses Stellung*, p. ix f; Walther Rehm, *Das Werden des Renaissancebildes in der deutschen Dichtung* (Munich, 1924); Brecht, *Heinse*, pp. 56, 61, 66; and Hans Nehrkorn, *Wilhelm Heinse und sein Einfluss auf die Romantik* (Goslar, 1904).

5. On Heinse's descriptions of works of art see Wilhelm Waetzoldt, *Deutsche Kunsthistoriker von Sandrart bis zu Rumohr* (Leipzig, 1921), pp. 117–131; Christian Schuster, *The Work of Art in German Fiction* (Philadelphia, 1948), pp. 55–65.

6. Cf. Israel Stamm, "The Empirical Character of *Sturm und Drang*," *Germanic Review*, 18 (1943): 11–23.

7. Heinse, *Sämmtliche Werke*, ed. Carl Schüddekopf and Albert

Leitzmann (Leipzig, 1902–1925), IX, 283. This edition is hereafter cited as Heinse.

8. *Ibid.*, pp. 298f.
9. *Ibid.*, p. 335.
10. *Ibid.*, p. 333.
11. *Ibid.*, p. 319.
12. *Ibid.*, p. 340.
13. *Ibid.*, p. 341. Compare Goethe's defense of Rubens, Chap. V.
14. Rubens is still mentioned with respect, however.
15. Heinse, VII, 56; cf. *ibid.*, pp. 65, 97.
16. *Ibid.*, p. 197.
17. *Ibid.*, pp. 115f. Describing Raphael's Madonna in Fuligno, he notes, quite characteristically: "How attractively the breasts swell out beneath the decorous red garment." (VII, 116; cf. pp. 81f.)
18. *Ibid.*, p. 321.
19. *Ibid.*, p. 219.
20. Heinse, IV, 402.
21. Heinse, VII, 231f.
22. *Ibid.*, p. 65.
23. *Ibid.*, p. 68.
24. *Ibid.*, p. 88.
25. *Ibid.*, pp. 135, 245.
26. The term "aesthetic immoralism" is the leitmotiv of Brecht's illuminating treatment of Heinse.
27. Heinse, IV, 122; III, 395.
28. Heinse, V, 197; cf. IV, 109.
29. Heinse, IV, 111.
30. *Ibid.*, pp. 288f.
31. *Ibid.*, p. 40.
32. *Ibid.*, pp. 262f, 392f.
33. *Ibid.*, p. 261.
34. *Ibid.*, p. 175.
35. *Ibid.*, p. 394.
36. *Ibid.*, p. 250.
37. *Ibid.*, p. 254.
38. *Ibid.*, p. 392.
39. *Ibid.*, p. 397.
40. See Klinger, *Dramatische Jugendwerke* (Leipzig, 1912–1913), ed. Hans Berendt and Kurt Wolff, II, 155, 225. The relatively pagan Moors in this drama enjoy a "natural," happy, erotic life, in contrast to most of the Christians (II, 231).
41. *Ibid.*, I, xliv.
42. Quoted by Jessen, *Heinses Stellung*, p. 220, from Heinse's *Nachlass*.

43. Heinse, IV, 185.

44. In one of Müller's idyls it is explicitly stated that the faun is really an "honest wine grower." *Idyllen*, ed. O. Heuer (Leipzig, 1914), II, 89. This edition is hereafter cited as *Idyllen*. Neither Müller's *Niobe* nor his *Iphigenie* is relevant to this study.

45. Cf. Willy Oeser, *Maler Müller* (Mannheim, 1928), pp. 19f.

46. See Werner Schaefer, *Maler Müllers Bedeutung* (Leipzig, c. 1928), p. 23.

47. *Idyllen*, I, 211.

48. *Idyllen*, II, 94f.

49. *Idyllen*, I, 279, 281; see also his poem "Dithyrambe" in the anthology *Sturm und Drang* (Berlin, [etc.], n.d.), IV, 11f.

50. *Idyllen*, I, 212.

51. See Andreas Müller, *Landschaftserlebnis und Landschaftsbild* (Hechingen, Germ., 1955), pp. 97–100.

52. See Alewyn's article "Mahler Müller und die heidnische Landschaft," *Neue Schweizer Rundschau*, 21 (1928): 217–219.

53. Cf. Schuster, *The Work of Art in German Literature*, pp. 103–106.

54. In *Prosaische Jugendschriften*, ed. Jacob Minor (Vienna, 1882), II, 119–139, esp. pp. 122f, 134.

55. Goethe, III, 241f. See Paul Zincke, *Georg Forsters Bildnis im Wandel der Zeiten* (Reichenberg in Bohemia, 1925), p. xix.

56. Forster's *A Voyage round the World* (London, 1777), II, 112.

57. *Ibid.*, I, 386, 303.

58. *Ibid.*, I, 263, 265.

59. *Ibid.*, I, 296.

60. *Ibid.*, I, 265.

61. *Ibid.*, II, 110f.

62. *Ibid.*, I, 256.

63. *Ibid.*, I, 269f, 289.

64. *Ibid.*, I, 270.

65. *Sämtliche Schriften* (Leipzig, 1843), IV, 235f.

66. *Voyage*, II, 54.

67. Stolberg's attack, originally published in the *Deutsches Museum*, is reprinted in part in R. H. Thomas' anthology *The Classical Ideal in German Literature* (Cambridge, Eng., 1939), pp. 113f.

68. See Forster's *Ausgewählte Kleine Schriften*, ed. Albert Leitzmann, in *Deutsche Literaturdenkmale*, XLVI–XLVII, 90.

69. *Ibid.*, p. 91.

70. *Ibid.*, p. 92.

71. *Sämtliche Schriften*, V, 236.

72. *Ibid.*, pp. 236f.

73. *Ibid.*, p. 246.

74. See Volk's *Die Entdeckung Tahitis.*
75. This poem is based on Bougainville's account. See Zachariae's footnotes to his own text and Volk, *Die Entdeckung Tahitis*, p. 71.
76. *Poetische Schriften* (Reutlingen, 1778), IV, 163. In contrast, F. L. Stolberg's "The Island" (*Gesammelte Schriften*, III, Hamburg, 1827, pp. 89f) is completely devoid of pagan elements.
77. *Poetische Schriften*, IV, 162.
78. *Ibid.*, pp. 171–174.
79. *The Island* (London, 1823), p. 25.
80. *Voyage*, II, 67.
81. *Typee* (Boston, 1922), pp. 266, 271.
82. *Ibid.*, p. 287, and after.
83. Melville may well have known Winckelmann's *History of Ancient Art* in the translation of G. Henry Lodge (Boston, 1849–1873). See Merton M. Sealts, Jr., *Melville's Reading* (Cambridge, Mass., 1950), pp. 103f. Neither Leon Howard's biography nor Jay Leyda's *The Melville Log* mentions Forster, however.

VII. Iphigenia and Italy: Goethe

1. Weimar Edition, section 3, vol. I, p. 290.
2. Goethe, I, 111: "Do you know the house? Its roof rests upon columns; the hall gleams, the room is radiant; and marble statues stand . . ."
3. See Fairley's *A Study of Goethe* (Oxford, 1947), esp. pp. 97–120.
4. See "Beherzigung," Goethe, II, 45.
5. *Ibid.*, p. 310: "If, Father of Love, there is sound on thy harp which his ear can make out, make his heart live again!"
6. *Ibid.*, p. 325:

> Only man alone
> Can perform the impossible:
> He distinguishes
> Chooses and judges.

7. Goethe, III, 278: "The man who overcomes himself can liberate himself from the power which confines all beings."
8. *Ibid.*, p. 275: "The cross stands, densely entwined by roses. Who has linked roses and the cross?" Cf. p. 281. See also Karl Viëtor, *Goethe* (Bern, 1949), pp. 83f.
9. See Geneviève Bianquis, *Etude sur deux fragments d'un poème de Goethe* (Nancy, 1926), pp. 14f. Professor Bianquis considers the links of the poem to Free Masonry, Rosicrucianism, and the religious thought of Lessing and Herder, but stresses especially its analogy to the ideas of L. C. de Saint Martin.
10. Goethe, XXIV, 770f.

11. Schiller's undated letter to C. G. Körner of early January 1802, quoted in Goethe, XXII, 306.

12. Goethe, XI, 116.

13. Goethe, VI, 148: "Seeking the land of the Greeks with my soul."

14. *Ibid.*, p. 198: "Preserve me, and preserve your image in my soul!"

15. See especially his *Geist der Goethezeit* (Leipzig, 1923–1957).

16. Cf. Franz Schultz, *Klassik und Romantik der Deutschen*, I (Stuttgart, 1935), 95–97, on *Stille* in Winckelmann and others.

17. Goethe, VI, 198f: "Let the race of men fear the gods! They hold power in timeless hands, and can use it as they see fit! Let the man whom ever they raised up fear them doubly! On cliffs and clouds chairs have been placed ready, around golden tables."

18. *Ibid.*, p. 199: "But they, they linger, eternally feasting at golden tables."

19. Goethe, XXIV, 405f.

20. Goethe, II, 295.

21. See Christoph Schrempf, *Goethes Lebensanschauung* (Stuttgart, 1905–1907), p. 239.

22. Goethe, VI, 242.

23. To Charlotte von Stein, June 8, 1787, Goethe, XIX, 84.

24. *Ibid.*, p. 29.

25. To Charlotte von Stein, June 8, 1787, *ibid.*, p. 84.

26. Goethe, XI, 95.

27. Letter of Nov. 1, 1786, Goethe, XIX, 23.

28. The word *rein* (pure) loses the predominantly moral meaning it had in *Iphigenia*.

29. Nov. 1, 1786, Goethe, XIX, 23.

30. Letter of Nov. 11, 1786, *ibid.*, p. 30.

31. Letter of Dec. 13, 1786, *ibid.*, p. 39.

32. See Herbert Koch, *Winckelmann und Goethe in Rom* (Tübingen, 1950).

33. Goethe stood close to the source of the Winckelmannian succession of seeking Greece in Italy. On earlier Italian journeys see Camillo von Klenze, *The Interpretation of Italy during the Last Two Centuries*. As one would expect, Goethe's letters from Italy are fresher and more vivid than the *Italian Journey*, which was written considerably later.

34. See letter to Herder and his wife, Dec. 2–9, 1786, Goethe, XIX, 37.

35. Goethe, XI, 112.

36. *Ibid.*, p. 110.

37. *Ibid.*, p. 115; cf. p. 238 on a "weaning" by Correggio.

38. *Schriften der Goethe-Gesellschaft*, II (Weimar, 1886), 124; see also p. 89. This volume is hereafter cited as *Tagebuch*.

39. See Goethe, XIX, 50; cf. p. 60 on the "hocus-pocus" in the Sistine Chapel.
40. Goethe, XI, 139.
41. *Ibid.*, pp. 134, 139.
42. *Ibid.*, pp. 133f.
43. Contrast Beutler's remarks, *ibid.*, p. 1021.
44. See Trevelyan, *Goethe and the Greeks*, pp. 111f.
45. Letter of June 8, 1787, Goethe, XIX, 85; cf. XI, 362.
46. March 22, 1788, Goethe, XI, 585.
47. *Ibid.*, p. 585.
48. Cf. Gustav Kestner, *Goethes Nausikaa* (Berlin, 1912); Eduard Castle, in *Aus Goethes Geist* (Vienna and Leipzig, 1926), pp. 211–236.
49. See Castle, *Aus Goethes Geist*, p. 224.
50. *Tagebuch*, pp. 73f; repeated in *Italienische Reise*, Goethe, XI, 45f.
51. See above, Chap. II, and E. Schmidt in *Tagebuch*, p. 376.
52. Palladio's works are cited as examples — *Tagebuch*, p. 89.
53. *Ibid.*
54. Goethe, XI, 462; cf. also p. 583.
55. *Ibid.*, p. 273.
56. *Tagebuch*, p. 133.
57. See Goethe, XI, 570, 527.
58. *Ibid.*, p. 603.
59. Letter of Jan. 6, 1787, to Charlotte von Stein, Goethe, XIX, 51.
60. Goethe, XI, 146.
61. *Tagebuch*, p. 240.
62. Goethe, XI, 165.
63. *Ibid.*, p. 172.
64. *Ibid.*, p. 601.
65. *Ibid.*, p. 603.
66. See *Götterlehre*, pp. 1–7.
67. See Goethe, XI, 352, and Trevelyan, *Goethe and the Greeks*, pp. 159–168.
68. May 17, 1787, to Herder, Goethe, XI, 352.
69. *Ibid.*, p. 436.
70. *Ibid.*, pp. 609–613.
71. On the comparable question of why he never visited Greece, see the contrasting views of Trevelyan and E. M. Butler (*The Tyranny of Greece over Germany*).
72. Above all his love of Christiane Vulpius, later his wife.
73. Goethe, I, 173: "Live happily, and thus the past shall live in you!"
74. *Ibid.*, p. 165: "In the heroic age, when gods and goddesses loved, Desire followed seeing, enjoyment followed desire."
75. *Ibid.*, p. 178.

76. Goethe, II, 110–114. See also his later poem "Das Tagebuch," *ibid.*, pp. 114–120.

77. *Ibid.*, p. 112: "The charming creak of the bed as it rocks back and forth."

78. See Emil Staiger's comment, Goethe, II, 640.

79. Goethe, I, 167: "And do I not teach myself when I explore the contours of her lovely bosom, guide my hand down along her hips? Then I really understand the marble rightly; I think and compare, I see with feeling eye, feel with seeing hand."

80. *Ibid.*, p. 171: "Glances of sweet desire, still moist even in the marble."

81. Rilke, *Sämtliche Werke*, ed. Ernst Zinn, II (Wiesbaden, 1956), 276: "Neither spirit nor ecstasy will we forego."

82. See E. Maass in *Jahrbuch der Goethe-Gesellschaft*, XII (1926), 68–92.

83. Letter of March 15, 1790, Goethe, XIX, 161.

84. Goethe, I, 221: "Sarcophagi and urns the pagan adorned with life: fauns dance about them, alternating with the chorus of Bacchantes; the goat-footed satyr, puffing out his cheeks, forces the hoarse note from the blaring horn."

85. *Ibid.*, pp. 223f.

86. *Ibid.*, p. 233.

87. Compare however the mood of the essay "Myron's Cow" (below, p. 215) and Faust's hatred of church bells, Goethe, V, 495, 498f.

88. Goethe, I, 227.

89. Goethe, II, 177.

90. *Ibid.*, p. 175.

91. Goethe, XX, 14.

92. Quoted by Calvin Thomas, *The Life and Works of Schiller* (New York, 1901), p. 288.

93. Cf. in Goethe's less vehemently anti-Christian poem "Great Is Diana of the Ephesians," the lines: "As if there were a god within the brain./There, behind man's silly forehead." (Goethe, I, 396.)

94. Goethe, I, 154: "Victims are sacrificed here, neither lamb nor bull but unexampled human victims."

95. *Ibid.*, p. 160: "The godhead rejoices in the repentant sinners; immortals raise lost children up to heaven, with arms of fire."

96. See Goethe, III, 213.

97. *Ibid.*, p. 233.

98. *Ibid.*: "Rather show the youth the value of nobly ripening age."

99. *Ibid.*, p. 195: "So that night become the beautiful half of life for you."

100. *Ibid.*, p. 207: "Of inspiring freedom and of commendable equality."

101. *Ibid.*, p. 202: "and meaningfully opened his mouth."

102. Goethe, I, 206.

103. _Ibid.,_ p. 207. The reference is to Friedrich August Wolf's theory that the _Iliad_ was made up of many poems and was the product of many poets.

104. Goethe, V, 379.

105. Goethe, III, 252: "Thus silently all enjoyed the abundance of blessedness."

106. _Ibid.,_ p. 260: "Alas! that the fair image shall so soon vanish from the earth, which far and wide rejoices in what is ordinary! That the fair body, the splendid, living structure shall be dissolved, abandoned to the devouring flame."

107. On its defect see _ibid.,_ p. 792 (Hellmuth von Maltzahn's commentary on "Achilleis"), and Otto Regenbogen, _Griechische Gegenwart_ (Leipzig, 1942), pp. 41f.

108. Goethe, V, 536.

109. Goethe, XV, 893.

110. _Ibid.,_ pp. 894–904.

111. Goethe, XIII, 150.

112. See Wolfgang Pfeiffer-Belli, _Goethes Kunstmeyer und seine Welt_ (Zurich, 1959); Meyer's own uninspired _Geschichte der bildenden Künste bei den Griechen_; and his manifesto against "religiopatriotic" German art (see below, pp. 221f).

113. Goethe, XIII, 295.

114. _Ibid.,_ pp. 305–307.

115. _Ibid.,_ p. 320.

116. Goethe, XXII, 348 (spring, 1804). Similarly, Schiller replaced the drunken porter's remarks, in his version of _Macbeth,_ by a hymn to the morning.

117. Letter of March 18, 1801, Goethe, XX, 847.

118. Goethe's essay appeared with other contributions in the volume _Winckelmann and His Century_ (1805).

119. Goethe, XIII, 417.

120. See Ernst Howald's excellent introduction to his edition _Winckelmann von Goethe_ (Erlenbach-Zurich, 1943).

121. Goethe, XIII, 422. As often, one is reminded of George's allusion to "the body godlike and the god embodied."

122. _Ibid.,_ pp. 420, 424.

123. _Ibid.,_ p. 425.

124. See Josef Körner, _Romantiker und Klassiker_ (Berlin, 1924), pp. 168, 200f.

125. See H. Hatfield, "Winckelmann: the Romantic Element," _Germanic Review,_ 28(1953):282–289.

126. Goethe, XIII, 438.

127. _Ibid.,_ p. 450.

128. Letter of April 20, 1805, Goethe, XX, 990.

129. Goethe, XV, 1035 (in notes to _Rameaus Neffe_).

VIII. *The Semblance of Paganism: Schiller*

1. Cf. Melitta Gerhard, *Schiller und die deutsche Tragödie* (Weimar, 1919), pp. 3–6.
2. See F.-W. Wentzlaff-Eggebert, *Schillers Weg zu Goethe* (Tübingen and Stuttgart, 1949), p. 11; also Reinhard Buchwald, *Schiller* (Leipzig, 1937), I, 240.
3. See Schiller, XI, 312f (Walzel's notes), and Walzel's article in the *Marbacher Schillerbuch* (Stuttgart and Berlin, 1905), pp. 42–57.
4. Schiller, XI, 103.
5. Zeller, *Winckelmanns Beschreibung des Apollo im Belvedere*, pp. 78–80.
6. Cf. Schiller, XI, xxvii, and Walzel in the *Marbacher Schillerbuch*.
7. Schiller, XI, 102f. See also p. 106.
8. *Ibid.*, p. 106. This note is struck again and again, most emphatically in "Die Götter Griechenlands."
9. *Ibid.*, p. 107; see Rehm, *Griechentum und Goethezeit*, p. 228.
10. All quotations of Schiller's letters are taken from Jonas' edition. Since it is chronologically arranged, I have not given references to volume and page.
11. Schiller, I, 156. Translated by Bulwer-Lytton thus: "Ah, flourish'd then your service of delight!/How different, oh, how different, in the day."
12. *Ibid.*, p. 329: "When the gods still were more humane, humans were more divine."
13. See Winckelmann, I, 163, as well as Lessing's essay "How the Ancients Represented Death."
14. Schiller, I, 328: "No holy barbarian gave judgment after the dread laws of specters."
15. *Ibid.*, p. 156: "Lovely beings from the land of fable."
16. *Ibid.*, p. 160: "Ah, that which gains immortal life in Song,/In mortal life must perish!" (Bulwer-Lytton). Thus the ending of the revised version of 1803. For this assertion, Schiller unfortunately sacrificed the contrast, at the close of the original poem, between severe truth as the modern ideal of life and beauty as the Greek.
17. Dec. 25, 1788.
18. May 25, 1792.
19. See Helene Lange, *Schillers philosophische Gedichte* (Berlin, 1905), pp. 5–7.
20. Cf. R. H. Thomas, *The Classical Ideal in German Literature*, pp. 105–119, and *Schiller und sein Kreis*, ed. Oscar Fambach (Berlin, 1957), pp. 40–73.
21. Cf. Melitta Gerhard, "Schillers Die Götter Griechenlands," *Monatshefte*, 38(1946):32–43, and her *Schiller* (Bern, 1950).

22. Schiller, XVI, 196.

23. *Ibid.*, p. 222.

24. Letter of March 9, 1789, to Körner.

25. *Ibid.* See also his letter to Humboldt of Oct. 26, 1795, again stressing his ignorance of Greek. Unless one believes that he was pathologically modest or coy, one is forced to take his word. See, however, Reinhard Buchwald's *Der junge Schiller* (Leipzig, 1937).

26. See Wentzlaff-Eggebert in *Schiller* (Stuttgart, 1955), pp. 328f.

27. Cf. Horst Rüdiger, *Übertragungen antiker Dichtungen* (Munich, 1944), p. 419.

28. Schiller, X, 105.

29. Schiller, I, 184: "The strength which swells in the muscles of the wrestler must appear in silent loveliness in the beauty of the god."

30. Schiller, XI, 236f.

31. To Goethe, letter of Aug. 17, 1795.

32. Schiller, XI, 248.

33. *Ibid.*, pp. 257f.

34. Cf. Walzel, *ibid.*, p. lxi.

35. Schiller, XII, 120. Inasmuch as the *Briefe* contain several transparent references to Goethe, it seems legitimate to think of Weimar here.

36. *Rousseau and Romanticism* (Boston, 1947), pp. 43f. As Schiller never really completed the work, he slighted the element of the sublime, which may partially account for Babbitt's interpretation.

37. Cf. Gerhard, *Schiller*, p. 252.

38. Schiller, XII, 103.

39. See J. G. Robertson's harsh but stimulating remarks in his *Schiller after a Hundred Years* (London, 1905).

40. See Julius Petersen, *Die Sehnsucht nach dem dritten Reich* (Stuttgart, 1934), pp. 34f.

41. Schiller, XII, 17f.

42. *Ibid.*, p. 5.

43. *Ibid.*, p. 33.

44. *Ibid.*, p. 116.

45. *Ibid.*, p. 30.

46. Cf. the letter to Goethe of Aug. 23, 1794.

47. Schiller, XII, 58.

48. *Ibid.*, pp. 59f.

49. Schiller, I, 191. Bulwer-Lytton translates it:

>   For ever fair, for ever calm and bright,
>   Life flies on plumage zephyr-light,
>   For those who on the Olympian hill rejoice.

50. Schiller, XII, 56.

51. See Berthold Vallentin, *Winckelmann* (Berlin, 1931).

52. Schiller, XII, 100.

53. *Ibid.*, p. 84.

54. See *Das Jahrhundert Goethes*, ed. Stefan George and Karl Wolfskehl (Berlin, 1910), p. 7.

55. Cf. Calvin Thomas, *The Life and Works of Schiller*, p. 283.

56. Schiller, XII, 24.

57. *Ibid.*, p. 120.

58. Schiller, I, 192. Bulwer-Lytton translates it:
> Safe from each change that Time to matter gives,
> Nature's blest playmate, free at will to stray
> With Gods a god, amidst the fields of Day,
> The Form, the Archetype, serenely lives.

59. *Versuch über Schiller* (Berlin and Frankfurt am Main, 1955), pp. 89f.

60. Cf. Rehm, *Griechentum und Goethezeit*, pp. 195, 213.

61. Schiller, I, 151: "Gaze on, and touch my relics now! At last thou standest here,/But art thou nearer now to me — or I to thee more near?" (Bulwer-Lytton).

62. *Ibid.*, p. 324: "His darkened senses are bound by the curse of the North." Von der Hellen (*ibid.*, p. 325) compares the poem with "Die Antiken zu Paris."

63. *Ibid.*, p. 140. Bulwer-Lytton translates it:
> Over the self-same green, eternally,
> (Let man's slight changes wither as they will,)
> All races which the wide world ever knew,
> United, wander brother-like! — Ah! see,
> The sun of Homer smiles upon us still!

64. Schiller, XII, 190f.

65. This useful word was first employed as a translation of Schiller's term, I believe, by Miss E. M. Wilkinson.

66. Schiller, XII, 179, emphasis added.

67. *Ibid.*, p. 182.

68. Winckelmann, I, 11.

69. Schiller, XII, 241, 181.

70. Schiller, I, 126: "Simply and quietly you take your way through the conquered world." The poem, written in 1795, was originally entitled "Natur und Schule."

71. Schiller, XII, 186.

72. Cf. *ibid.*, p. 249, and Walzel's introduction, Schiller, XI, lxxix.

73. Schiller, XII, 229.

74. *Ibid.*

75. Schiller, I, 154: "That the beautiful passes away, that the perfect dies." In "Die vier Weltalter," too, the passing of the age of beauty is lamented. I, 13f, and 291.

76. *Ibid.*, p. 269.

77. Schiller, II, 135: "Must not the artist himself bring the seedling from abroad, and borrow from Rome and Athens the sun, the air?" Cf. p. 136.

78. Of July 26, 1800.

79. Cf. Gerhard, *Schiller und die griechische Tragödie*, and Florian Prader, *Schiller und Sophokles* (Zurich, 1954).

80. Schiller, XVI, 285, 287.

81. See Schiller, XII, 328–330. This undated fragment, found among Schiller's literary remains, may well have been written in the 1790's, but as it is similar in spirit to "Über den Gebrauch des Chors in der Tragödie," it seems convenient to discuss it here.

82. *Ibid.*, pp. 329f.

83. *Ibid.*, p. 330.

84. Schiller, XVI, 123.

85. *Ibid.*, p. 124.

86. *Ibid.*, p. 126.

87. *Ibid.*, p. 128.

88. On this point see Prader, *Schiller und Sophokles.* However admirable the breadth of Schiller's religious views, there seems to be a consensus that the mixture of "myths" in the *Braut* is aesthetically unfortunate.

89. See Schiller, *Sämtliche Werke* (Berlin, 1926), XXII, 5f. Karl Hoffmeister dated this fragment 1801. See his *Nachlese zu Schillers Werken* (Stuttgart and Tübingen, 1840), III, 274. I am grateful to the Schiller National Museum for this information.

90. Carefully read, his letter to Humboldt of Oct. 26, 1795, does not contradict this statement. For a skillfully presented argument that Schiller was separated from the Greeks by a great gulf, see Theodore A. Meyer, "Der Griechentraum Schillers und seine philosophische Begründung," *Jahrbuch des freien deutschen Hochstifts*, 1928, pp. 125–153.

91. Letter of Dec. 17, 1795. In part, Schiller's attitude may be explained as a reaction against Friedrich Schlegel's "Über die Diotima." But see also his rejection of Pindar, letter to Körner, Oct. 25, 1794.

92. To Christian Reinhart, March 16 [?], 1803. This and the following passage are quoted by Walzel in the *Marbacher Schillerbuch*, p. 44.

93. Letter of Feb. 17, 1803.

94. Letter of July 3, 1796.

95. See "Schiller und das Barockdrama," in *Götterstille und Göttertrauer*, esp. pp. 96f, 99.

96. Cf. his letter to Goethe, Jan. 5, 1798, and Max Asmus, "Schiller und Julian," *Zeitschrift für vergleichende Litteraturgeschichte*, New Series, 17 (1909): 71–114.

97. "Schillers Geistesart," *Abhandlungen der preussischen Akademie der Wissenschaften*, Philosophisch-historische Klasse, no. 13 (Berlin, 1941).

98. Goethe, XIII, 422.

99. See, for example, Schiller, I, 129, 199; XII, 227f.

100. See I. Feuerlicht, "Vom Wesen der deutschen Idylle," *Germanic Review*, 22(1947): esp. pp. 210–212. Spranger pertinently notes ("Schillers Geistesart") that it is curious to consider this tale idyllic.
101. Letter of Feb. 10, 1790.
102. Letter of May 26, 1794.
103. Cf. Meyer, "Der Griechentraum Schillers," p. 129.
104. This term was apparently coined by Rehm.
105. Schiller, II, 124: "Oedipus tears out his eyes, Jocasta hangs herself, both guiltless; the play has come to a harmonious conclusion."
106. Cf. Spranger, "Schillers Geistesart," p. 69.
107. Letter of Dec. 25, 1795.
108. *Ibid.*
109. See Karl Schmid, Goethe, XX, 1039.

IX. The Greek Gods and Christ: Hölderlin

1. Goethe, IX, 608.
2. Hölderlin suffered a serious but not total collapse in 1802; in 1806, his condition having further deteriorated, he was committed to a clinic for a year. Thereafter he lived with a private family, distraught but harmless.
3. *Sämtliche Werke*, ed. Friedrich Beissner (Stuttgart, 1946–1961), II, 167. This edition is hereafter cited as Hölderlin.
4. Hölderlin, II, 170. See also II, 213: "It is nothing, evil."
5. Hölderlin, I, 257:
   You cold hypocrites, speak not of the gods!
   You are sensible! You do not believe in Helios,
   Nor in the Thunderer and the Sea-god.
6. His biographer Wilhelm Böhm concluded that the poet suffered from schizophrenia. (*Hölderlin*, 2 vols., Halle, 1928–1930, II, 670f.)
7. See especially the poems "An unsere grossen Dichter" and "Dichterberuf."
8. See Böhm, *Hölderlin*, I, 21–34.
9. Hölderlin, I, 38, 87.
10. *Ibid.*, pp. 85, 90.
11. *Ibid.*, p. 88.
12. *Ibid.*, p. 75.
13. See Rehm, *Griechentum und Goethezeit*, p. 322.
14. Hölderlin, IV, 191.
15. *Ibid.*, p. 190.
16. Hölderlin, I, 126:
    In the presence of the gods
    You uttered the decision
    To found your realm on love.
17. *Ibid.*, p. 125: "You are like none/Among your brethren."

18. *Ibid.*, p. 180:
I yearn for the distant land
For Alcaeus and Anacreon
And I would rather sleep in the narrow house [the grave],
With the saints in Marathon.

19. *Ibid.*, p. 480.

20. *Ibid.*, p. 199.

21. Thus Beissner's note, *ibid.*, p. 480.

22. *Ibid.*, p. 204.

23. *Ibid.*, p. 267: "In the arms of the gods I grew to manhood."

24. See *Die Lyrik Hölderlins* (Frankfurt am Main, 1921), p. 134.

25. *Ibid.*, p. 140, footnote.

26. One of Hölderlin's last, fragmentary poems was devoted to the Madonna.

27. Hölderlin, II, 745.

28. See Georg Stefansky, *Das hellenisch-deutsche Weltbild* (Bonn, 1925), p. 154.

29. Hölderlin, VI, 432, undated letter of fall 1802.

30. Hölderlin, II, 145.

31. Hölderlin, III, 96.

32. Hölderlin, II, 228: "they wished to found a realm of art. But in this effort they neglected the national element and Greece, the fairest, wretchedly went to ruin." Possibly Hölderlin was indirectly referring here to the "unpolitical" attitude of German intellectuals.

33. Hölderlin, I, 255.

34. Contrast the line "poor in deeds and rich in thoughts" in "To the Germans," Hölderlin, II, 9.

35. See Ronald Peacock, *Hölderlin* (London, 1938), pp. 64, 68.

36. See his remarks on translating Sophocles (Hölderlin, V, 193–202, 263–272) and his letter of Dec. 4, 1801 (VI, 425f). See also Lothar Kempter, *Hölderlin und die Mythologie* (Horgen-Zurich and Leipzig, 1929), pp. 77, 83.

37. See Paul Böckmann, *Hölderlin und seine Götter* (Munich, 1935), p. 116.

38. Hölderlin, I, 230.

39. Hölderlin, II, 94.

40. *Ibid.*, p. 153.

41. Hölderlin, VI, 126, 684f.

42. On the relation of Hölderlin's novel to Heinse's *Ardinghello* see Pierre Grappin, "*Ardinghello* et *Hyperion*," *Etudes Germaniques*, 10(1955): 200–213.

43. F. T. Vischer called Hölderlin a "Werther of Greece"; see the *Marbacher Schillerbuch* (Stuttgart and Berlin, 1905), p. 285, quoted in Hölderlin, III, 430.

44. *Ibid.*, pp. 153–156.

45. *Ibid.*, pp. 7, 20. Like most of the leading German Hellenophiles, Hölderlin never visited Greece; he depended on travelers' accounts.
46. See Romano Guardini, *Hölderlin* (Munich, 1955), p. 365.
47. Hölderlin, III, 90.
48. *Ibid.*, p. 143:

> And their blissful eyes
> Gaze with quiet
> Eternal clearness.

49. *Ibid.*, p. 58.
50. Hölderlin, IV, 11.
51. See Böckmann, *Hölderlin und seine Götter*, pp. 257f.
52. See Friedrich Schlegel's suggestion, perhaps only half serious, that a modern myth be founded on Spinoza (below, Chap. X).
53. Hölderlin, II, 4.
54. *Ibid.*, p. 5: "Where is thy Delos, where thy Olympia/That we all may find each other at the supreme festival?"
55. *Ibid.*, p. 91.
56. *Ibid.*, p. 93: "Only at times can man endure divine abundance./ Life thereafter is a dream of them."
57. *Ibid.*, p. 94: "For the greater became too great for joy linked to the mind." In context, this enigmatic line seems to mean that men were no longer able to endure the joy of direct communion with the gods, as the Greeks had done.
58. See Böckmann, *Hölderlin und seine Götter*, p. 350.
59. Hölderlin, II, 103: "Does Ionia blossom; has the time come?"
60. *Ibid.*, p. 111: "Let the people look toward Hellas, and with tears and thanks/Let the proud day of triumph become gentle in remembering."
61. *Ibid.*, p. 150.
62. *Ibid.*, p. 152.
63. Similarly, in "At the Source of the Danube" Hölderlin emphasizes that though the relation between ancient and modern is based on "ceaseless love," the two must be "well separated." *Ibid.*, p. 127.
64. *Ibid.*, p. 139.
65. Cf. Wilhelm Michel, *Hölderlins abendländische Wendung* (Jena, 1923), pp. 5–53.
66. Hölderlin, II, 221f.
67. *Ibid.*, p. 222. By "aorgic" Hölderlin seems to mean "formless, wild, undisciplined" in contrast to the organic.
68. Hölderlin, VI, 422, letter of June 2, 1801.
69. *Ibid.*, pp. 425f, letter of Dec. 4, 1801.
70. The treaty of Lunéville.
71. Hölderlin, II, 132.
72. *Ibid.*
73. See *ibid.*, pp. 131, 708.

74. *Ibid.*, p. 137.
75. Hölderlin, VI, 419.
76. My discussion is based on the first version.
77. Hölderlin, II, 153: "What is it that fetters me to the old, blissful coasts, that I love them still more than my native land?"
78. *Ibid.*
79. *Ibid.*, p. 154.
80. *Ibid.*
81. *Ibid.*, p. 155.
82. *Ibid.*, p. 755.
83. *Ibid.*, p. 155.
84. My discussion is based on the "fair copy" made for the landgrave by the poet. For variants, revisions, and so forth, of all poems, see Beissner's edition.
85. See Karl Schwartz, *Landgraf Freidrich V von Hessen-Homburg und seine Familie* (Rudolstadt, 1878), I, 87, and elsewhere. On "Patmos" see esp. Robert Beare, "Patmos, dem Landgrafen von Homburg," *Germanic Review*, 28(1953): 5–22.
86. Hölderlin, II, 165.
87. *Ibid.*
88. *Ibid.*, p. 168.
89. *Ibid.*, p. 171; see p. 172.
90. *Ibid.*, p. 170.
91. See Romano Guardini, *Hölderlin: Weltbild und Frömmigkeit* (2nd printing, Munich, 1955), p. 543.
92. "Der veste Buchstab": cf. the "feste Burg" of Luther's "battle hymn of the Reformation."
93. See Eduard Lachmann, *Hölderlins Christus-Hymnen* (Vienna, 1951), p. 113.
94. See Beissner's comment (Hölderlin, II, 795).
95. In his *Hölderlin*, passim.
96. See Lachmann, *Hölderlins Christus-Hymnen*, p. 55.
97. Hölderlin, VI, 439, 1101.
98. Guardini, *Hölderlin*, p. 350.
99. *Werke*, ed. Norbert von Hellingrath (Munich and Leipzig, 1913–1923), VI, 404, 469; see also Butler, *The Tyranny of Greece*, p. 237.
100. Hölderlin, II, 306: "Far about us, with intellectuality, is the old legend,/And new life comes again from mankind."
101. Hölderlin, II, 187: "But too much love, where there is adoration, is dangerous, woundeth the most."

X. Christianity versus Aesthetic Paganism: Some Romanticists

1. See "Fragmente zur Philosophie und Literatur," ed. E. Behler, *Neue Rundschau*, 70 (1959):12. The *aperçu* dates from 1809.

2. See Curtius' "Friedrich Schlegel und Frankreich," in *Kritische Essays zur europäischen Literatur* (Bern, 1950), pp. 78–94, and René Wellek's *A History of Modern Criticism, 1750–1950*, II (New Haven, 1955), chap. 1.

3. Herder, I, 293f.

4. Herbert Bloch suggested this point to me.

5. August Emmersleben, *Die Antike in der romantischen Theorie* (Berlin, 1937), p. 6.

6. See Werner Mettler, *Der junge Friedrich Schlegel und die griechische Literatur* (Zurich, 1955), pp. 46–97.

7. See Siegfried Reiter in *Euphorion*, 23 (1921): 226–233.

8. *Friedrich Schlegels Jugendschriften*, ed. Jacob Minor (Vienna, 1882), I, 5. This edition is hereafter cited as Minor.

9. Minor, I, 2, 8f.

10. *Ibid.*, p. 12.

11. *Ibid.*

12. *Ibid.*

13. *Ibid.*, p. 13.

14. *Ibid.*, p. 15.

15. *Ibid.*, p. 78.

16. *Ibid.*, p. 125.

17. *Ibid.*, pp. 158f.

18. *Ibid.*, p. 159.

19. See "Caesar und Alexander" (1796), in *Sämmtliche Werke* (Vienna, 1822–1825), IV, 263–312, and Minor, I, 127f. This edition is hereafter cited as Schlegel.

20. See esp. Minor, I, 129.

21. *Ibid.*, p. 152.

22. *Ibid.*, p. 110.

23. Minor, II, 220f.

24. See Schlegel's *Literary Notebooks, 1797–1801*, ed. Hans Eichner (London, 1957), p. 35, no. 181.

25. Minor, I, 121.

26. *Ibid.*, p. 114.

27. *Ibid.*

28. *Ibid.*, p. 115.

29. *Literary Notebooks*, p. 27, no. 91.

30. Minor, I, 140.

31. *Literary Notebooks*, p. 159, no. 1567. See also two "hymns" (actually sonnets) of 1801, to Diana and Isis, Schlegel, IX, 27f.

32. Minor, I, 333f.

33. *Literary Notebooks*, p. 107, no. 981.

34. Schiller, I, 269: "Scarcely has the cold fever of Gallomania left us/When a burning one, Graecomania, breaks out."

35. Minor, II, 179.

36. Minor, I, 128, 142.

37. Minor, II, 361.
38. *Ibid.*, p. 227.
39. *Literary Notebooks*, p. 193, no. 1951.
40. See *Rousseau and Romanticism*, p. 263.
41. Minor, II, 226.
42. Minor, I, 59. Schlegel also repeats Winckelmann's point that the man who cares for female beauty only may be moved entirely by sensuality (*ibid.*, p. 66; Winckelmann, I, 244).
43. See Carl Enders, *Friedrich Schlegel* (Leipzig, 1913), pp. 156–165.
44. *Lucinde* (Munich, 1922), p. 19.
45. See *Die Auffassung der Liebe* (Halle, 1922), p. 376.
46. *Lucinde*, p. 78.
47. *Ibid.*, p. 15.
48. *Ibid.*, pp. 140f, 169, 136.
49. *Ibid.*, p. 169.
50. *Ibid.*, pp. 189–198.
51. *Ibid.*, p. 50.
52. *Ibid.*, p. 43; cf. pp. 50f.
53. *Ibid.*, p. 152.
54. *Ibid.*, p. 167.
55. See above, p. 106.
56. *Lucinde*, pp. 138f.
57. *Ibid.*, pp. 58f.
58. *Ibid.*, pp. 62f; see Oskar Walzel, *Das Prometheussymbol von Shaftesbury zu Goethe* for the background of literary association.
59. *Lucinde*, p. 65.
60. *Ibid.*, p. 181.
61. *Ibid.*, p. 201.
62. *Ibid.*, p. 204.
63. Schlegel is presumably indebted to Novalis for the basic imagery of this passage. See I. Rouge, *Erläuterungen zu Friedrich Schlegels Lucinde* (Halle, 1905), p. 125.
64. See Kluckhohn, *Die Auffassung der Liebe*, p. 639.
65. See *Adel des Geistes* (Stockholm, 1945), p. 440.
66. Minor, II, 358.
67. See Liselotte Dieckmann in *Comparative Literature*, 7 (1955): 306–312.
68. Schlegel is apparently referring to the highly speculative "Nature Philosophy" of such men as Schelling.
69. Minor, II, 366.
70. See Strich, *Die Mythologie*, II, 46f.
71. Minor, II, 372.
72. See J. M. Raich, *Dorothea von Schlegel und deren Söhne*, I (Mainz, 1881), 98.
73. Even if one finds Schlegel's "hymn" to Diana convincing, it is

an isolated attempt. Prometheus and Hercules, in *Lucinde*, are avowedly mere allegorical figures.

74. *Sämmtliche Werke* (2nd ed., Vienna, 1846), VIII, 354.
75. Schlegel, X, 89f.
76. See Rehm, *Götterstille und Göttertrauer*, esp. pp. 151f.
77. Schlegel, X, 90.
78. Schlegel, I, 26.
79. *Ibid.*, p. 16.
80. *Ibid.*, pp. 18f.
81. Schlegel, II, 274; cf. p. 285.
82. *Ibid.*, pp. 319, 274.
83. *Ibid.*, pp. 256, 274.
84. *Ibid.*, pp. 285f.
85. Schlegel, X, 210f.
86. See Strich, *Die Mythologie*, I, 395.
87. Minor, II, 254f.
88. *Ibid.*, p. 255.
89. *Ibid.*, p. 233.
90. See *A History of Modern Criticism*, II, 72.
91. For a detailed discussion see Robert Gundacker, "August Wilhelm Schlegel und seine Einstellung zu J. J. Winckelmann" (unpubl. diss., Vienna, 1932).
92. *Sämmtliche Werke*, ed. Eduard Böcking (Leipzig, 1846–1847), IX, 4. This edition is hereafter cited as A. W. Schlegel.
93. See his *Vorlesungen über schöne Literatur und Kunst* in *Deutsche Literaturdenkmale des 18. und 19. Jahrhunderts*, XVII, 142. This edition is hereafter cited as *DLD*.
94. *Ibid.*, p. 340.
95. *Vorlesungen über dramatische Kunst und Literatur* (Heidelberg, 1809–1811), I, 68. This edition is hereafter cited as *Dram. Vorlesungen*.
96. A. W. Schlegel, IX, 239.
97. *Dram. Vorlesungen*, I, 24.
98. Cf. *ibid.*, pp. 24–26.
99. A. W. Schlegel, IX, 250.
100. *DLD*, XVII, 349.
101. *Ibid.*, p. 22.
102. *Dram. Vorlesungen*, I, 16.
103. *DLD*, XVII, 349.
104. *Ibid.*, pp. 347f, 350.
105. Tieck also contributed to this extremely important little book.
106. See Gerhard Fricke, in *Festschrift Paul Kluckhohn und Hermann Schneider gewidmet* (Tübingen, 1948), pp. 345–371, esp. pp. 346f, 354.
107. Vico and Herder had begun the process.

108. *DLD*, XVII, 340.

109. A. W. Schlegel, IX, 93.

110. A. W. Schlegel, I, 88.

111. A. W. Schlegel, IX, 93.

112. *DLD*, XIX, 84f, 206.

113. *Nachtwachen von Bonaventura* (Potsdam, 1920), p. 225.

114. *Ibid.*, pp. 228f. See Heine's "The Gods in Exile" and Heinse's sentences on the present lot of the Olympians, quoted above, p. 76.

115. First printed in the *Athenaeum*, 2(1799):131.

116. A. W. Schlegel, X, 365f.

117. It was widely believed that Wackenroder had become converted to Catholicism and was making propaganda for the Church; Schlegel carefully kept his distance from this tendency. See Wellek, *History of Modern Criticism*, II, 72, and Schlegel's very bitter epigram on his brother Friedrich's conversion, A. W. Schlegel, II, 38.

118. A. W. Schlegel, IX, 254.

119. See also his extremely dull elegy "Die Kunst der Griechen," A. W. Schlegel, II, 5–12.

120. A. W. Schlegel, XII, 321–383.

121. Cf. A. W. Schlegel, IV, 283.

122. Novalis took the *History of Art* with him to Jena in 1790. See *Schriften*, ed. Paul Kluckhohn (Leipzig, c. 1929), IV, 472, 475; III, 63. (This edition is hereafter cited as Novalis.) Of course any alert young student of the time would be likely to be acquainted with Winckelmann's general ideas.

123. Novalis, III, 13.

124. *Ibid.*, p. 68.

125. *Ibid.*, p. 343.

126. *Ibid.*, pp. 140f.

127. Novalis, II, 406.

128. *Ibid.*, p. 90.

129. Novalis, III, 160.

130. Novalis, I, 208.

131. Novalis, III, 265f.

132. Novalis, II, 404f.

133. Novalis, III, 68.

134. Besides the examples quoted in the discussion, see esp. "Zehre mit Geisterglut meinen Leib, dass ich luftig mit dir inniger mich mische und dann ewig die Brautnacht währt" (Novalis, I, 56). In certain hymns of the Pietist tradition, to which Novalis was deeply indebted, erotic imagery is indeed used, but it seems sentimental rather than passionate, at least in comparison with his. Zinzendorf, for instance, may write of the "ardent glow of love" of Christ's wounds, but the effect is very different. See J. R. Thierstein, *Novalis und der Pietismus* (Bern, 1910), esp. pp. 59, 82.

135. Novalis, I, 59: "I am wandering across [the frontier of death], and every hurt will some day be a spur to rapture. Only a little time, and I'll be free, and lie, drunken with bliss, in love's embrace." Compare with the eighth line of this poem the sentence quoted in the second "Hymn": "Sie wissen nicht, dass du [der Schlaf] es bist der des zarten Mädchens Busen umschwebt und zum Himmel den Schoss macht" (*ibid.*, p. 56).

136. Novalis, I, 66: "Downward to the sweet bride/To Jesus the beloved."

137. *Ibid.*, p. 57.

138. See esp. the seventh "Song," *ibid.*, p. 74f.

139. See Grete Lüers, *Die Sprache der deutschen Mystik des Mittelalters im Werke der Mechthild von Magdeburg* (Munich, 1926), esp. pp. 16–21, and J. M. Clark, *The Great German Mystics* (Oxford, 1949), pp. 101f.

140. See Bruce Haywood, *The Veil of Imagery* (The Hague, 1959), p. 150: "It must be emphasized that at no point is erotic imagery subordinated to the Christian."

141. See Robert Minder, *Ludwig Tieck* (Paris, 1936), p. 104.

142. Cf. Novalis, II, 397; III, 82f, 297, 327.

143. *Sämtliche Werke*, ed. Prussian Academy, Section 1, XI (Weimar, 1935), 56–75.

144. *Ibid.*, p. 59.

145. *Ibid.*, p. 64.

146. *Ibid.*, p. 60.

147. *Ibid.*, pp. 71–73.

148. *Ibid.*, p. 72.

XI. Aesthetics and Culture: Humboldt

1. On Heyne's great influence see P. B. Stadler, *Wilhelm von Humboldts Bild der Antike* (Zurich and Stuttgart, 1959), pp. 17f.

2. See his *Briefe an F. G. Welcker* (Berlin, 1859), p. 102, letter of March 18, 1823.

3. Cf. Walther Rehm's remarks in *Europäische Romdichtung* (2nd printing, Munich, 1960), pp. 212f.

4. See Werner Schultz, *Die Religion Wilhelm von Humboldts* (Jena, 1932).

5. Cf. Stadler, *Humboldts Bild der Antike*, p. 13.

6. Letter of July 31, 1813, in *W. und C. von Humboldt in ihren Briefen* (Berlin, 1906–1916), IV, 83.

7. See Howald's *Wilhelm von Humboldt* (Erlenbach-Zurich, [1944]), p. 48.

8. Letter to F. A. Wolf, Jan. 23, 1793, in *Gesammelte Werke*, V (Berlin, 1846), 18.

9. *Gesammelte Schriften*, Section 1: *Werke*, ed. Albert Leitzmann, I (Berlin, 1903), 261. Humboldt's emphasis. Leitzmann's edition is hereafter cited as Humboldt.

10. Humboldt, I, 269f.

11. *Ibid.*, p. 274.

12. *Ibid.*, p. 277.

13. *Ibid.*, pp. 274f.

14. *Ibid.*, p. 422.

15. *Ibid.*

16. See Robert Leroux, "L'Esthetique Sexuée de G. de Humboldt," *Etudes Germaniques*, 3(1948):261–273.

17. Winckelmann maintained that those who perceive beauty only in women are stirred by sex: Winckelmann, I, 244.

18. See Rudolf Haym, *Wilhelm von Humboldt* (Berlin, 1856), p. 150.

19. By Guhrauer, according to Haym, *Wilhelm von Humboldt*, p. 224, footnote.

20. See Stadler, *Humboldts Bild der Antike*, pp. 118f.

21. Letter of Oct. 22, 1803, in *Briefwechsel zwischen Schiller und Wilhelm von Humboldt* (3rd ed., Stuttgart, 1900), p. 307.

22. Letter to Goethe of Aug. 23, 1804, *Goethes Briefwechsel mit W. und A. von Humboldt* (Berlin, 1909), pp. 183f.

23. *Ibid.*, p. 186.

24. *Ibid.*

25. *Ibid.*, pp. 184f.

26. See Stadler, *Humboldts Bild der Antike*, p. 140.

27. Humboldt, IX, 35.

28. *Ibid.*, pp. 43f.

29. *Ibid.*, p. 45: "What, being sheer truth, escapes the mind,/Radiates from it [the *Gestalt*] in high sensuous clarity."

30. Humboldt, III, 136f.

31. *Ibid.*, p. 152.

32. *Ibid.*

33. *Ibid.*, p. 153.

34. *Theologische Jugendschriften*, ed. H. Nohl (Tübingen, 1907), p. 23, quoted in Walter Kaufmann, *The Owl and the Nightingale* (London, 1960), p. 124.

35. Humboldt, III, 142, 157.

36. *Ibid.*, p. 141.

37. *Ibid.*, p. 162.

38. Friedrich Paulsen, *Geschichte des gelehrten Unterrichts*, II (Berlin and Leipzig, 1921), 204.

39. *Goethes Briefwechsel*, p. 197, letter of April 12, 1806.

40. Humboldt, IX, 92.

41. *Ibid.*, p. 67: "yearning for the sacred hills/Around which quiet grandeur hovers eternally."

42. *Ibid.*, p. 17: "And from the sense of grandeur rises the peace of the mollified bosom/Longing for deeper peace down in the grave."

43. See Otto Harnack, *Wilhelm von Humboldt* (Berlin, 1913), p. 115.

44. Goethe, XIII, 1152. See below, Chap. XII.

45. *Goethes Briefwechsel*, pp. 232f, letter of Oct. 31, 1813.

46. See esp. his *Briefe an eine Freundin*, ed. Albert Leitzmann (Leipzig, 1909).

47. Humboldt, IX, 90:

> I am a poor pagan man
> Who cannot stand churches;
> I live in the ancient past,
> So I've chosen loneliness for my part.
> The men of today, they don't please me;
> They fetch a wondrous light from Heaven;
> The ancients, they drew it from their own breast
> And let it down into the sadness and joy of life.

48. O. R. Brosius' arguments that Humboldt moved rather close to Christianity in later years (*W. von Humboldts Religion*, Berlin, [1929]), are convincingly refuted by Werner Schultz in *Die Religion Wilhelm von Humboldts*.

49. *Briefe an F. G. Welcker*, p. 102, letter of March 18, 1823; see also p. 79 (Dec. 15, 1822).

50. *Ibid.*, p. 102.

51. Haym, *Wilhelm von Humboldt*, p. 580, cites Gentz, *Schriften*, ed. Schlesier, V, 291, 300.

52. Humboldt, IX, 349: "Thus since in Hellas' works the highest earthly goal has been achieved, we should no longer heed the lure of alien tones." See also pp. 375f.

53. *Ibid.*, p. 213.

54. See the comments of Humboldt's editor Albert Leitzmann in his *W. von Humboldts Sonettdichtung* (Bonn, 1912), pp. 6of.

55. Humboldt, VII, 659.

56. *Ibid.*, footnote.

57. One sonnet, devoted to the Fall, is not available in print. (Leitzmann included only a fraction of the sonnets in his edition.)

58. *Briefe an eine Freundin*, II, 405.

59. Various scholars have noticed a strain of sensuality in Humboldt's own nature. It appears most clearly in the extraordinarily realistic, even brutal, descriptions of sexual bondage in his narrative poem "The Greek Slave" (1822), Humboldt, IX, 93–151. See also VII, 653–655.

60. *Ibid.*, pp. 609, 611.

61. Humboldt, III, 199, 200f.

62. *Ibid.*, pp. 197f.

63. *Ibid.*, p. 206.

64. Humboldt, VII, 612.

65. See his "History of the Decline and Fall of the Greek Free States," where Humboldt expresses concern about the decline and fall of his native Prussia after the battle of Jena.

66. Humboldt, VII, 609.

67. *Ibid.*

68. Humboldt, III, 195.

69. Humboldt, VI, 548.

70. See Eduard Spranger, *W. v. Humboldt und die Humanitätsidee* (Berlin, 1909), p. 456.

71. Humboldt, III, 197f.

72. Humboldt, VII, 614f.

73. *Ibid.*, p. 616.

74. Humboldt, III, 184.

75. See Haym, *Wilhelm von Humboldt*, pp. 273–277.

76. See Eduard Spranger, *W. v. Humboldt und die Reform des Bildungswesens* (Berlin, 1910), p. 166.

77. Paulsen, *Geschichte des gelehrten Unterrichts*, II, 292.

78. Humboldt had already shifted from education to diplomacy, but the spirit of his reforms prevailed.

79. See Spranger, *Reform des Bildungswesens*, p. 167.

80. *Ibid.*, p. 171.

81. Paulsen, *Geschichte des gelehrten Unterrichts*, II, 311.

82. *Ibid.*, pp. 344f.

83. Spranger, *Reform des Bildungswesens*, pp. 254f; Paulsen, *Geschichte des gelehrten Unterrichts*, II, 292.

84. Haym, *Wilhelm von Humboldt*, p. 277.

85. Paulsen, *Geschichte des gelehrten Unterrichts*, II, 286.

86. Cf. *ibid.*, esp. II, 637–692.

87. Compare the conclusions drawn by Spranger in his *Reform des Bildungswesens*.

XII. *The Return of Helen: Goethe*

1. See Curtius' *Torso* (Stuttgart, 1957), pp. 163f.

2. Goethe, X, 695.

3. *Ibid.*

4. *Ibid.*, pp. 143f; cf. p. 139.

5. *Ibid.*, pp. 318f.

6. *Ibid.*, p. 321.

7. See his discussion of the festival of Saint Roch below.

8. *Goethes Unterhaltungen mit Müller* (Stuttgart, 1898), p. 63, conversation of June 8, 1821.

9. On March 11, 1832, Goethe, XXIV, 770f.

10. *Ibid.*, pp. 771f.

11. *Ibid.*, p. 732.
12. *Goethes Unterhaltungen mit Müller*, p. 238, June 8, 1830.
13. *Ibid.*
14. Goethe, XXIV, 467, Feb. 28, 1831.
15. See Mann's "Zu Goethe's Wahlverwandtschaften" in *Die neue Rundschau*, 36(1925):391–401.
16. *Briefe* (Weimar Edition, Section 4) XX, 26, March 7, 1808. This section of the edition is hereafter cited as *Briefe*.
17. C. F. von Reinhard, *ibid.*, p. 230, letter of Dec. 2, 1808.
18. *Ibid.*, p. 26.
19. Goethe, XIII, 644.
20. *Ibid.*, p. 1152; compare pp. 98, 204f, and 234.
21. *Gespräche* (Leipzig, 1909–1911), II, 15, Dec. 31, 1808.
22. *Briefe*, XXIX, 13, Jan. 16, 1818, to Boisserée.
23. Goethe, IX, 588, no. 667.
24. *Ibid.*, p. 608, no. 807.
25. See Goethe's letter to Boisserée, March 3, 1831, *Briefe*, XLVIII, 156.
26. *La Réligion de Goethe* (Strasbourg, 1949), p. 123.
27. Goethe, I, 612.
28. *Gespräche*, I, 534.
29. *Ibid.* For two examples of quite untypical neutrality between romanticism and classicism, see *Gespräche*, IX, 181, 238.
30. Goethe, I, 615:
       And so, once and for all, I want
       No beasts in the pantheon!
       The ugly elephant-trunks . . .
31. Goethe, IX, 602, no. 763.
32. Goethe, XIII, 846.
33. Goethe, XXI, 885, letter of Dec. 31, 1829, to Zelter.
34. For a further discussion see H. Hatfield, "Towards the Interpretation of *Die Wahlverwandtschaften*," *Germanic Review*, 23(1948): 104–114.
35. See Oskar Walzel, "Goethes *Wahlverwandtschaften* im Rahmen ihrer Zeit," *Goethe-Jahrbuch*, 27(1906):166–206.
36. Goethe, IX, 262.
37. *Gespräche*, II, 62, undated.
38. On him see esp. Eduard Firmenich-Richartz, *Die Brüder Boisserée*, I (Jena, 1916); Oscar Seiler, *Die Brüder Boisserée in ihrem Verhältnis zu den Brüdern Schlegel* (Vienna, 1915).
39. Sept. 11, 1815, quoted by Firmenich-Richartz, *Die Brüder Boisserée*, p. 119.
40. Letter of Oct. 1814, quoted by Firmenich-Richartz, *ibid.*, p. 204.
41. Goethe, XIII, 688.
42. *Ibid.*, p. 705.

43. *Ibid.*, p. 679.
44. Goethe, XII, 476.
45. Goethe, XIII, 708.
46. *Ibid.*, p. 710.
47. *Ibid.*, pp. 715f.
48. *Ibid.*, p. 724.
49. See Erich von dem Hagen, *Goethe als Herausgeber von "Kunst und Altertum" und seine Mitarbeiter* (Berlin, 1912), p. 190.
50. Goethe, XIII, 845.
51. *Ibid.*, p. 730.
52. To Georg Sartorius, July 20, 1817, Goethe, XXI, 238.
53. Goethe, XIII, 736.
54. Goethe, III, 287.
55. Cf. *ibid.*, pp. 339, 385.
56. *Ibid.*, p. 299.
57. Goethe, IX, 608, no. 806.
58. Goethe, III, 299: "I will praise the living element/Which longs for a fiery death."
59. *Ibid.*, pp. 397f.
60. *Ibid.*, p. 406:

> Jesus felt purely and conceived
> Of only one god, quietly;
> Whoever made him into a god himself
> Vexed his sacred will.

61. On this point see Ernst Beutler's comments in his edition of the *Divan* (Wiesbaden, 1943), pp. 768–772.
62. Goethe, III, 333, 297. One is reminded of Brother Martin's comments, in *Götz von Berlichingen*, on poverty, chastity, and obedience. See also hits against priests in the *Divan* (III, 327, 333).
63. Goethe, VIII, 43.
64. See Arthur Henkel, *Entsagung* (Tübingen, 1954), *passim*; and Erich Trunz's comments in his edition of Goethe's *Werke* (Hamburg, 1948–1960), VIII, 590.
65. Goethe, VIII, 172.
66. *Ibid.*, p. 179.
67. *Ibid.*
68. *Ibid.*, p. 131.
69. Cf. Henkel, *Entsagung*, p. 150.
70. See Weimar Edition, Section 1, I, 467.
71. See Henkel, *Entsagung*, esp. Appendix I.
72. Goethe, II, 405: "Freedom awakes in every breast,/We all protest with a will."
73. See Camus' *Speech upon the Award of the Nobel Prize*, trans. Justin O'Brien (New York, 1958), pp. viii f.
74. See Beutler's introduction to *Faust*, Goethe, V, 738.

75. *Ibid.*, p. 370: "The forms are great, and great the memories."

76. The remark was made apropos Lord Byron. See *Gespräche* (2nd ed.), IV, 56, Dec. 3, 1828.

77. Goethe, V, 378.

78. *Ibid.*, p. 422.

79. *Ibid.*, pp. 360, 372.

80. See Walter F. Otto, *Dionysos* (Frankfurt am Main, 1933), chap. XIV, "Dionysos und das Element der Feuchte," esp. pp. 148f, 159.

81. Thus Barker Fairley, *Goethe's "Faust"* (Oxford, 1953), p. 82. Stuart Atkins, in *Goethe's Faust* (Cambridge, Mass., 1958), p. 190, writes of Homunculus' end as a *Liebestod*.

82. Goethe, V, 409: "Thus let Eros rule, the initiator of all life!"

83. *Ibid.*, p. 404.

84. *A Study of Goethe* (Oxford, 1947), p. 191; see also his *Goethe's "Faust,"* p. 85.

85. To W. v. Humboldt, Oct. 22, 1826, Goethe, V, 643.

86. To preserve him from "everything ordinary": *ibid.*, p. 456.

87. *Three Philosophical Poets*, pp. 179f.

88. Goethe, V, 457: "Who has neither achieved a name nor has a noble goal/Belongs to the elements: so depart!"

89. See Renato Poggioli's brilliant essay "Naboth's Vineyard or the Pastoral View of the Social Order," *Journal of the History of Ideas*, 24(1963):3–24, esp. 11–19.

90. See Konrad Burdach, in *Sitzungsberichte der preussischen Akademie*, 1912, pp. 627–659, 736–799.

91. See Goethe's remarks to K. E. Schubarth, Nov. 3, 1820 (Goethe, V, 640).

92. Faust has been made particularly irritable by the ringing of a chapel bell, which, as Atkins well says (*Goethe's Faust*, p. 248), "reminds him of a religion which he has consistently regarded as hostile to life itself."

93. Goethe, V, 505:
This world is not unresponsive to the effective man
Why does he need to roam off into eternity?
What he perceives, he can firmly grasp.
Thus let him wander through his day on earth;
When spooks walk, let him go his own way
And find torment and happiness in striding forward —
He, unsated every instant!

94. Conversation of June 6, 1831, *ibid.*, p. 664.

95. To Eckermann, June 6, 1831, *ibid.*, 663.

96. See Werner Kohlschmidt, "Klassische Walpurgisnacht und Erlösungsproblem in *Faust II*," in *Form und Innerlichkeit* (Munich, 1955), pp. 97–119.

97. Nov. 3, 1820, Goethe, V, 640. The words "des alten Herrn" are ambiguous in German, and anything but reverent in tone here.

98. Goethe, V, 518. As often, Goethe's optimism recalls Leibniz.

99. *Ibid.*: "Thus it is omnipotent love/Which forms everything, cherishes everything."

100. The word *Liebe* and its variations appear some fifteen times in this scene; its effect is reinforced by words like *Wonnebrand*, *Gotteslust*, and *Seligkeit*.

101. To Lavater, July 29, 1782, *Briefe*, VI, 20.

Index